SHOEBOX

Baby

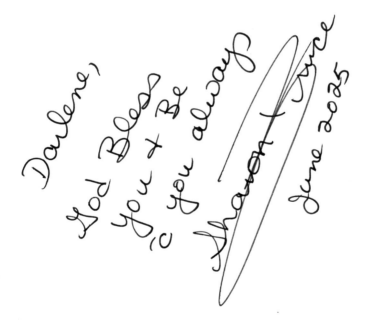

Darlene,
God Bless
you + Be
c you always

Sharon Bruce

June 2025

SHARON BRUCE

Shoebox Baby
Copyright © 2023 by Sharon Bruce

Tellwell Talent
www.tellwell.ca

ISBN
978-0-2288-9065-2 (Hardcover)
978-0-2288-9064-5 (Paperback)
978-0-2288-9066-9 (eBook)

DEDICATION

To these amazing women: Grace Fenton, Sue Fenton Wixson and Ruby McLoed Lavigne. Each of you displayed strength, courage, love of life and family, and a wonderful sense of humour.

TABLE OF CONTENTS

PREFACE

This book has been a work in progress for over four decades. Getting to know the family members and gathering their stories has been fascinating.

I want to acknowledge and thank the people who have encouraged, assisted and pushed me in this painstaking and wonderful endeavor.

My husband Norm Bruce, Diane Belanger Armstrong, Connor Wixson, Gundi Sheppard, Arlene Sorsa, Janice Lessard, Glenda Wilson and my children and friends.

PART 1

CHAPTER 1

Arrival of the Shoebox Baby

There was something about that turbulent winter night that sent a deep chill through Grace like no other. She felt the howling bitter ocean wind coming through the walls of the weather-worn shack she called home. Newspapers stuffed between the boards did little to keep the chill out of the air. Grace hoped that the meagre fire in the wood stove and the few old grey woollen blankets would keep her five children warm enough, and she longed for her husband Marshall.

In May of 1929, at the start of the Great Depression, Marshall and his brother Alexander were laid off from the local mine. They had to leave Pictou and found work in the sawmill in Yarmouth, three hundred miles away on the other side of the province. Poverty became the norm and food was as scarce for the Fenton's as for most families. Grace was thankful they were still able to pay the rent on the home they lived in, even though it could be considered more of a shack than a house. So many families were homeless, and several of the less fortunate had died on the streets.

In the following three years, Marshall and Alexander could only find short-term, menial jobs that compensated minimal wages. The Fenton family was already impoverished and barely able to survive before the Depression. Marshall sent money home from Yarmouth but because Yarmouth was so far away, he had only been home once in those three years. In May, Marshall returned home because Audrey had contracted scarlet fever and the doctors suggested that Grace ask Marshall to come.

"That's a night I'm not goin' ta forget," Grace said out loud as she rubbed her protruding abdomen.

Grace sat down in the old paint-worn rocking chair and vividly recalled the last time her husband was home. Marshall had not replied to the telegram she had sent him, which stated, "Audrey has scarlet fever . . .very ill . . .Dr. Smith urges you to come home." Instead, he quickly gathered a few of his belongings and headed straight home. When he walked into the kitchen, Grace was sitting at the table.

Looking up at him, she rubbed her eyes and blinked several times.

"Tis that you Marshall, or am I seein' things?" Grace excitedly hollered.

Marshall ran up and embraced Grace and gave her a long, passionate kiss.

"Tis me. I'm only home for a bit. How's our Audrey doin'? I can't stay longer than a few days," Marshall whispered in her ear.

"A few days is better than no days," said a thrilled Grace. "I wish you woulda replied to me telegram. I sent you anodder one tellin' you that Audrey seems ta be on the mend. The fever broke day afore yesterday. So far none of the other children are showin' signs of scarlet fever."

Marshall wasted no time going into the bedroom to see Audrey. "Heard you was feelin' a mite bad, Girly?" he said as he sat on the bed.

"Yup Fadder. I was feelin' poorly but I'm feelin' a mite better now," replied a weak Audrey.

Marshall tapped her leg and said, "Glad ta hear that me girly."

When the rest of the children saw their father, they hooted and screamed with delight. Although they only ate watered-down chicken stew and biscuits for supper, you would have sworn it was a king's feast the way Marshall went on about how delicious it was.

That evening when the children were in bed, Marshall and Grace made up for lost time in their bedroom. After three days, Marshall headed back to Yarmouth.

Grace never dreamed that at the age of 28 she would have five children and another one on the way. She was almost in her sixth month of pregnancy. They could barely feed the five children they had, so she did not know how she was going to provide for another one. Marshall did not know that Grace often went without food to ensure her five children were fed.

Somehow, she had this profound feeling deep inside that this child would be special. Not in an extraordinary way . . . *hmmm*, she just could not wrap her mind around it, but she knew something was brewing and about to bring forth a new era.

Letting her mind wander back to her yesteryears was an activity Grace seldom permitted herself to do. She felt that reminiscing was a waste of time since it would not change a damn thing, nor was it any good to dwell on such nonsense.

It seemed her children were having to grow up way too fast since the Great Depression hit the country. Fran, the oldest, had just turned 11 years old, and was a great help with the other children. Often, she had her head in the clouds, dreaming about movie stars she had seen in a magazine at her friend's house.

The oldest boy, Critch, was her second child and a strong lad, for being all of ten years old. He used to love helping his dad make barrels for the Annapolis Valley Apple Cider Company. Now he had the role of being the "man of the house." This role was a heavy weight for a boy of his age.

Marg, the third child, was a handful at times. She was way too interested in boys for a nine-year-old girl. Seven-year-old Arthur, the fourth child born, was a scallywag who kept getting into scraps with other boys. Then there was Audrey, who was a surprise baby . . . much like the one Grace was now pregnant with. Audrey was full of piss and vinegar. It was hard to keep up with that five-year-old.

Grace allowed herself to relish her memories, and then, as if a cold pail of water hit her, she stood up and declared with disgust in herself, "Enough tomfoolery! I have no time for such thinkin's."

Wrapping her thin, barren shawl tightly around herself, Grace slipped outside, into the snowstorm that was raging, to get a few more pieces of driftwood. The pile of wood was getting low and she knew she would have to send Critch and Marg out in the morning to gather more along the ocean shore. Grace hated to do that in such frigid weather, because the winds coming off the water made it almost unbearable, but she had no choice. Keeping the woodstove burning was not only a necessity to keep some warmth in the drafty home, but it was also the only source of heat she had to cook with.

"There somethin' a stirrin'. I gotta feelin' in me bones," she whispered to herself as she waded through the foot of snow that had fallen onto the path leading to the back door. Grace moved the snow away from the door and re-entered the house.

She brushed the snow off the wood and put it into the wood stove. While she was bending over, she felt a sharp pain in her lower abdomen. It was a grabbing pain and she bent over moaning. "No not now . . . this can't be happenin' . . . no, no . . . soon. No, this wee one can't be a comin' now," Grace muttered.

Taking a long deep breath helped her to calm herself and regain her composure. She knew the signs of labour and she could not deny it.

She went into the children's bedroom and shook Critch roughly, saying in an urgent tone, "Get up Critch and fetch the doctor. I'm a birthin' this wee one tonight."

Critch moaned, "Oh Maw, not now. I'm so tired."

Grace shook him again and raised her voice, "Critch, get your butt out of that bed now! I'm a birthin' this baby!"

Suddenly it dawned on Critch what his mother was saying, so he jumped out of bed and quickly got dressed.

Fran and Marg were awakened by their mother's elevated voice. "Come me girlies, it's time. I need your helpin'. You know what to do. You has been with me at many a birthin's. Be quiet. No sense wakin' up the other two youngens."

Frantically Fran blurted, "But Maw this baby's not a'pose to be birthin' yet!"

Grace gave Fran a reassuring pat on her shoulder and said, "It will all be fine me girly. Don't matter one-bit ifin the baby's not a'ppose to be birthin' now. He or she is a-comin'!"

Throughout the past few years, the girls had assisted their mother in the village with other births. They saw a stillborn birth and an infant who died shortly after being delivered. Those situations bothered the girls deeply. It took them days before they could even talk about them. Grace wished she could spare her daughters from being present at this birth, but she had no choice; she needed their help. If this infant survived even the delivery it would be a miracle.

As a second labour pain hit, Grace was jolted back to the present situation. She decided that she would prepare for a live birth and do whatever she could for this baby.

"Girly." Grace pointed at Fran. "Fetch that shoe box you've been a keepin' your treasures in. Empty it and put a heap of cotton battin' in it. Find the mineral oil and keep it handy."

"Maw what can I do?" asked Marg.

Because Grace did not want this baby born into chaos, she calmly gave Marg instruction. "You know that eye dropper in the eye medication bottle, fetch it and git some clean towels. Boil the kettle and put the eye dropper in the mug with boilin' water, after you worsh it. Keep warm water in the kettle ta worsh the baby."

One hour later, Critch and the doctor rushed into the chilly home. They brushed the snow off that had accumulated on their clothing and removed their coats and boots. The doctor rushed to Grace and discovered that her water had already broken.

"This one is too early Grace, but nevertheless let's get this baby delivered," urgently spoke the doctor.

The doctor had arrived just in time to deliver the little, tiny girl, who weighed and looked no bigger than a pound of butter. Her legs and arms were the size of Grace's baby finger, and her head was the size of a small apple. The wee baby did not cry when she was born. As the translucent-skinned little one took her first breath, she made a small mouse-like squeak.

Fran was standing at the end of the bed with an unfolded clean towel draped over her hands. The doctor held the baby in one hand and passed her to Fran.

As soon as he did, Grace urgently yelled, "Hurry but be a mite careful and git that wee girly worshed up. Warm up the oil a bit and cover her with it. Git her inta the shoe box with the cotton battin' and open the warmin' oven. Put the box inta it . . . do it right quick!"

With pity in his eyes, the doctor told Grace, "This baby will be dead before the morning. There is no sense fussing over her."

The maternal instinct to protect her new little one swiftly rose in Grace. "I birthed her and I'm her Maw. Ifin she is a-livin', I'll fend to her."

Since the infant had to be fed every hour, Grace stayed up the rest of that night. Grace pumped her breasts manually and filled the eye dropper with her milk to nourish her little shoe box baby. Fran and Marg were sent off to bed because they would have to help care for the other two younger children during the day.

Between the two girls and Grace they managed to keep the infant fed, care for the other children and keep up with the chores. Several days later the baby was still alive and seemed to be doing okay as far Grace could tell. At least she was still feeding and soiling the cotton batting. Of course, the wee child had a long way to go before she was out of the woods. Whether she lived or died, Grace felt it was important for her shoe box baby to be named. The least she could do for her new child was give her a name that could be put on a cross or gravestone.

"Well children, what should we call this wee one? We gotta give her a good name!" urged Grace.

"I know Maw. Let's call her Susan, after that pretty lady Susan Hayward. That one in the picture shows!" declared Fran.

"Then Susan it is, and I'm a likin' the name Adelta. Yup, Susan Adelta Fenton suits her just fine," said a smiling Grace.

One month later, on December 15th, 1936, Grace sent a telegram to Marshall: "Baby born early stop on November 13th stop baby Susan doing good stop all is well here."

CHAPTER 2

Polio Strikes

The winter of nineteen hundred and thirty-six and thirty-seven dragged on. The freezing temperatures and relentless snowstorms seemed endless. These were especially difficult times for a family who had so little. Since the birth of Suzie, the family was kept busy trying to feed themselves, keep the home warm and attend to the wee life in the shoe box whose nursery was the warming oven.

Fran and Marg were kept home from school to help attend to the baby. The supply of driftwood had to be kept stocked, so Critch also stayed home.

In preparation for his wood gathering he put on his patched, oversized, thin winter coat, his newspaper-soled gum rubber boots, a scarf that once belonged to his father, and mittens given to the family by the Salvation Army.

Just before he left the house, Grace would wrap Critch's scarf snug around his head and neck and say, "Don't doddle. Ifin you get cold, light a small fire but mind you don't burn all the wood. Be back afore sundown. You know me and your fadder are glad fer a child like you. Be careful me boy!"

Then she would hand him the pork lard sandwich she had made him and wrapped in newspaper. Grace knew he should have more to eat but a whole pork lard sandwich was a double portion in their home during these difficult times.

Critch did not notice the tears running down his mother's cheeks as she shut the door behind him, nor did he hear her whispered prayer: "Please me Lord, be with me boy. Keep him safe and bring him home."

Off he would go, no matter what the weather, pulling the wooden sled in search of driftwood on the frosty, windy ocean shoreline. He always tried to get extra driftwood to sell for food.

The winter months often found Grace struggling to provide her children with the necessities in life. The applesauce preserves, canned carrots and peas, stored potatoes, and turnip she had put away in late autumn only lasted a few months.

Occasionally Marshall's brother, Joseph, would come around and bring a few pounds of pork lard, a small bag of flour, baking soda, one jar of molasses and a few cans of corned beef. These items were used sparingly so they would last longer.

Marshall did send Grace whatever money was left over after he paid his room and board. The meagre amount barely paid the bills, let alone provided enough food for the children.

On a day that the cupboard had only baking soda left in it, Grace was in a panic because she knew the children would not eat. Hunger pangs were no stranger to this mother, nor to her children. Sometimes she was able to get some potato peels from the grouchy old farmer down the road; the children never knew that the potato peel soup she made came from the farmer's pig swill bucket. Grace had recently heard that the farmer had passed away though, so that slim supply of food was no longer available.

"Oh, me God, we sure are in need of some food. Ifin you could see your way clear to helpin' me git some fer me youngin's I'd be some grateful," prayed Grace before she started her chores.

In the afternoon, a man and woman dressed in Salvation Army uniforms showed up on her back step.

As she opened the back door, the man smiled and said, "Good afternoon. We are from da Salvation Army and we was just passin' by and thought we'd bring you a few things. This winter has been a mite hard on everyone."

Before Grace could greet them, he tipped his hat and said, "Good day to you Ma'ma." The woman with him smiled and they left as swiftly as they came.

When Grace looked down, there were two boxes full of groceries.

"Thank ya!" she hollered after them, and lifting her head heavenward with tears streaming down her face, she whispered, "And thank me Lord."

How the Salvation Army was aware of Grace's dilemma remained a mystery. All she knew was that God had answered her prayer.

When the spring came, it was not long before the warm salty breezes of summer washed across the small village. Grace felt a sigh of relief that she and her six children had made it through another winter.

Her joy was short-lived when an outbreak of polio swept through the region. Grace did everything she could to keep her children safe. She followed the sheet of health rules suggested by the county, that had been left on the doorstep outside. She made sure everyone in the house washed their hands several times a day, and the children stayed away from other children in the village. They remained at home and were only allowed to play in the yard. Regardless of her diligent efforts, polio found its way into their home.

One morning, Suzie, who was now eight months old, had not woken at her usual time. Fran went to check on her and as soon as she saw the wee toddler she started screaming, "Maw come quick! Somethin's wrong with the wee one."

The frantic tone in Fran's scream made Grace rush into the bedroom. Suzie had vomited all over herself. Her face was flushed and moist. She was whimpering and running a fever. Grace's heart pounded hard in her chest. Dread washed over her whole being.

Grace's voice trembled as she instructed Fran, "Go fetch Dr. Smith and tell the others not to come in here."

Quickly, Grace fetched a basin of water to clean the baby up and change her. The whole time, Suzie whimpered, and tears were spilling out over her closed eyes and running down her cheeks.

"It's ok, me tiny girly . . . it's ok. Maw's here," comforted Grace as she cuddled and rocked her. It seemed like the doctor was taking forever.

Doctor C.B. Smith arrived and confirmed her fear. Polio had easily found its way into Suzie's wee fragile body.

The doctor wrote out strict instructions. "Keep baby by itself away from other children. Do not allow any of the family to be away from the house and do not allow any visitors for two weeks or until advised to do so. Keep the child on a pillow well supported. After soreness goes out (you can touch her without her wincing or crying), rub it and massage whole area, moving all joints. All bowel movements and urine from baby or any secretions from nose and mouth must be burned. Careful washing of hands before and after attending to baby is important."

The three oldest children, Fran, Marg and Critch were put in charge of taking care of the two other younger children, Arthur and Audrey.

The children were instructed by the doctor and Grace to keep their distance from the baby and their mother. Grace would insist the children go outside when she had to go into the kitchen. The doting mother was the only one who handled all of Suzie's clothes, diapers and feeding utensils.

After a few days of cool bathing, the fever subsided. Suzie was no longer whimpering or wincing when her diaper was changed, so Grace began to massage her limbs and move her joints. During the second week, Grace noticed that Suzie's right arm and leg were not as strong as her left limbs. As she pushed on the baby's right foot there was little resistance. When she held a cracker out to Suzie by her right side, Suzie's right arm did not move. While Grace held Suzie up and supported her to stand, Suzie was leaning over to one side. She could barely believe, after all her wee girly had been through, she may be crippled as well. Sweeping Suzie up in her arms, Grace tightly hugged her and wept silently.

Dr. Smith's examination confirmed her fears. Baby Suzie had infantile paralysis on her right side.

During Dr. Smith's visit, he noticed that Grace was flushed and sweaty. She seemed to be experiencing some pain and stiffness when she bent over to pick up the baby's blanket.

The doctor asked, "How are you feeling? This seems to have taken its toll on you."

"I'm a mite tired. I haven't been sleepin' much," replied a weary Grace.

"Grace let's have a look at you now and don't argue," he insisted.

After Dr. Smith examined Grace, he asked Fran to make him and her mom a cup of tea. The baby was made comfortable and the rest of the children shooed outside when the tea was ready. Grace did not have time to think about why her back was so sore when she was taking care of Suzie. Grace assumed that all she needed was a few good nights sleeps and she would be fit as a fiddle.

When Grace sat across from Dr. Smith, she could see the apprehension in his eyes. Grace knew what the look meant and asked, "I got the Polio, don't I'?"

He nodded his head in agreement, "It appears you do. I believe it has affected your spine and your back muscles. That may be why you are having trouble straightening up when you bend over."

Tears filled her eyes and ran down her cheeks. Dr. Smith handed her his hanky and gave her a few moments to digest what he had revealed to her.

Grace heard the children playing outside and it brought her back to her senses. "Ok . . . it is what it is. I don't have time to coddle me self with this brood. What can I expect?"

Dr. Smith answered, "Your back should stop hurting in a few days. I will check back on you in a week or two. We will know more then."

Grace interrupted him and said, "Will I be able ta keep a walkin'?"

"I don't know. Sometimes the effects of polio are not permanent. With some, the damage shows up slowly through the years. Then there are those who get hit with a vengeance within weeks," he informed Grace.

"Well, that's that! I have ta keep a walkin' and fend to me family," she stated.

Grace wrote Marshall and told him about baby Suzie's bout with polio. She also filled him in on the home front happenings with each child. What she did not mention was that her back was left weak and hurting from polio and baby Suzie appeared to be paralyzed on her right side.

After such a gruelling and frigid winter and difficult spring, Grace and her family embraced the summer months. The warm weather and sunshine felt liberating. It meant that the family could once again spend time on the beach of the shoreline.

Watching her children run and play on the shoreline reminded her of her childhood with her own sisters and brothers. It did Grace's heart good to see them in the spacious outdoors and fresh air, instead of the confined quarters of their small home.

Grace loved to feel the light sting of the salty ocean spray on her face and the breeze tossing her hair. Whenever she stood on the shoreline her spirits were lifted and her soul refreshed as she watched the tide roll in.

Not only was summer a time to play, but it was also a time to work and gather food. During this season it was not as difficult to feed the family. The orchard just down the road often had apples that fell off the trees and over the fence. The children would gather them and take them home. Clams and seaweed were plentiful and could be found along the ocean shore. The boys would occasionally bring home fish that they had so proudly caught. A small garden that Grace and the girls had planted provided them with potatoes, turnips, carrots and peas.

Little did Grace know that she would need all the strength and stamina she gained from that summer to face an autumn like none she had ever known.

CHAPTER 3

Marshall and Alexander

The beginning of autumn was a busy season for the Fenton family. With school starting, gathering extra wood, harvesting the garden, putting down preserves, and keeping up with her chores, Grace had no free time for herself. Usually, when the children were in bed, she tidied up or did more laundry. When she went to bed, she was asleep within seconds of her head hitting the pillow.

One evening, she was too tuckered out to do anything extra. She decided that the laundry would still be there in the morning and there were no pressing matters to deal with, so she made herself a cup of hot tea and sat in the rocking chair. As she sipped on her tea, she wondered how her husband was doing and when he would be home next. Marshall had not been home since May. The cost of the train fare to go home was too expensive and the mill was so busy that they had four shifts running each day, therefore, no time off was allotted.

Grace did not realize it, but she was going to see her husband sooner than she expected.

In the middle of November, Marshall and Alexander showed up unannounced at home. Grace was shocked to see them. As soon as she set eyes on them, she knew why they had returned home. Both appeared to be sick. They had lost weight, were pale, sweaty, and had chronic coughs. These were signs of tuberculosis.

Grace made the men a strong cup of sweet tea and rushed out the door in search of Critch, who was in the back yard playing with

Arthur. When Critch saw the serious look on his mother's face, he knew something was wrong.

"Maw, what's a matter?" he yelled out.

An out-of-breath Grace responded, "Run and fetch Dr. Smith. Hurry, your fadder lookin' a mite poorly."

While she was waiting for the doctor, she firmly told the other children that they were not to come into the house until she told them they could. Fran was instructed to take young Suzie outside with them. It was a good thing that autumn day was on the warmer side and the sun was shining.

When Dr. Smith arrived, he examined both men and confirmed Grace's fear. Both men had contracted pulmonary tuberculosis. Since they shared a room at the boarding house in Yarmouth, one had passed the highly infectious disease to the other. It was common knowledge that the disease was highly contagious.

The first thing Dr. Smith told the three adults was, "This home is going to be quarantined. Grace, you will have to nurse both men. Alexander, you cannot go home. I am going to try to make arrangements for you both to be sent to the Kemptville Sanitorium. In the meantime, I am going to give Grace strict instructions and you two men are to follow them. Are either of you coughing up blood?"

Both men feebly shook their heads. "No."

"Good, that buys us a bit of time, but I need to know immediately if either of you are spitting up blood. Do you understand me? This is extremely serious." Doctor Smith was adamant.

Dr. Smith also ordered both men be put on complete bed rest and given plenty of fluids. They were to eat small meals six times a day, whether they wanted to or not.

Grace was given instructions to soak blankets in Pine-Sol and hang them in a squared-off section of the home where the men's beds would be. Blankets were in short supply in the Fenton home and the doctor was aware of it so he told Grace that he would supply the blankets for the Pine-Sol wall and a few extra. The floors and all surfaces in the house had to be scrubbed with Pine-Sol.

Grace was to wash her hands before and after tending to the men. A clean rag or handkerchief was to be worn over her mouth and nose, to help prevent her from catching the disease. The children were not to have any contact with the men. Grace was to limit her contact with the children also.

Even though she had no idea how she would accomplish this feat, since the house was so small, she was determined that no one else in the home would come down with the dreadful tuberculosis.

The men had to use Grace and Marshall's bed. There was no room for another bed in the house. Old blankets were placed on the kitchen floor for Grace to sleep on. This would be very hard on her back but there was no alternative.

The children had not seen their father for a long period of time, and they were extremely disappointed that they were not permitted to visit with him. Fran and Marg had tears in their eyes when Grace explained the situation.

Critch was so upset that he yelled, "Damn!" and stormed out of the house.

Even though the doctor may not have approved, that evening Grace made a small opening in the wall of blankets and each child took their turn chatting with their father for a bit. When it came to Suzie's turn, Grace held Suzie and introduced her to her father.

"Suzie me girly this is your fadder. Marshall this is our wee Suzie, I told you 'bout in me letters."

"She is a wee thing for sure. Is she a cripple?" Marshall asked.

Grace nodded her head in affirmation.

"Guess the family best take care of her then," he sadly declared. Then he closed his eyes.

Grace was sure she had seen a tear running down Marshall's cheek.

The two months that Grace cared for her husband and his brother were physically and mentally exhausting. At first, the men were demanding. They were constantly calling her into the bedroom to get them something or do something for them. As the days went by, they grew weaker and seldom called for her attention. They both started spitting up blood a month after they arrived home. Dr. Smith visited the men once a week and he was making every attempt to have them admitted to the Sanitorium. They had to wait until beds became available in Kemptville.

Grace was constantly telling the children to be quiet. In the small surroundings, it was almost impossible for her to avoid proximity with the children. It was gruelling for Fran, Critch, and Marg also, because they had to care for the other children.

The meals Grace put together were meagre but at least they helped to keep hunger pangs away. Having the preserves and a bit of extra food she had managed to put away for the winter was a blessing, but she knew her supply was dwindling. Stretching and rationing food was something Grace had grown accustomed to.

Hanging the extra laundry out in the freezing cold was excruciating on her hands. Once the laundry was frozen stiff, she would bring it in to thaw. There were always puddles of water and Pine-Sol on the floor. Most of Grace's waking hours were consumed with cleaning. If she was not washing bed linen, blankets, and clothes, she was wiping off surfaces and the floor. Three or four time a day she was emptying a chamber bucket and cleaning it. The smell of Pine-Sol permeated everything. Grace was convinced that the scent of Pine-Sol had damaged her sinuses and it would be the only scent she would ever smell. In the evening Grace would fall asleep from exhaustion, only to be awoken by one of the men coughing. She did not remember the last time she had a full night's sleep.

One week before Christmas, an ambulance from the Kemptville Sanitorium pulled up into the driveway in front of the Fenton home. Marshall asked that his brother be taken out of the house on the stretcher first. He wanted a few minutes with Grace before he left.

"Grace my love, I put some money away in the bottom drawer of the dresser in a sock. It ain't much luv but it will help yah. Always rememberin' I love you, my girly. Take good care of the youngins and yourself," Marshall said seriously, and he blew a kiss to her.

Grace pretended to catch it and put it in her heart. She had loved this man for years, but she felt the last couple of years apart had almost made them strangers. The man who came home sick was a man she did not know. During his illness he was demanding and harsh. Although Grace understood that affliction could change a person, she never expected that her Marshall could be transformed by anything.

Standing outside in the bitter cold, with her threadbare winter coat on, Grace watched as they loaded her husband on the stretcher into the ambulance. She did not know if she would ever see him again. As the ambulance pulled away, she waved. It was so cold you could hear the tires crunching on the snow packed road. Grace stood there util the vehicle was out of sight. This was one of those moments where she did not even try to stop her tears from flowing down her near-frost-bitten face.

While she felt physically, mentally, and emotionally drained, she was grateful that she did not have any signs or symptoms of tuberculosis. Everyday Grace had pleaded with God to protect her, the children and tiny Suzie.

CHAPTER 4

Bill

Grace hoped that 1939 would be a better year. Lord only knew she needed a reprieve from the calamities that kept hitting her family.

The Christmas that had just passed was skimpy. All Grace could give her children for gifts were hankies she had made from an old, stained apron. Chicken stew, with a few potatoes, carrots, peas and the last of the canned corn was their Christmas meal. The last jar of applesauce was opened for dessert.

Even though that Christmas seemed just like any other day of the week she was thankful that her children had not come down with tuberculosis, and that her husband was getting medical help, albeit he was too far away for her to visit.

One night in March, she sat in her rocking chair in the kitchen, with a cup of tea to warm herself by the woodstove. The children were all settled in their beds. Their beds were potato sacks filled with straw, with sheets and blankets from the Salvation Army laid on top. The boys slept in one bed, the girls in a separate bed, and baby Suzie in a dresser drawer on the floor. Pillows were an extravagance and there were only two in the house. One Grace kept for herself and the other was used to prop up Suzie.

Grace should have been hanging clothes to dry on the clotheslines that crossed the kitchen, and making soup for the next day, but her weary and sore body just wanted rest.

That night she was not thinking about her children or her husband; her thoughts kept returning to the man she had met at the corner store. He noticed she was struggling with a fifty-pound bag of flour purchased with food stamps from the Salvation Army.

He introduced himself, "Hello, pretty lady. My name is Bill McLoed. Can I give you a hand?"

Even though she was hesitant to accept his offer, she did because she knew she might not be able to manage the bag of flour with her sore back. Bill carried the flour home for her.

The proper thing to do after such a kind gesture was to invite him in for a cup of tea. Though the children kept interrupting, the two new friends were able to chat and learn more about each other in the few hours of their visit. Bill was married and had six children of his own and was an electrician at the local mine. Finding Bill so easy to talk with, Grace shared more about herself than she intended.

Thanking her for the tea and the fine company of such a courageous and pretty lady, he got up to leave. Grace blushed like a teenager and thanked him once again.

As he left, he smiled and said, "You have not seen the last of me. I will be back."

Grace questioned if she was attracted to Bill because she had not had a man treat her so sweetly for so long, or if she was just grateful for his help.

Whispering under her breath, she reprimanded herself, "Bill is married and has six children of his own. I'm bein' just plain foolish. School-girly dreams and just foolishness."

It was as if Grace had forgotten she too was married. *What am I thinkin? I has a husband*, she thought to herself, as she attempted to quench the new emotions rising in her.

Quickly she got up and pulled out a pad of paper and a pencil and wrote a letter to Marshall, to get her focus back on her husband. She wanted to connect with her spouse, even if she did not have anything new to tell him. Deep inside she desperately yearned for that deep loving relationship they had once shared. Grace knew this letter, like the previous ones she had sent, would go unanswered. Letter-writing was never one of Marshall's strong suits, but before he was ill, he had made attempts to keep in touch. Grace knew he was extremely weak and writing a letter may be too much for him.

The response she received was from one of the doctors. Regardless, she was eager to know how he was doing.

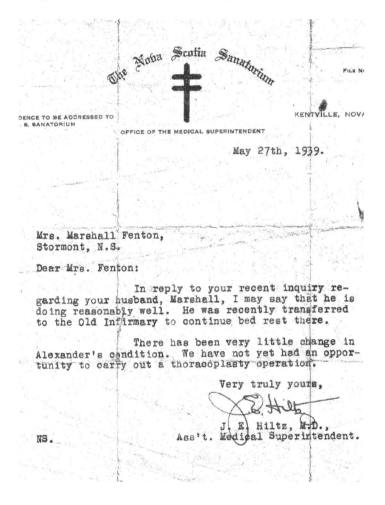

The Nova Scotia Sanatorium

FILE Nº

DENCE TO BE ADDRESSED TO
. S. SANATORIUM

KENTVILLE, NOV/

OFFICE OF THE MEDICAL SUPERINTENDENT

May 27th, 1939.

Mrs. Marshall Fenton,
Stormont, N.S.

Dear Mrs. Fenton:

      In reply to your recent inquiry regarding your husband, Marshall, I may say that he is doing reasonably well. He was recently transferred to the Old Infirmary to continue bed rest there.

      There has been very little change in Alexander's condition. We have not yet had an opportunity to carry out a thoracoplasty operation.

      Very truly yours,

J. E. Hiltz, M.D.,
Ass't. Medical Superintendent.

NS.

She sighed and folded the letter, putting it in her jewellery box as she had done with the rest of the correspondences from the sanitorium.

Painful muscle spasms and stiffness, though less frequent, continued to plague Grace. Whenever she noticed she was slightly leaning forward, she would force herself to straighten up, correcting her posture.

Grace and the older girls faithfully followed Dr. Smith's instructions for Suzie's care. Once a day they massaged her right leg and arm and moved them to encourage joint involvement. It had been six months since polio struck Suzie, and she did not seem to be regaining strength. It was obvious she had some feeling in her leg because she would cry when they moved it. However, when they moved her arm, it was limp and not a sound was heard from her.

Dr. Smith asked them to continue the regime. He suggested that Grace look into electric shock treatments for the affected limbs, once Suzie was a bit older.

Though Suzie was not walking, she excelled at learning to talk. To keep Suzie engaged with the family, she was tied to a wooden chair during the day. She tended to lean to the left and fall over if she was not tied on the chair. The children would entertain her with their antics, especially Critch. He could get her laughing and he got the biggest kick out of her high-pitched laugh.

Overall, she was a happy little one. Audrey taught her to say "Maw" and "Fadder", but Suzie would say "Fadd." Holding objects with her left hand came naturally to her, but she made quite a mess when she drank her milk from her tin cup. Since the other children laughed when she did this, Grace suspected she did it on purpose. Though milk was a precious commodity and the thought of it being wasted bothered Grace, she could not help but giggle under her breath at all six of them.

For an eighteen-month-old toddler, Suzie was physically behind her peers, but was doing well considering her difficult and premature start in life.

"Maw, I'm gettin' tired of changin' these stinkin' diapers. When are you goin' to teach Suzie to use the chamber pail?" whined Fran.

Grace sternly replied, "Land sakes, Suzie would fall int the pail, and she can't be usin' the outhouse. She is too wee. She can't even crawl yet. Stop your whinin', girly! Just be glad she's not your size."

Toilet training was not going to be an easy task with Suzie's limitations, but Grace was determined that Suzie would learn and progress as much as possible.

Keeping to his word, Bill McLoed visited the Fenton family at least two days a week. He stayed for an hour or two for a cup of tea and a chat with Grace. The children were growing to like Bill, although Grace was not sure if it was Bill they liked, or the cinnamon candy he brought them. When he left, Grace would find extra food items that miraculously appeared in the cupboards.

On one of his visits, Grace finally mustered up the courage to ask, "Bill, does your wife know you've been a-comin' 'round here?"

"Well sweet lady, what she doesn't know won't hurt her. Besides, we aren't doing anything wrong. Just visiting," said a smiling Bill.

They both knew they were walking on shaky ground. Though she knew she should tell him not to come around anymore, she just could not do it. The adult company, extra provisions and male attention were a welcome treat for her. She had to admit she was growing very fond of Bill.

CHAPTER 5

Home Visit

In early summer Grace received a letter from the sanatorium. Her husband was insisting on a home visit.

Grace gathered the five older children around, "Your fadder is comin' home for a bit. He wouldn't be happy if he knew Bill was comin' 'round."

Marg piped up, "Ya 'cause Fadder's your husband and Bill is—"

Grace cut her off quickly. "Bill is just Bill. He is a friend, that's all. Your fadder might not understand. Could get him thinkin' the wrong thing and that's not good fer him."

"What kind of thinkin', Maw?" asked Arthur.

"Never ya mind, ya ninny. You're too young to be a thinkin' 'bout it," said Critch.

Grace's eyebrows went up. She could barely believe what her oldest son had just said, but ensuring her children did not mention Bill's visits took precedence over dealing with Critch.

The family cleaned up the house as best they could. The wet Pine-Sol-soaked wall of blankets was hung. Clean sheets and blankets for Marshall's bed had been hung outside and smelled of the salty ocean breeze.

The children had their weekly bath the night before. It was such a chore to make sure all six children were bathed. The large, galvanized steel wash tub was brought in the kitchen. Pots of water were heated on the wood stove. One-third of the tub was filled with cold water and just enough hot water was added to make it lukewarm. The first two in the tub were Audrey and Suzie. Suzie could sit on Audrey's lap while Audrey held her. Audrey enjoyed this because Suzie splashed the water and giggled.

Grace was amused by the girl's antics, but she knew the water was cooling off. Sternly she said, "Enough, me girlies. Stay still so I can worsh you up! The rest of the youngin's need a bathin' also. I swear you all were playin' in a pigsty. You're so filthy."

By the time both were bathed, Grace was soaking wet. Suzie was the first to be taken out of the tub and dried. Audrey was dried with the same towel. Worn and holey, the four towels the family shared belonged in a rag bin, but the family had to make do.

The rest of the children took their baths according to their ages: Fran, Critch, Marg and then Arthur. By the time Arthur had his bath, not only was the water dirty, cold, and full of soap scum, but he also had to dry off with a soaking wet towel.

Arthur was disgusted. "Ah Maw, do I have to get into that pig swill? I'm cleaner than that there water."

Grace gave him a stern look and retorted, "Get your butts inta the tub afore I paddle your behind. Least you're not gonna smell like a pig. I don't has time for such whinin'."

When the bathing ritual was completed, all children smelled clean like lye with a hint of lemon. The homemade soap consisted of pork fat, ashes from the stove and lye. If lemons were not too expensive, Grace would purchase one and add the juice and the zests to the batch of soap. This soap was also used to wash the clothes. It may not have been as good as the new detergents on the market, but it cleaned the clothes when used on the old scrub board.

Marshall arrived home a week after she received his request in the mail. Each family member was dressed in clean clothes in anticipation of his arrival. Most of their clothing was stained and well-worn but at least they were clean. Grace took her only half-decent dress out of the closet the night before. The dress was worn so thin that there was a two-inch hole right in the front. As she ran her hand over the material, she knew there was no way it could be mended, because the material was too thin to hold the stiches.

"Can't get my knickers in a twist over it," Grace decided. "I will put on me best apron. That'll do. Not like the king or queen is visitin'."

She pulled her long grey-streaked brown hair in a bun and went outside where the children were lined up to greet their father.

The ambulance pulled up and the children cheered and clapped. Marshall was helped of the ambulance by the attendant. The first sight of him took Grace's breath away. Marshall's face was of a greyish pallor with sunken cheeks and wrinkles. Grace wondered who this old man was, haggard, weak, and thin. Surely this wasn't her thirty-four-year-old husband, once a sturdy and strong young man.

The children all excitedly yelled, "Hi Fadder," and waved.

Marshall was not aware of what was happening, so the attendant helped Marshall turn around. He whispered into his patient's ear, "Wave. Those are your young'uns saying hi."

Feebly, he waved to his children.

Once in the house, the attendant helped Grace get Marshall into bed. When Marshall was settled, he fell asleep within minutes.

Grace stood over the bed, looked down on him and then turned her face heavenward. "Please don't let me husband die 'til he's laid eyes on all the kids."

That evening before bed, Grace made a small opening in the wall of blankets, as she had done when he was home before. Each child stood and filled their father in on the events of their lives. Even though Marshall's speech was low and weak, they were comforted by hearing his familiar voice.

"Be good for your maw while I'm gone. Make Fadder proud!" Marshall would say to each one. He was not a man of many words, nor was he prone to show his affections verbally, but the children had always understood and knew that he loved them.

When it came to Suzie's turn, Grace held her up and Suzie gleefully yelled out, "Fad. Fad," and waved to Marshall.

With a weak smile on his face, Marshall waved back. "She ain't grown that much. She's still a wee girly. She seems happy enough! Is she slow . . . I's mean in her thinkin'?" Marshall asked as he struggled to breathe and talk.

Grace proudly replied, as she hugged and kissed Suzie, "No. I think her mind's good. Suzie seems to be a smart little gaffer."

The next moment, when Grace looked over at Marshall, he was sound asleep. The long trip had exhausted him. Quietly she went into the kitchen and instructed the children to go outside.

During the first two days that Marshall was home, he mainly slept except when Grace woke him up for his meals. By the third day he had a bit more strength. Grace was able to help him sit up for longer periods of time and catch him up on the comings and the goings of friends and family. They spoke about the rumours of war overseas. Germany, Italy, and Japan had formed an alliance. It appeared that they were going to attempt to take control of smaller countries in Europe. World War One had ended just a little over two decades ago. The country was just recovering from the Great War and the Great Depression. Nova Scotia was even slower in its recovery. If war broke out, Grace and Marshall could not imagine how destitute Canada, and especially Nova Scotia, could become. They were genuinely concerned about their children's future.

On the fourth day, once all the children were tucked in bed for the evening, Marshall whispered to Grace, "Come lay with me for a bit me girl."

Grace could not resist his pleas. This time she found it so difficult to lay with her husband. Afterwards, she sat alone in the dark in her rocking chair and cried. Tears flowed down her face, not only because of the dreadful state her husband was in, but also because she knew she no longer loved him, as a wife loves her husband.

The rest of the evening Marshall's coughing increased, and he spat up blood. By the morning he had a fever. Grace knew what she had to do. A telegram went out to Kemptville Sanatorium about Marshall's condition, and an ambulance came to return him to what he began to know as his second home.

Grace knew deep down in her heart that she would never see him alive again. A huge wave of sorrow swept over her. She would miss and mourn not the man he currently was, but the man he used to be.

CHAPTER 6

Tucker

The rest of that summer was sweltering. Even the cool breeze coming off the ocean brought little relief. It was, however, good clothes-drying weather. As Grace was hanging clothes on the clothesline, Suzie was beside her playing in the grass. Out of nowhere, came a medium-sized, scruffy, long- haired, brown dog. It wandered up to them and made itself comfortable lying down beside Suzie.

Suzie looked startled at first, but soon started to pet the mangy dog and said, "Nice puppy, puppy, puppy."

Grace's first instinct was to chase the dog away, but the mutt looked up at her with gentle and mournful eyes. Those huge, brown eyes tugged at Grace's heart.

Squatting down beside Suzie and the dog, she asked, "Where did you come from, feller? You sure look a might dirty and thin. Guessin' I could find a wee bit of food fer you." Then she called to Fran, who was standing on the back porch step, "Fran, fetch a small bowl of the porridge left over from breakfast, and a bowl of water."

Fran turned and saw the dog. "Oh Maw . . . a dog. Where did he comes from?"

"Never you mind. Just git what I asked you fer, girly."

Fran came running back with the items her mother asked her to get. The other four children followed.

"Stop and walk . . . you're gonna scare the poor beast. Stand back a bit and give him room. Fran gives me the porridge and water," said Grace.

The children watched as the dog wolfed down the porridge and lapped up the water, until the bowl was empty. When he was finished, the poor wretch laid back down beside Suzie. Suzie once again started to pet the filthy, matted dog. The children could not contain their joy over this unexpected visitor. They knelt and started to pet the dog.

"Take turns, or you'll give the poor thing a fright," scolded Grace.

"It sure a lookin' tuckered out, Maw," Critch declared.

Grace replied, "Yuppers, he sure does.".

"Wonder who it's a-belongin' to, Maw?" asked Marg.

"Not sure, but he needs some tending to," responded Grace.

Arthur tapped his mother on the shoulder and asked, "Can we keep it, Maw, please?"

Then the rest of the children joined in the pleading, "Please Maw . . . Please Maw . . . Please Maw."

"Stop your beggin'. We can if no one comes a lookin' fer it. You have to clean it up and take care of it. It's tuckered out ya know. I don't have time to tend to a dog," explained Grace.

"We will. We will," the children screamed as they jumped up and down. Even Fran forgot her composure and joined in with the others.

"We gotta give it a name," stated Audrey.

They all grew quiet to think about a name. Suzie continued to pet the dog as she quietly repeated, "Tucker puppy. Tucker puppy."

Everyone stopped and looked down at Suzie and the dog.

"Tucker . . . it should be called Tucker!" yelled out Marg.

Suzie echoed, "Tucker, Tucker, Tucker."

So that day, Tucker, the male mongrel, became a part of the Fenton family.

By autumn, three-year-old Suzie was able to drag herself along the floor on her bum by pulling herself with her left arm. It wasn't crawling, but she managed to get underfoot and scoot along at a good pace. Grace was worried the poor wee one would get splinters in her bum from the rough wooden floors, but she dared not stop her development if this is how she would be able to move about.

It became evident that Tucker was becoming not only a loyal family dog, but also Suzie's watchdog and protector. Wherever she went, he followed close behind. He ensured she was never out of his sight for long, whether she was in the house or outside in the yard.

One August afternoon, Suzie was nowhere to be found in the house. Grace felt her stomach churn as she dashed around the house looking for her.

"Suzie, girly, where are you?" shouted Grace. She looked under her bed, under the wobbly wooden table and the wired-up wooden chairs. Since the house was so small, it took Grace only a few minutes to search it. Her girly was not there.

Critch was out gathering driftwood. Grace had sent Fran and Marg to the corner store for molasses. Audrey and Arthur were in school. Unable to acquire help from the others, she ran outside.

Frantically, Grace repeatedly yelled, "Suzie, where is you? Suzie girly, answer Maw!"

She couldna' gotta that far, thought Grace.

"What ifin . . . oh me God . . . the shore . . . oh me God, the high tide is a-comin' in!" she screamed out loud as she dashed towards the ocean shore.

Grace had a lump in her throat. As she ran her feet were sinking in the dry white sand with every footstep. At one point she lost a shoe but scarcely noticed. Going back to look for it would be a waste of precious time that she could not afford. Grace felt like she was going in slow motion even though she was moving at a good speed. When she reached the beach, she saw the foam from the waves washing up on the shoreline. The tide had just started to come in. She stopped and frantically looked up and down the shoreline. In the distance she saw Tucker struggling with something he was pulling along in the sand.

She rushed toward Tucker, then stopped dead in her tracks when she heard Suzie screeching, "Tucker, stop it! Let me go. Tucker stop! Me britches is full of sand!"

A drenched and stinky Tucker had his teeth planted firmly in the back of Suzie's soaking wet, seaweed-covered britches. He was pulling a resistant Suzie to safety.

Grace was furious at herself and at Suzie. How did she let Suzie out of her sight long enough for her to get this far on the beach? Why did Suzie leave the house when she knew better? Grace ran to them and slumped to the ground on her knees, covered her face and sobbed so hard that she scared her child and the dog. Tucker began to howl, and Suzie started to cry.

When the shock wore off and she came to her senses, Grace stopped crying and started to nervously laugh. What a sight the three of them must have been. A drenched dog, a sandy, soaking-wet three-year-old, and a shoeless disheveled mom.

Grace patted Tucker. "Good boy, Tucker. You saved me wee girly!"

As she scooped up Suzie, she tightly hugged her.

"Maw . . . ouch," whined Suzie.

On the way back to the house, Grace remembered her lost shoe. She found it at the edge of the water. If the high tide had come in, her shoe would have been washed out to sea. New shoes were a luxury she could not afford.

Once Grace was able to think straight, she questioned Suzie, "What were you doin' down here, girly?"

"I was swimmin'. In the swim hole," proudly declared Suzie.

The swimming hole was a hole the children had dug on the shore. They built walls inside of it with large rocks and packed the sand in between. It was approximately three feet deep. When the low tide was out it held a little under one foot of water. As the high tide came in the hole filled. The children had to repack the walls after high tide. This swimming hole was made for Suzie. Even though they had to lift her in and out, it was a place where they could keep an eye on Suzie while she played in the water.

When Grace, Suzie and Tucker reached the house, Grace pulled Suzie away from her chest. She looked straight into Suzie's eyes and in a harsh and firm voice said, "Don't you ever go out of da home without Maw, Fran, Critch, or Marg! Do you hear Maw!"

Suzie started to cry and shake at the reprimand. Her maw had never spoken to her in such a stern manner before. Grace was at odds with herself. She wondered if she should have given Suzie a paddling for her dangerous escapade, but she felt the ordeal was enough for one day. She didn't have the strength to punish Suzie further. The whole episode, as well as carrying Suzie back to the house, was exhausting, and caused painful spasms in her ailing back.

CHAPTER 7

Winter Blows In

Bill McLoed was a frequent visitor at the Fenton home after Marshall went back to the sanatorium. Although he and Grace had become romantically involved, they had not become intimate. When the children were not around or were not looking, they sneaked in a kiss or hug.

Bill could not help but notice Grace was putting on weight. He knew the reason because his wife had borne six children.

"Gracie, are you in a family way?" Bill inquired, one evening.

Tears welled up in Grace's eyes and she nodded and murmured, "'Tis Marshall's baby. We laid together when he was home."

Putting her head down and covering her eyes with her hands, she began to sob. "I'm in a family way ag'in. I shoulda said no. I just couldn't say no to me husband."

Taking Grace in his arms and gently rubbing her back, Bill softly said, "It'll be alright. I'll take care of you and the children."

His gentle manner and kindness made Grace cry even more. When the tears subsided, Grace put the kettle on, added more wood to the fire and started tidying up the kitchen. Puttering gave her those few minutes she needed to calm herself down, so she could think clearly. Bill sat in silence, at the kitchen table watching Grace. It was apparent to him that she needed to gather her thoughts.

Grace poured the boiling water into her mother's brown and chipped teapot. She placed two melamine mugs and the teapot on the table.

"I'm sorry, Bill. I got no milk or sugar," Grace apologized, as she sat down and poured the tea.

"Black tea is just fine," he replied.

"How is you gonna tend to me when ya have a wife and kids?" inquired Grace, nervously twisting her stained apron in her hands.

"My wife and I have not been happy for a long time. I want to move in with you and your family, Gracie," proclaimed Bill.

Grace shook her head. "No! You can't. Not while me Marshall's still alive! What about your young'uns? No, no. It ain't good!"

Grabbing Grace's trembling hands tenderly, Bill reassured her, "Gracie . . . we will work it out. Not now but someday."

Out of Grace came an uncontrollable, deep sigh of relief.

On September 1st, 1939, Nazi Germany invaded Poland and triggered World War Two. When the news came over the radio, Bill and Grace were in shock and wondered how it would affect Canada and their personal lives. They had no idea at the time that Canada would prosper economically from the war. The war efforts would require resources that Canada could produce, such as lumber, minerals, and food. New industries would emerge, and old ones would reopen.

The war seemed so far away and surreal to the Fenton home, but as Canadian troops left for Europe from Halifax two weeks after the war was initiated, reality struck home. Some of Bill's friends and family members were in the first deployment of soldiers.

Every evening before they went to sleep, Grace reminded the children to pray for the Canadian troops and for the war to end. The anxiety that came with the threat of the Germans bombing Canada was always in the back of their minds. Although Grace was not a practicing church member, she was raised in a Baptist home, and she believed in the power of prayer.

Winter seemed less harsh to the Fenton family that year. The air was still frigid, the nasty freezing wind still blew off the ocean, and snowstorms came and went. But that winter Grace did not have to worry about scrounging for food. Bill kept to his word and took care of her and her family by providing food and wood for the woodstove.

Grace had no idea where he acquired the wood, and she did not ask. One day, an old, rusty, red Ford truck filled with birch and pine logs drove up to the house. Two scruffy disheveled men with long beards, unloaded the truck. Critch and Arthur piled the wood at the back door.

"Maw . . . I never seen such a bunch of wood. It's like we got a forest near the back door," laughed Critch. "I'm guessin' I don't have to get driftwood."

Grace smiled at Critch. "I'm guessin' you don't, but don't go a-thinkin' you'll be doing nothin'. You gotta split some of those logs and make kindlin'. I'll find you work, so don't you worry."

On Christmas Eve, Grace told the children, "Go git one of your stockin's and hang it on a chair. Mind you, Audrey and Arthur, put only one stockin' out. If you git greedy and put two, Santa may leave you coal."

Grace could not help but snicker because these two had tried this for the past few years.

"Aw Maw . . . me stockings are dirty. Do you think Santa will still give me something?" inquired a concerned Arthur.

Grace responded, "Oh, deary me. He might pass out and we'll find him layin' on the floor in the mornin'."

The rest of the children laughed and mercilessly teased Arthur about his stinky feet and socks.

Over the past several Christmases Grace had not felt very festive, but this year Bill's generous contributions lifted her spirits. Not only had he bought all the stocking stuffers for the children, but he also provided them with a goose and all the trimmings for their Christmas meal.

Bill asked Grace what he should get the children for Christmas, and she firmly said, "I don't want to spoil them young'uns. Then they be expectin' it. An orange for each and a pencil would do them just fine."

Oranges were too expensive for Grace to afford, and the children seemed to always be needing a pencil. Bill insisted they all should have a candy cane as well. She gave in and let him purchase the items.

"Off to bed, Audrey and Arthur. Fran, put wee Suzie to bed," instructed Grace. "You older ones can help git things ready fer Christmas supper."

Critch got busy plucking the goose, Grace was preparing the stuffing, and the two girls were washing the dishes when Grace heard a dripping sound.

"Shushim! Listen. Land sakes is the ruff leakin'?" Grace looked up, searching for a wet spot on the rough, planked wooden ceiling.

The three children also heard water dripping. They wandered around the room looking up at the ceiling.

Splash! Critch stepped into a puddle of water. "Maw . . . it's here. It ain't the ruff."

Critch held up Arthur's drenched stinky sock that was hung over the back of a chair.

"Oh, fer Pete' sakes. That silly young'un. Critch, wring that out!" ordered Grace.

Fran and Marg were giggling in the corner. Critch burst into laughter. "I guessin' he didn't want to be killin' Santa. Guessin' he took us seriously. Now it ain't just stinkin' but it's wet too. Smells like Tucker on a rainy day."

They carried on about Arthur and his soaking wet stocking, while they did their evening chores with periodic fits of laughter.

On Christmas morning, the children were so surprised as they reached into their stockings and each pulled out an orange, a pencil and a candy cane.

"Santa musta be rich this year," Audrey squealed.

"A ball . . . a ball," yelled Suzie.

"No, tis not a ball, wee one. Tis an orange. You eat it," stated Grace.

Suzie tried to take a bite out of it. "Yuck . . . yucky . . . yucky."

"Wait. I'm gonna peel it for ya," laughed Marg.

"I'm so glad I worshed me stocking," declared Arthur.

Arthur's proclamation set Grace, Critch, Fran, and Marg into fits of laughter.

In years gone by, the children's Christmas gifts were hand-made by Grace. One year she made small rag dolls. The boys' dolls were soldiers with helmets, crafted from grey socks. Christmas supper was whatever was in the cupboards. Even if that were only porridge with a bit of molasses in it. This indeed was a Christmas full of joy, wonderment, and full bellies.

Since Bill had to be with his own family that Christmas, he told Grace he would see her on the 26th. The day after Christmas, as he promised, he was back in their kitchen, stomping the snow off his feet and making a grand entrance, yelling, "Ho, Ho, Merry Christmas."

The children surrounded Bill, the young ones hugging his legs and the older ones shaking his hand. Gratitude for Bill's generosity flowed in the room.

Grace couldn't help but feel guilty when she thought of Bill's family. Yet she was also relieved and comforted to have a good man in her life, who provided for her and the children. They stepped over the line and became intimate a few days after Christmas. Part of her believed she owed him, so she gave in to his advances. Another part of her wanted to hold Bill just as much he wanted to hold her. She hoped Marshall would never find out. Grace knew it would kill him.

Grace was gravely concerned that Bill's wife would discover their secret before Bill had spoken to her. One day, while at Sobeys Groceteria, Grace overheard a woman saying, "Six children and her husband still alive. What a whore!"

CHAPTER 8

Adjustments

On January 30th, 1940, Bill was visiting, and he and Grace were laughing and joking when a knock came at the door. It was a man from the telegram office. He handed Grace a handwritten note from the telegram he received, from the Kemptville Sanatorium. Marshall had passed away.

Kentville

Mrs. Marshall Fenton   Jan 30th 1940

Regret husband passed away this morning Telephone instructions Undertaker Hiltz Kentville

Dr A. F. Miller

Funeral Expenses   Jan. 30/1940
Cost of casket placed on train at Bridgetown for Antigonish including all services. $150.00

Charges from Bridgetown to Antigonish $22.50
Charges from Antigonish to Isaac Harbor 30.00
                            Grave digging   7.50
Share of cost $35.00   Total 210.00

After reading the telegram out loud, Grace's legs gave out from under her. Bill gently scooped her up in his arms and sat her on a chair. Kneeling in front of her, he brushed her hair away from her face and kissed her forehead softly. When he was certain she would not pass out, he got up and put the kettle on. "A strong cup of tea is what you need."

"Sorry Bill . . . I'm not sure why I'm feelin' so poorly right now."

"Well, you will be having a baby in a month or so and you just found out your husband died. I think that would be the reason, Gracie girl."

"I know, but I was expectin' it someday. After the last time I seen him, I was sure he would never be comin' home ag'in," she whispered.

They made the funeral arrangements over a couple of strong cups of tea. Bill generously paid the two-hundred-and-ten dollars for the funeral and burial.

On Friday, February 2nd, at 2:30 p.m., Grace, her children, and a few of Marshall's family members piled into the small Salvation Army Citadel. Seated on the old wooden chairs, they waited for the captain, who was an ordained minister, to arrive to perform the service. Grace glanced at Marshall's family. It was obvious from their nasty looks that they were displeased that Grace was pregnant. She knew they were not impressed by the way the children were dressed. They were dressed in the best clothes they owned, which looked like items fit for a rag bag, but at least they were clean. The children bathed the night before and Grace insisted they comb their hair for the funeral. Grace wore her best dress with her apron over it to hide the stains and the hole.

She was not sure why, but she felt embarrassed by their disapproval. *Marshall's kin folks had done no visitin' when he was in the sanatorium. They hardly comed around to see us a'fore that. They had no uses for me. They knew 'bout Suzie and didn't do no vistin' to see her,* Grace thought,

Bill did not attend the funeral, because as Grace said, "Folks gotta enough to wag tongues 'bout."

Grace's reflecting was interrupted when Captain Dowis entered the room and began what turned out to be a very loud and somber "hellfire and brimstone" sermon. The older children were especially

42

upset and had trouble containing their sorrow. Several times, Grace had to remind Fran and Marg to hush. They were sobbing so loud that the captain gave them a disapproving look. Grace felt she needed to be strong and shed no tears in front of her children. Audrey was struggling with Suzie who sat beside her, squirming, and chattering. Audrey's shushes were louder than Suzie's babbling. Arthur was bored and sat sideways on his chair staring at the relatives.

"Oh Lordy, will dis ever end," Grace whispered under her breath.

When the funeral finally came to an end, she paid the captain. Grace knew she should thank him for the service, but she was feeling so out of sorts from the lengthy guilt-ridden sermon that all she wanted to do was get home. Briefly she spoke to Marshall's family and left in such haste she almost left Suzie behind.

Grace wanted to leave Pictou now that Marshall was dead. She had enough of the sneers and gossip, and she was terrified of encountering Bill's wife when she went to town. To avoid running into her, Grace would send one of the three older kids to do errands. Grace also knew people thought the baby she was carrying was Bill's.

Grace discussed her concerns and fears with Bill, as they lay in each other's arms late one night. Bill understood the dilemma that Grace was experiencing. He too was concerned about the inevitable conflicts that would arise amongst his family and the Fenton family, once the full truth was revealed about Grace and Bill's relationship. That night Bill and Grace made plans to move to Antigonish, approximately fifty miles away. There was a coal mine there and he would make an application for employment.

"What's goin' to be happenin' to your family?" inquired Grace.

"That's my problem, Grace. My wife has had suspicions for a while now. I will deal with it. Don't you worry your pretty little head over it," Bill reassured her, as he rubbed her shoulders.

Grace could not help but worry about it. She felt like she was stealing a man from his family. Grace then decided she had to stop thinking about Bill's family and concentrate on her own.

Over the following two weeks Grace and the children packed up their belongings.

The children asked too many questions and rightly so. "Where are we goin' Maw?" "How comes we movin'?" "When is we movin'?"

Grace and Bill had chosen not to give the children information that they might reveal to friends, neighbours or classmates. All Grace would tell them was, "You will like it. 'Tis a surprise."

They filled a few wooden boxes and several cardboard boxes Critch found behind the Groceteria. Grace had no idea when they would move or how, but she knew she had to get packed in case this baby decided to make an early appearance. As far as she could tell, she was due around the end of March.

Bill did not come around as much because he had business to take care of connected to the move. He had been gone over a week and Grace was afraid Bill had changed his mind. Her thoughts were reeling for days around the possibility that she had been a fool.

"How could a man like Bill love a mess like me? I'm just plum dumb . . . six kids, one's cripple, one in the oven . . . What man with any sense would be a-wantin' such a brood? Maybe he woke up and knew he's done with the lot of us." Grace worked herself up into a state of turmoil. Her nights were restless and her appetite lacking.

The children kept asking where Bill was and why he was not coming over. Grace let her anxiety get the best of her and blurted out, "Maybe he's not comin' back. Maybe he's fed up with the lot of us!" She rushed into the bedroom, threw herself on the bed and sobbed.

Grace pulled herself together after a short time and was sitting at the table mending socks when there came an unexpected knock at her door. To her surprise and delight, Bill walked into the kitchen. He had been away for ten days. In her haste to get into his arms, she knocked over the basket, tripping on the well-worn socks scattered on the floor.

"Oh Bill." She let the wave of relief wash over her and down her cheeks, as Bill held her.

"Gracie, did you think I wasn't coming back?" He took her face in his hands and looked straight into her watery, blue eyes. He knew his answer. "Oh, my sweet Gracie. I should have got word to you."

Bill looked around at the piles of boxes, the home in disarray. "I see you are packed and ready to leave."

Grace nodded as he pulled her towards the table to sit down. "Grace, we need to talk."

Grace was trembling as she turned her face towards the ceiling with her eyes closed. She thought, *here we go. My nightmare's 'bout to happen.*

Bill took both her hands in his. "Gracie, I told my wife about us. She has made it clear to me that she will never let me have a divorce. She does not believe in divorces. She sees it as an unpardonable sin." He took a deep breath and said, "So we can never get married, like we had hoped."

Looking into Bill's eyes, Grace said, "'Tis that what you wanna talk 'bout?" Then she started to laugh with relief. Bill was puzzled.

"I was thinkin' you was gonna leave and stay with her."

"No . . . no. I want us to still be together, but I need to be clear, marriage is not an option," declared Bill.

Marrying Bill would have been a dream come true, but at that point in her life it was not essential. Grace just wanted to be with him, married or not.

"So where was you fer the last ten days?" she asked.

Bill winked and said, with a huge smile on his face, "I was in Antigonish. I found a house for us and got a job in the coal mine. I was getting things prepared to start our lives together."

CHAPTER 9

Somethings Amiss

At the beginning of March, the same old, rusted, red Ford truck pulled up to the house with the same two scruffy men who delivered the wood in the fall. They loaded all the Fenton's belongings and the worn-out, meagre furniture.

Bill arrived in a shiny blue Plymouth car, just before the truck left.

He handed the men a piece of paper with the Antigonish home address on it and some cash. "Make sure you fellows go straight to the house. I will pay you the other half when the job is done. That way I can make sure you don't stop and have a few drinks before."

"You sure know us, Billy Boy," laughed one of the men. "See you at the new place in 'bout an hour."

The children were so excited to have a ride in Bill's car, especially the ones who had never ridden in a vehicle. Grace could not remember the last time she had been in a car. They headed to their new home with four children and Tucker piled in the back seat. Audrey sat in the front between Bill and Grace, with Suzie on her knee.

It was a cool, sunny March Day and the snow was starting to melt.

Looking in the side-view mirror, Grace thought, *Goodbye Pictou. I'm a-hopin' in Antigonish, life is better.*

The children babbled on so much that finally Bill sternly said, "Enough talking. I can't concentrate on the road. Hush up now. We will be there soon."

When they arrived in Antigonish, Bill kept on driving. Grace sent him a questioning look.

"Just wait. You will see where we are going," said Bill.

About one mile south of Antigonish, Bill pulled off the main road on to a side street. Just around the first corner he pulled into a snow-covered driveway behind the old red Ford truck. Bill's two friends were almost finished unloading the truck.

The children piled out of the car and stood in front of a two-story home. It looked sturdy, though the windows were dirty, and the paint was peeling in spots. Compared to the small run-down three-room home they had left behind, it looked like a mansion. Grace was in awe at the size of it.

When they entered the house, Critch said, "Look Maw, no cracks in the walls and no newspaper to keep the wind out!"

"You right, it will be a mite warmer," Grace replied.

Grace walked up to a living room wall and pulled on a piece of old torn wallpaper.

"I know it's an old home, Gracie, but we can fix it up," Bill said nervously as he watched Grace.

"Oh, Bill, 'tis perfect! A good scrubbin' and lick a paint will make it just fine."

Even though the house needed some tender loving care, Grace and her children had never lived in such a wonderful place.

Tucker went out to explore the yard as the children explored the house. In the kitchen were a large wood stove and a pantry. The living room was spacious enough for a couch and a few chairs. A big, galvanized bathtub sat in the bathing room. The only running water was in the kitchen and it was cold water. Grace was used to that. The second floor had three bedrooms, one larger than the others. All the walls were covered with translucent flowery green wallpaper. Grace smiled as she visualized the children yanking off the peeling wallpaper. The oak floors were scratched and grey from wear in spots that had borne heavy foot traffic over the years. The upstairs rooms had floor grates open to the downstairs, allowing the heat to rise and flow through them. The house was probably a grand love-filled home, many years ago.

"Yup, plenty room for dis family!" Grace said aloud.

Yet Grace had a gnawing feeling that something was amiss. A cold chill ran down her spine as she entered the main bedroom. The same chill came and went when she entered the bedroom across from it. She knew it was not from the frosty air in the unheated place.

There was a ton of work to be done so Grace did not have time to investigate her feelings any deeper. First priority was asking Bill to light the wood stove to warm up the place. The next two weeks were a flurry of cleaning, unpacking, and getting their new home in order before the baby came.

The day Grace announced, "'Tis looking a mite good. If I do say so," was the day she went into labour. In the early afternoon, her labour pains started. Bill was at work in the mine and a doctor was not close by. Since this was her seventh child, Grace realized she would probably have a quick delivery. Four hours later, the two older girls assisted Grace with bringing the new baby into the world.

The baby not only looked healthy but also sounded healthy. When he was born, he cried so loud that Fran thought all Antigonish could hear her infant brother. This baby was not placed in the warming oven, nor would his bed be a dresser drawer. This little one had a crib.

Marg cleaned the baby, diapered him, and wrapped him in a blue blanket that had been Arthur's when he was an infant. Fran cleaned up the room from the birth. Proudly, Grace placed the baby in the crib she had purchased at the Salvation Army Thrift Store in Antigonish.

As Grace sat in the old familiar rocking chair beside the crib, she told Marg, "The young'uns can come in now."

When the bedroom door was opened, the rest of the children rushed in and gathered around the crib to see the new baby. All except Suzie who waited so she wouldn't get stepped on. She was not going to be excluded from the happy event, so she dragged herself to the crib and pulled herself up, holding on to one of the crib rungs. Suzie teetered and Audrey reached out to catch her.

Suzie firmly said, "No. I do it." Biting into the sheet and mattress and holding onto the crib with her left arm, she stood and leaned against the crib. "See Audrey, I'm standin' too," proudly declared Suzie, as she joined in the joyful family occasion.

The children tossed around several names, but it was Critch who got to name the new baby. Critch chose Howard Marshall. Grace asked where he got the name Howard.

Critch replied in a matter-of-fact fashion, "I don't know. I just like it."

"'Tis a good strong name," agreed Grace.

When Bill arrived home, the house was all a-buzz over the new baby boy. He had barely walked in the door when Critch took Bill's lunch pail from him and scooted him off to see the new arrival. Bill liked the name, and he agreed the baby looked like a strong little fellow. The unemotional tone of his voice surprised Grace.

Over the next few weeks Bill appeared indifferent towards Howard, although he was not unkind. Grace wondered if he was yearning for his own children and if his children missed him. Occasionally when Bill watched Grace's younger children playing, he would grow quiet and have a distant look in his eyes. Grace knew that if he wanted to talk about his children, he would bring it up. Otherwise, it was a topic not to be discussed.

Now and again, when Grace was in her bedroom with the baby, she felt the hair standing up on her arms and a chill run down her spine again. When she thought she saw a shadow of a woman in front of her, near the curtains, she would close her eyes and shake her head. It was gone when she opened her eyes. Strange things had been happening in the house since the birth of the baby. Some of Howie's baby items had gone missing. The wooden bench in the upstairs hallway did not seem to stay in the place she put it. At first, she thought the children were moving the bench, but one time there was no one home but Grace, Howie and Suzie, and the bench was moved to the corner. The children kept talking about a lady who they saw out in the yard. By the time Grace went outside to investigate, the lady disappeared. When she asked the children where the lady was, they would shrug their shoulders and say, "She was just here." Tucker was also acting strange. Unexpectedly he would run upstairs and start barking. They would find Tucker in Grace and Bill's bedroom, barking at the curtains. Something was definitely amiss!

CHAPTER 10

Mystery Lady

Grace was in the kitchen preparing breakfast when a scream from upstairs echoed through the house followed by, "Maww, Maww Maww . . ." Grace was so alarmed that she dropped the spoon in the pot of hot porridge she was stirring. She raced up the stairs and to the girls' bedroom. Sitting on the floor was her wee Suzie, face pale, lips quivering, pointing to the old cracked floor-length mirror on the closet door.

"Girly, what you all worked up and hollerin' 'bout?" a winded Grace questioned.

"Maw, sheee . . . was here . . . in the mirror." Suzie's voice was trembling.

Grace saw only Suzie's reflection in the mirror. She sat on the floor beside her daughter, pushed Suzie's bangs out of her eyes and rubbed her back. Gently she said, "Calm down, wee one. Tell me, who was here?"

Suzie was breathing rapidly, and her eyes were as big as saucers. "Maw, 'twas that lady. That lady who's been a watchin' us when we are out back playin'."

"Tell me's what she's a lookin' like. Does she look like Maw?"

"No, Maw, she's a mite perdy with long black hair. You has short hair."

"Don't you think I is perdy?" teased Grace.

Suzie's eyes rolled upward, and she shook her head, "Maw, no 'cause you just a maw!"

Grace was amused by her daughter's explanation. Since Suzie had calmed down Grace continued to discuss the lady in the mirror. From what Grace could understand from four-year-old Suzie's description, the lady had long black hair down to her waist. She was tall and wore a long flowing white cotton dress, the long sleeves trimmed with lace. She was bent down to tie up her shiny black boots. Then she stood up and brushed off her dress as if though it had dust on it. She looked directly at Suzie and extended her hand as though beckoning Suzie to come to her. That is when Suzie started to scream.

Suzie just kept repeating, "Maw, I don't like her. She makes me 'fraid!"

They were interrupted by Fran hollering from downstairs, "Maw, the porridge is burnin'!"

"Land sakes!" Grace said as she scooped up Suzie and ran downstairs to a kitchen filled with black smoke. The outside door was opened, and Fran and Marg waved tea towels in the air to clear the smoke.

Grace fed the children toast and jam and sent them off to school.

All that day Suzie clung to Grace. Every time Grace turned around; frightened Suzie was underfoot. As the hours passed, Suzie seemed to relax, and she was her giggly self by the time the other children came home from school.

Grace did not mention Suzie's episode to Bill. She figured he would think Suzie was just concocting stories. Prior to this incident, Grace had seriously questioned whether this lady was in fact a ghost. She had heard many ghost stories throughout her life, colourful threads woven into the fabric of Nova Scotian culture. Yet she had never seen one. After Suzie's encounter she had to reconsider her interpretation.

The next day Grace and Fran went about their daily household chores once the four older children headed out to school. Grace kept baby Howard and Suzie close at hand, walking on pins and needles, wondering when the ghost lady would appear again. It seemed this ghost lady had an interest in Suzie and her siblings.

The morning passed without incident. In the early afternoon, Grace told Suzie she would be taking her nap in the living room on the couch. Prior to this no one was allowed to sleep on the new couch with the floral upholstery, so Suzie was delighted. A dresser drawer was used as a makeshift crib for the baby, in the living room. Grace covered Suzie with an old quilt, the baby with a blue knit blanket, and tucked them both in for their afternoon nap.

In the kitchen Grace got a bucket of water to wash the floors. When she returned, she checked on both of her sleeping children. The baby's blanket was not on him.

Wondering if Suzie had taken the blanket, Grace gently lifted the quilt, but the blanket was not there.

That's a mite strange . . . I was sure I covered the baby up with the blue blanket, she thought.

Fran entered the room as Grace was searching for the blanket. "Maw, what's you doin'?"

"I was sure I put a blanket on Howie. Can't find it. Go fetch me anudder one, girly."

Fran left to do as her mother asked. She returned with the blue knit blanket. Grace glanced at the blanket, then at Fran, then back at the blanket.

"Where did you fetch that from?" asked a bewildered Grace.

"Maw, it was in the crib upstairs."

"Is you sure it was in the crib?"

"Yuppers . . . right there layin' in the crib as you put it." Fran sensed that her mother did not believe her. "Honest, Maw. It was there!"

"Fran, I believe you. Now fetch me the Pine-Sol for me worsh water to clean the floors," instructed Grace, trying to change the subject.

Once again Grace experienced unexplained chills running down her spine. Frantically she glanced around to see if the mystery lady was visible. "Ghost lady, I know you moved the baby's blanket. Stays away from me younguns," she said firmly yet with a quiver in her voice.

The rest of the day they carried on but not as usual. Grace did not let the baby or Suzie out of her sight at all. Fran kept complaining that Suzie was getting in her way. Fran knew her mother was not acting like herself but felt she could not pry.

Bill worked late that day and he arrived home after dark. His supper was in the warming oven. The older kids were in bed. Grace had put Suzie back on the couch to sleep and Howie in the dresser drawer beside her. Just as Grace sat down in the living room, Bill entered through the back door. He went straight into the kitchen and didn't find Grace there. "Gracie, where are you?"

"I'm in the livin' room, Bill," she whispered loudly, trying not to wake the two sleeping young ones.

Bill could barely hear her. He turned the corner into the living room and stopped suddenly at the sight of a disheveled Grace, the baby in the drawer and Suzie on the couch. "What in the world is going on here?" he asked.

"Shush. You will wake 'em," whispered Grace. She pointed to the chair beside her to indicate Bill should sit. Bill was famished, but he could tell Grace was upset so he sat down and waited for her to fill him in on what was going on. Grace told him about the mystery ghost lady; how the children had seen her in the yard; how she had seen a shadow of a woman near the curtain upstairs; how Suzie had seen her in the mirror and about how today the baby's blanket was moved from downstairs where Grace had covered Howie with it, to the crib upstairs.

"Bill, I got a real bad feelin' 'bout this ghost lady. I'm 'fraid she could hurt these two young'uns." Grace's shaky voice concerned Bill.

"Grace, you should have told me about the ghost lady. I suspected something was wrong. You've been preoccupied lately." Bill took both her hands as he often did to comfort her. "We will figure this out. I do believe you and the kids. When I was young, I seen a ghost at the old mill in Pictou." Bill told her the story, then had his supper and headed to bed. He told her they would discuss the situation more in the morning when his head was clearer. Grace slept on the couch that night, dozing in and out of sleep, Suzie in her arms, Howie in the dresser drawer next to her.

The next morning Bill told Grace, "I think we need to find out the history of this house. Find out what the ghost lady wants. If we can figure out why she is here, we may be able to do something about it.

We really can't move right away, and I know we will not find another home this size for rent this low."

An exhausted Grace agreed with Bill. "I guessin' so. We will make do for now."

The ghost lady did not make another appearance, nor did she make her presence known for the following two days.

One afternoon, three days after the blanket incident, Bill was at work, Fran was in town purchasing blackstrap molasses and yeast. Critch, Marg, Audrey, and Arthur were at school and the baby was fast asleep in his crib at the end of Grace and Bill's bed. Grace and Suzie laid down to take a nap. They snuggled up in bed under the warm heavy grey and brown quilt, which Grace had made many years ago. Suzie fell fast asleep within moments and was softly snoring. Grace ran her hand delicately over Suzie's face, taking in the beauty of her peaceful wee resting child. As Grace pulled the quilt up around her shoulders, she noticed that the black yarn quilting knots were beginning to rot and fall out. Her mind was on replacing the quilting knots when that cold chill ran down her spine and the hair on her arms stood up. She tensed up and felt nauseated. There was no doubt that the mystery lady was present. Grace forced herself to sit up. She stared at the foot of the bed in horror. Bending over the baby's crib was the mystery woman. Terror gripped Grace. *Who is she? What does she want? Why is she here?* Thoughts were whirling through her mind. Grace was frozen in place for a few seconds.

She wanted to snatch Howard up and tell this ghost woman to leave, but all she could do was weakly utter, "What do you want? Who is you?"

The ghost woman looked up at Grace and scowled. Her green eyes were not only filled with anger but also grief. It sent shudders throughout Grace's body, and then the lady vanished.

Once Grace was finally able to move, she jumped out of bed, grabbed her sleeping baby and held him protectively to her chest. Grace sat down on the bed, for fear that her legs would give out from under her. Her heart was beating so loudly in her ears that she did not hear Fran come into the bedroom.

"Maw . . . you look as white as da sheet. Maw, you, ok? Maw, I will fetch you a glass of water." Fran was in a panic. She grabbed a glass of water that was on the bedside table. "Here, Maw . . . drink dis!" She handed the glass to her mother, but then rapidly grabbed it from Grace's hand. "No, Maw . . . don't drink it! Sometin's wrong with it."

Grace and Fran could see white powder floating in the water. Some of the white substance had settled at the bottom of the glass. They stared at each other in horror. Fran returned the glass back to the bedside table and hastily sat on the bed and snuggled up to her mother. "Maw, what's happin'? 'Tis weird stuff goin' on here. Maw, I'm 'fraid."

"So am I, so am I, girly." Grace wrapped one arm tightly around Fran, while still clutching the baby.

Could that be arsenic in the glass of water? Was the ghost lady trying to get rid of me? thought Grace as she exhaled a deep, nervous sigh.

Grace told Fran to pick up Suzie, who was now wide awake and trying to get past them to get off the bed.

Suzie was not impressed because she was stubbornly independent. "No, Fran! I do it meself," squealed Suzie.

"Suzie, 'nough, girly! This time let Fran carry you," ordered Grace.

They fled down the stairs into the kitchen. Fran put Suzie down on the floor and got the dresser drawer to put Howie in. Grace pulled a chair to the cupboards and stepped up on the counter. She reached up and ran her hand along the upper cupboards. She almost knocked over the bottle of arsenic she was searching for. The bottle was missing the screw-on cap. She continued to blindly feel around for it, but it was not there! Grace always screwed the cap on tightly after she used it in the mice trap that were strategically hidden around the house. As she stepped down from the counter, she told Fran, "Stay here. I be right back."

Grace headed upstairs to her bedroom and searched for the bottle's cap. Behind an old vase on the nightstand she found the cap hall-full of arsenic powder. Grace knew that no one, not even Bill, knew where that arsenic was stored.

CHAPTER 11
Developing a Plan

When Critch, Marg, Arthur and Audrey got home from school, they were all hyped up about the duck-and-cover bomb drills they had practiced at school. Marg was horrified at the thought of ever using the manoeuvres. Arthur enjoyed the drills since it kept him from doing math. Audrey found it interesting and drove the teacher crazy with her many questions of why they had to practice and when they would use it.

"Maw, ifin we hear the sirens go off we have to get under our desks and roll up in a ball," explained Audrey. "In case them their bombs are droppin'."

Marg trembled and said, "Let's hopin' we never has to do that."

"Yah. Ifin we are in the hall, we gotta git against the wall and drop and curl up like a possum," exclaimed Arthur. "As ifin it's gonna keep us from gittin' blown to bits."

"That's 'nough, Arthur. You're scarin' the girls," Grace interrupted. "Go and git changed and do your chores."

"Ah Maw, can't we play outside for a bit," asked Audrey.

"No, not tonight. Get about your chores now!" Grace realized her tone was sharp, but she wanted the chores done so they could have a family meeting after supper.

The children's chatter about dropping to the floor and hiding under their desks was a sober reminder of the war. So much was happening at home that Grace had barely thought about the war overseas. Arthur was right, Grace thought grimly. If a bomb went off close to the school, there would probably be casualties. Maybe some of the children would survive and be protected from falling debris if they were under their desks. Grace shuddered at the thought of their town being bombed by the Germans, but she had more pressing matters on her mind, and getting supper prepared was one of them.

When Bill arrived home, Grace took him aside and told him about the incident with the ghost lady. They both agreed it was time to make a safety plan.

After everyone finished their meal, the boys rose to leave the table, but Bill said in a serious tone, "Everyone stay where you are. We need to have a talk."

The boys reluctantly sat back in their chairs. Usually when Bill said this, one of them was in trouble.

"I didn't do it!" proclaimed Arthur. "'Tis one of the girls did it."

"No, we didn't!" Marg stood up and yelled back at Arthur.

"Stop your tattle-taling, sit down and tell me more about this lady you've been seeing," asked Bill.

They looked at each other and then back at Bill.

"What do you need to know, Bill," asked Critch.

"Tell us when and where 'bouts you saw the lady," said Grace.

Soon everyone started talking at once. The air was filled with a collective excitement and nervousness.

"Stop. One at a time. Critch, you go first," insisted Grace.

"We was outside over yonder at the back. I know we're not 'pose to be there. Anyways we was. The lady was standin' there and watchin' us playin' tag," explained Critch. "I think we saw her a few times at the same spot."

Audrey, Arthur, and Marg agreed with Critch.

"Was she doing anything else besides standing there?" inquired Bill.

"No, she was just a watchin' us. Oh . . . wait. One time when Suzie scooted up towards her, she stepped forward," replied Marg. "She looked kinda like Maw when we are doin' somethin' we're not 'posed to."

"Yup, she sure did. Suzie got her little butt outta there fast," agreed Critch. "She might a been there 'bout ten minutes maybe. Then she was gone. Kinda like she just disappeared." Critch suddenly realized what he had just said, "Oh . . . wow. Is she a ghost?"

Fran started to speak, and Grace put her hand on Fran's arm and shook her head. The afternoon episode must be kept a secret for the time being. The other children would be scared to death and their imaginations would make matters worse.

"My turn, my turn," Suzie interrupted. "I seen her in the mirror."

"We know you did. Critch, we do suspect she is a ghost. Now, children, I am going to tell you what I found out today," explained Bill.

Marg and Audrey covered their mouths in horror and their eyes were wide open.

Arthur boastfully said, "I know'd she was a ghost."

"Calm down, girls, and listen." The children shushed and Bill began to tell the story he had uncovered. "Apparently, a young couple built this house. They had a baby boy. The little boy went missing just before his second birthday. They feared he wandered into the forest and a bear, or another animal got him. Some people thought a stranger had taken the child. There were a lot of rumours going around. The mother was devastated and wandered around the woods and the town, in her long white nightgown and laced-up black boots, calling for her little boy. She did this for years. Most of the town folks knew who she was and often would help her return home."

"How do ya know dis Bill," asked Grace.

"John, the old miner. He has been here for sixty years. He said this happened way back, many years ago," Bill responded.

"What happen to the mother?" asked Fran.

"She lost her mind. Her husband put her in the lunatic asylum, in Halifax, then sold the house and moved. He heard the mother came down with tuberculosis and died a few years after she was placed. It seems the mother is the ghost that has been haunting this house since her death."

"Bill, what are we gonna do?" asked Grace, anxiously.

Everyone started talking at once, expressing their desire to move out of the house. Bill halted the chatter: "We can't move, well at least not now. While your mother and I figure out what we are going to do, you children are never to be alone in any room or alone in the yard. Stay in twos no matter what you are doing."

"Even when we are doin' our business in the outhouse?" said smarty pants Arthur.

Bill gave Arthur a stern look. "Not right in the outhouse but someone should be standing outside the outhouse door. You need to tell me or your mother if you see her again. Now go and do your homework and get ready for bed. This ghost lady does not seem to want to hurt any of you. So, you can rest easy."

When the older children were upstairs, the boys thought this was a great adventure and discussed different ways they might get the ghost lady to talk to them and reveal her secrets. The girls were not impressed with the boys' plans. They just wanted the ghost gone.

Bill and Grace discussed the situation further when the older children and Suzie were in bed. They sat in the living room, Howie asleep on Grace's lap.

"We are missing something," Bill was convinced. "The ghost lady started showing herself when the children were in the back yard. I just got a feeling we are missing something Grace. Maybe we can figure out why she is not at peace."

It was dusk when Bill ventured into the back yard. He remembered Critch saying "Over yonder at the back" where they weren't supposed to be. Bill thought he must have meant at the back of the lot near the woods. Bill made his way to the tree line and, exploring the area, he noticed something dark on the ground. He got on his knees and swept the grass aside. There he found a few rotting boards which he moved to one side. What he found underneath startled him! Bill left it uncovered. He marched into the house and up to the boys' bedroom.

"Critch, come with me," he ordered. Critch was familiar with Bill's stern tone of voice. He immediately jumped out of bed and followed Bill down the stairs, through the kitchen and into the backyard.

"Critch, is this where you saw the ghost lady?" Bill pointed towards the boards he had laid out.

"Yup. It sure is." Critch took a few steps closer to the boards.

"No, Critch, don't go any closer," Bill yelled. Then he explained, "Critch, there is a deep hole there. I think it is an old well. I won't be able to check it out until it is daylight. Now back to bed, boy. We have work to do in the morning."

CHAPTER 12

The Well

The next day, Bill and Critch further investigated the deep hole. "It looks like an old well. I wonder . . . Critch, fetch that long rope from the pantry." As Critch ran to the house Bill yelled after him, "Bring the flashlight too."

Bill could not shake the feeling that this well had something to do with the mysterious ghost lady. He did not think it was a coincidence that the ghost lady first appeared by this hole. "The only way to put my mind at ease is to take a look and see what, if anything, is down there," he said to himself.

Critch returned with the rope and flashlight. Marg, Audrey, and Arthur were hot on his heels. They wanted to know what the rope and flashlight were for.

"Kids, I don't want you too close to this hole. Stand back everyone, except Critch. You come here," instructed Bill.

Bill and Critch got on their knees and Bill shone the light in the hole. "Yes, it is an old well. Whoever covered this over did a piss poor job," declared Bill, shaking his head in disapproval.

"Yup, for sure. Bill, did you see that shiny thing? Shine the light over dat way and down," Critch pointed.

"Something is shiny down there. Might be pyrite, a rock that looks like gold but isn't," explained Bill. "Well, the only way to know for sure is if one of us goes down and has a look."

"I will go. I can do it," Arthur said as he ran toward the hole.

"Stop, Arthur. I am a bit too big and may cause it to cave in. I think Critch should go down since he is older and has his wits about him. Do you mind going down if I rope you off good?" Bill asked Critch.

"Ah Critch gits to have all the fun," moped Arthur.

"I will do it, Bill," quickly agreed Critch. He saw this as a great adventure.

While the crew was investigating the hole in the back yard, Grace and Fran were cleaning up the kitchen from breakfast. Grace could not stand it anymore. "Das it, Fran. Grab Howie. Suzie, you come too. We are gonna see what's a happenin' out there."

Grace held Suzie's hand to steady her, so she could walk. Suzie was now able to walk with support. Fran wrapped Howie in a blanket, and they headed to the tree line in the back yard. As Grace approached the group, she hollered, "Bill, tis it an old well like you been thinkin'?"

"Land sakes, Gracie, don't yell. All Antigonish can hear you! Yes. It is an old well. I am going to tie a rope around Critch and lower him down. He has the flashlight because we noticed something shiny way down there. Don't you worry. I will make sure he is tied up good and the rope is anchored to that big beech tree over there," said Bill, pointing to the tree.

"I'm trustin' you to keep me boy safe." The idea of her son going down in an old well terrified her. "What if he gets stuck or what if the walls cave in?'"

Ignoring Grace, Bill secured one end of the rope to the tree and made a sling around Critch's legs so he could be lowered down. The rope came up the front of him so he could hold on to it. Bill handed Critch the flashlight. "Ready boy? Try not to touch the sides too much. If for any reason you aren't comfortable, tell me. I will pull you up."

Critch nodded. "I'm ready Bill."

"Arthur, you can come behind me and help me hold the rope to lower your brother down and then to bring him back up," said Bill.

"Alright. I finally git to do somethin'." Arthur proudly took his place behind Bill.

Slowly Bill and Arthur released the rope as they lowered Critch into the old well.

"Stop, I see the shiny thing. It's kinda stuck in the wall," Critch's voice echoed from the depth. "Gives me a minute."

Critch put the flashlight in his mouth and used his two hands to scratch away the dirt around the object carefully as not to dislodge chunks of the earth wall. The buried object was part of a gold chain. He pulled on it gently, but it didn't move. So he yanked on it and it fell out of his hand to the bottom of the well.

"Oh no. I dropped it! Lower me down some more," Critch bellowed.

Bill and Arthur continued lowering him. Occasionally, Bill would yell down the hole, "You still doing fine?"

As they were about to run out of slack in the rope, Bill called, "Hey, boy. Are you ok?"

Critch didn't answer.

Bill yelled again, "Critch, answer me! Are you ok?"

Still no answer. Bill tensed with panic.

Grace ran to the hole and knelt at the edge. "Critch Marshall Fenton, you answer me right now. Is you ok?" she screamed as loud as she could.

"Yes, I'm fine. I found sometin' for sure," he screamed back. "Gives me a minute. Pull me up when I tug on the rope."

Everyone heaved a huge sigh of relief.

Grace felt that same cold chill run down her spine. The hairs on her arms were standing up. She glanced around to see if the ghost lady had appeared. The ghost lady was not visible, but Grace knew she was present. Just as Grace was about to demand that Bill pull her boy out of the well immediately, Critch tugged on the rope. Slowly Bill and Arthur hauled him up. When Critch emerged from the well, everyone held their breath in anticipation.

"What's you find, Critch?" asked Arthur, expressing the excitement they all felt.

"Just wait till you sees what I got," Critch announced as he pulled himself out of the well's entrance, stood up and brushed the dirt out of his hair and off his clothes.

"Look at dis!" He first pulled the gold medallion and small chain out of his pocket. He handed it to his mother. "Dat ain't all."

From inside his shirt, he pulled out a small human skull. "Der's more bones down der too, Maw," he said.

The girls screamed and ran to their mother. Arthur wanted to hold the small skull.

Staring at the objects, Bill said, "I knew it. I knew there was something in the well. I bet you it is the bones of the two-year-old that went missing years ago. That is why the ghost lady was standing here. Give me the skull." Bill held out his hand. "Ok, everyone back to the house. Kids stay in the house 'til I get back. I need to go into town and talk to an officer at the RCMP office. Critch, get yourself cleaned up. You're coming with me."

Bill gave Grace a hug and kiss. He whispered in her ear. "I think we solved the mystery of the ghost lady. Maybe she will be at peace now."

Grace leaned into his ear and said, "I sure hope so. She was here when Critch was in da well. I was fearin for him."

Grace opened her hand and examined the medallion. It was engraved with an image of a woman holding a child. The necklace was small enough for a child. She held the necklace out to Bill. "Better take this with you. I don't want no dead young'un's stuff in me home."

The RCMP from Antigonish sent a crew of officers to retrieve the rest of the remains from the well. The officer in charge wondered why Bill searched the bottom of the well. Bill never told them the whole story. He knew some folks would never have believed the ghost story.

The bones of the ghost lady's son were removed, and railway ties were placed over the well opening. Bill built a small fence around it to protect the children.

The family never saw the ghost lady again. Grace believed that she was now at peace.

CHAPTER 13

The Diagnosis

Weeks after the discovery of the bones in the well, Grace was still on edge, although there had not been any more visits from the ghost lady. The family returned to their normal routines without living in fear.

Spring came and went, bringing blooming wildflowers such as daisies, devil's paintbrushes, rose bushes and Queen Anne's lace, which grew profusely in the field and backyard. The chokecherry trees were magnificent with their fragrant white blossoms.

Summer was the time to pick wild blueberries, strawberries, gooseberries, and sugar plums. The children did not mind picking berries, except for Fran, who wanted to spend her time in town with a young man she had recently met. Berry-picking meant Grace would turn those delicious berries into homemade jams. Sugar was rationed, because of the war, but she had saved a few months' worth of ration coupons for her preserves. Grace made the bitter chokecherries into sweet, delicious jelly that made one's mouth water as it was cooking.

Grace showed her children how to identify the shiny, deep green mint leaves that grew in the woods near the house. They were harvested and dried for tea. Dandelion coffee was made from roasted and ground-up dandelion roots.

Suzie tried to do her share of picking and gathering. Critch would carry her to a strawberry or blueberry patch or amongst mint leaves and sit her down. Grace had to remind her that she needed to fill the bowl, not just her stomach. The fruits of the fields and woods were plentiful, so Grace did not mind if the children ate while they picked, if they picked more than they ate. That skill Suzie had not developed yet.

Many summer days were spent on the beach. The salty smell of the ocean was the sweet aroma of home to Grace. She was one of the sixth generation of Nova Scotians. The ocean was in her blood. Those beach days were filled with swimming, building sandcastles, and gathering clams. The boys collected firewood and they roasted the clams over an open fire on the beach. It was a treat like no other for the family.

When the children weren't playing on the shoreline, they were in the nearby woods playing hide-and-seek, building forts, or searching for nature's treasures. Suzie was not able to join the other children when they played in the woods. She could not scoot on her bum on the forest floor, there were too many rocks and branches. She could only walk if an older child or adult stood on her right side and put their arm around her waist to help her keep her balance. After she stepped her left foot forward, the person supporting her would have to use their foot to push her right foot forward. Suzie had to bear all her weight on her left leg. Her right leg was weak and lacked muscle mass. This was a painstaking chore for Suzie and the helper.

Grace decided it was time to investigate the shock treatments Dr. Smith had recommended for Suzie three and a half years prior. Grace made an appointment with a doctor in Antigonish. That day, Bill was on an afternoon shift at the mine, so he drove Grace and Suzie to the appointment. Suzie was thrilled that she was the center of attention and got to go for a car ride.

"Where we's goin?" asked Suzie.

"To see a doctor 'bout you crippled leg and arm," answered Grace.

"He's gonna get me walkin', Maw. Maybe he can fix me arm too." Suzie was optimistic.

"Not sure what he can do . . . We will see!" Grace had heard of other children who had permanent paralysis from polio, but she was determined that if there was something that could help her girly, she would do her best to make it happen. At the top of Grace's mind was her desire to give Suzie a life as normal as she could have.

When they got to Dr. McLellan's office, the nurse led Grace, Bill, and Suzie straight to an examination room. The smell of disinfectant was strong, the black-and-white checkered floors were shiny, and the table that contained jars of cotton batting, gauze pads, Q-tips, and other medical items was glistening clean. A spotless white sheet covered the examination table.

The nurse pointed to two white-padded chrome chairs and said, "Have a seat. Dr. McLellan will be right with you."

Grace sat down and Bill placed Suzie on Grace's knee. Bill took one look at the immaculate white chairs and decided to remain standing. Suzie reached out and tried to grab items off the nearby table.

"Suzie don't be touchin' stuff," scolded Grace.

Dr. McLellan walked in. He introduced himself and shook Bill's hand. Bill introduced Grace as his wife and pointed to Suzie, saying that she was his stepdaughter. Grace blushed when Bill introduced her as his wife, because she knew she was not his wife legally, but she did love how it sounded when Bill said it.

Dr. McLellan turned to Suzie. "Who is this sweet young lady on her mother's lap?"

"I'm Suzie Fenton!" Suzie proudly declared.

"Suzie, I am pleased to meet you. What can I do for you today?"

"I wanna you to help me walk and use me arm," Suzie said, as she grabbed her floppy underdeveloped right arm to show the doctor.

Dr. McLellan was well acquainted with polio. He had seen many children and some adult patients afflicted by the dreadful disease.

"Mom, could you put Suzie up on the examination table please." The doctor picked up a reflex hammer and his stethoscope, while Grace put Suzie on the table.

After examining Suzie, he said she had good reflexes in her left leg and left arm. The muscles in her left arm and leg were extra strong from working double time to compensate for the two lost limbs. Suzie had hypotonia on the right side of her body. Her leg had poor muscle tone and some nerve damage. Her right arm had no muscle tone and neuropathy (also known as dysfunctional nerves). She was underdeveloped physically. Her weight and height were like that of an average two-and-half-year-old. As far as he could tell her mental and emotional development were typical for a four-and-half-year-old, or indeed, almost five-year-old; Suzie corrected him on that matter.

After discussing his assessment of Suzie, Dr. McLellan shared his recommendations. "Suzie may benefit from shock therapy. There are machines available that you can use at home with instructions in the box. Suzie should have treatments every day. It is best if you keep her on a schedule for her treatments. You can purchase the Home Medical Apparatus at the local drugstore in town. I am afraid it is expensive but it could help her gain muscles tone in her leg so she could walk independently. It may also revive the nerves in her leg. I am not sure about her arm, because it seems to be severely damaged, but we could try. I would also suggest you give her a shot glass of red wine twice a day, to help with her circulation. Give her one shot glass after breakfast and one after supper. She must have something in her stomach before drinking the wine. Alcohol can be hard on the stomach, especially for one so young."

Then Dr. McLellan turned to Grace. "Mrs. McLoed. I noticed when you brought Suzie over to the examination table you were walking a bit bent over. When you did straighten up, you seemed to be in pain."

"Oh, I had polio the same times as me Suzie. It got me in the back. Me back does gives me troubles," explained Grace.

"Mrs. McLoed, what if your husband takes Suzie out to the waiting room and I examine your back." Grace began to object, but Dr. McLellan put his hand up and continued, "It will only take a few minutes. If we do it know you won't have to come back into town for another appointment this week."

Grace reluctantly agreed to the examination. When Dr. McLellan finished his assessment, he invited Bill back into the examination room. The doctor asked the nurse to watch Suzie while he had a conference with her parents. "Mrs. McLoed, your upper and middle back muscles are weak from your bout of polio. There also appears to be some nerve damage. Although I recommend shock therapy for many of my polio patients of all ages, I do not feel it would be beneficial for you. It could damage your spinal cord. There really is little that can be done, and I am sorry to tell you this, but your back will get progressively worse. You probably will eventually be walking bent over at a forty-five-degree angle." Dr. McLellan demonstrated the position. "I can give you a prescription for morphine to alleviate the pain."

Bill put his hand on Grace's shoulder and gave it a gently reassuring squeeze. She put her hand on his. With tears in her eyes, she asked the doctor, "How long 'fore I's bent over?"

"I cannot say. It could be a year, or it could be fifteen years. No one can predict that. You may have to use a wheelchair one day. It's important that you keep moving as much as possible. Do not let yourself get to the point where you are in severe pain before you take the morphine if you want it to work properly. Make sure you get a good night's sleep every night. I am sorry I couldn't give you better news." Dr. McLellan then left the room to give Grace and Bill a moment to digest his diagnosis before they left the office.

"Gracie my girl, we will figure it out." Bill reassured her as he always did. "We will talk about it this evening. As for now, let's get Suzie, then pick up some red wine, your prescription, and that shock box, or whatever it is called." Grace felt emotionally and mentally numb from the news she had just received, so she was thankful that Bill took charge.

CHAPTER 14

Shocking Experience

Bill was stunned at the price of the shock treatment box. It cost $10.60 for the box and battery. That amount of money could buy one week's worth of groceries, but Bill knew how much Suzie's therapy meant to Grace. Bill paid for the box, the morphine and wine, and kept his thoughts on the price to himself.

On the ride home, Grace was quiet, but Suzie talked enough for all three of them. She babbled on about how clean the Dr.'s office was and how pretty Nurse Betty was.

"Suzie didn't the Dr. give you a lollipop?" asked Bill.

"He sure did give me one . . . an orange one," replied Suzie.

"Suzie, go ahead and lick on that lollipop 'til you get home please," pleaded Bill.

When Bill looked at Grace, she mouthed *thank you*.

When they arrived home, Grace put her anxiety aside to focus on preparing supper. Suzie was excited about the new apparatus and told her siblings about it.

"Can we try it after supper, Maw?" she asked.

"Tomorrow, Suzie. Bill and me has to figure it out first," answered Grace.

That night when the younger children were tucked into bed, Bill placed the shock treatment box on the kitchen table. He opened it up and read the directions inside the lid out loud:

"Directions for using the D.D. Home Medical Apparatus with Mesco Dry Cell Battery.

The small switch to the left of base is used to put the battery in operation. The cell is working only when this switch is on the contact stud, consequently the life of the cell will be prolonged by taking care not to turn it on until everything is ready for the application, and to turn it off promptly when through. The rheotome, or current interrupter, should commence to hum or vibrate as soon as the switch is turned on its stud; if it does not do so, draw in towards the coil and release it suddenly. The contact screw should be adjusted so that the vibration will give an even, continuous hum or buss; it should never be turned so far as to press the vibrating spring against the coil. Three different currents are obtained from the apparatus: the mildest of primary current (alone) by placing the cord tips in the contact holes marked 1 and 2. By placing the tips in 2 and 3 the secondary current (alone) is obtained, and by placing them in 1 and 3 the combined currents are given out. No. 1 is negative, and either 2 or 3 positives when used with No. 1. Nos. 2 and 3 together give alternating pulsations. The strength of all the currents can be varied by moving the regulator or core-shield of the coil; the further out the shield is drawn the stronger the currents become.

One cell will last from 4 to 12 months, according to the length and frequency of applications. We furnish a copy of 'The Electropathic Guide' and the following accessories with each Battery.

Two metallic tube hand Electrodes, 2 Conducting cords with tips, 2 Improved sponge Electrodes, 1 Foot Plate Electrode, 2 Insulating Wood Handles for attachment to the two metallic hand electrodes or the two sponge electrodes, or to one of each - Moisten the sponges to use them and have them as nearly dry as possible when put away in the box.

To take out the Battery, loosen the screws with clamp. It's the flat upright pieces; the Battery cell can then be lifted out of the plated cup, on lifting the latter, which is hinged to an upright position. In replacing the Battery, notice that the Carbon Pole belongs and fits to the flat upright at the back of the base, and the Zinc pole fits the upright nearest to you.

The battery will last many months with proper use. Price of extra cells, 60 cents each. Apparatus complete, $10.00."

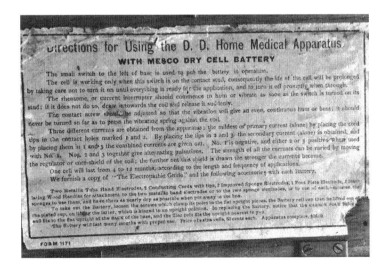

Occasionally, Bill paused and pointed to the items the directions were describing.

"My land sakes . . . good thing you're an electrician, Bill," declared Grace. "I'da never be able to figurin' how it works."

Once Bill had deciphered how it worked, he got Grace to wet the sponges and wring them out. Bill put the sponges on the probes and set the machine to the lowest dosage of electric shock. As an electrician, Bill was no stranger to getting zapped by electricity occasionally.

"Here we go," said Bill as he turned it on. "SON OF A BITCH!" Bill yelled out in pain, as the shock coursed through the probes and into his leg. "That current is strong enough. If this doesn't awaken Suzie's muscles and nerves, nothing will."

Grace looked at him in horror. "I hope the wee thing can handle it. I'm a guessing we owes it to her ta try."

"It's a good thing she is having some wine before. I hope it takes the edge off the pain," said an empathetic Bill.

The rest of the evening the couple discussed the prognosis Grace had received from the doctor. Grace cried on and off during their conversation. She felt bad that Bill had a crippled stepdaughter and may also have a crippled wife.

Bill reassured her, "We will take things as they come. I love you, Gracie, my girl. I am here for the long haul."

Yet knowing that Bill had already left one woman made Grace wonder what was going to keep him with her when things got tough. How could she be sure he would stay? These questions were running through her mind that night as she lay in bed beside Bill, who was snoring.

The next morning Suzie could not wait for breakfast to be over so she could try out her new machine. "I'm gonna be walkin' cause of me machine," she told her siblings at the breakfast table. "Me arm's not goin' to be tiny anymore."

"Suzie, it's goona' take time. Maybe a long time," explained Grace. "Now drink the wine I gave ta you."

Suzie took the small shot glass, put it to her lips and after the first taste said, "Yuck! That's yucky, Maw." She spat and sputtered. Her face was scrunched into a grimace. Her siblings laughed at the sour face Suzie made.

"Drink it now. It's not 'ppose' to taste good but 'tis good fer you," insisted Grace. "Hold your nose and drink it down. Then go wait fer me in the livin' room."

Suzie pinched her nose and gulped the bitter liquid down, wiped her mouth and tongue off on her sleeve and headed to the living room to wait for her mother. Grace wanted the wine to take effect on Suzie, so she took her time helping the two older girls clean up from breakfast. When Grace brought the Medical Apparatus into the living room Suzie was asleep on the couch. She prepared the machine and shook Suzie awake.

"'Tis time Suzie," said Grace. "I see the wine made you a mite sleepy, girly." Grace smiled, then her voice become solemn. "Now Suzie, do you remember the doctor told you dis will hurt?"

Grace told Suzie to pull her night gown up. Grace put one of the dampened sponge electrode rods on her calf and the other one above her knee.

"Yup I do. I can do it, Maw, if it helps me getta walkin'," Suzie asserted.

"Let's do it. I'm gonna turn it on after I count to three. Take a deep breath, Girly, when I say three."

Grace started to count, and Suzie got ready to take a deep breath on the count of three. As soon as Grace turned the machine on Suzie let out an excruciating high-pitched scream and then she started to wail. Grace turned the machine off and grabbed her sobbing child.

"Shhh, girly, I know it hurts, but if you gonna walk we has ta do dis," Grace said, consoling Suzie.

"Maw . . . no no . . . it hurts me bad . . . please no no . . . it hurts me bad. Maw," begged Suzie between sobs.

The other children ran into the living room to see what the ruckus was all about. As usual, Arthur was the first to speak. "We swore Maw was killin' you! For Pete' sake, Suzie, don't give us a fear like that agin'! Be a big girly now."

Grace jumped to her feet and angrily waved the children out of the room. "The gang of you go outside now. Leaves us be."

Seeing Suzie in such agony made Grace sick to her stomach. She would bear the pain for her little girl if she could, but Grace had to keep her perspective. If Suzie had any chance of walking this had to be done. Grace took a deep breath, fought back tears, and sat down beside Suzie. Calmly she said, "We' do it one more time and then you can have some hot chocolate. I put a big heap of chocolate in it fer you."

Suzie was still trembling from the trauma she had experienced ten minutes earlier. She looked at her mother with pleading, tear-filled eyes and bit her trembling lip. Diverting her eyes from Suzie's face, Grace took a deep breath to gain the courage to continue. Grace was trembling as she turned on the machine and once again applied the probes to Suzie's leg. Again, Suzie screamed and cried, blood dripped from her bottom lip as she was biting down on it so hard. Grace put Suzie on her knee, wiped the blood that was running down her chin and rocked her in her arms. The treatment and wine had exhausted Suzie. Within a few minutes, Suzie was asleep in Grace's arms, still, but softly whimpering.

"Lord gives me and me Suzie strength. I don't know how me girly will be able to take dis every day," Grace prayed as tears streamed from her eyes, landing on her sleeping child's head.

CHAPTER 15

Learning a Lesson

The next week of shock treatments was excruciating for Suzie and Grace. Grace decided she would give Suzie a bit more wine in the morning and a wet face cloth to bite down on. The probes were leaving burn marks on Suzie's leg, so Grace had to make sure she did not apply the probes in those areas. It took a few days for the burns to heal and fade. After each treatment session, Grace applied cold cloths to the burns and rubbed some Minard's Liniment on sections of her leg that were not burned. (Minard's Liniment was made with camphor, ammonia water and medical turpentine. It was believed to help sore muscles, relieve pain and stimulate the circulation).

During the daily shock sessions, Tucker stood outside near the living room window howling. When the sessions were completed, Grace let Tucker into the house. Tucker rushed to Suzie, jumped up on her and licked her face. Then he'd lay on the floor beside her, and they slept for at least two hours.

After the first two weeks of shock treatments, Suzie seemed to have more tolerance to the pain. Therefore, Grace increased the number of shock applications on Suzie's leg. Suzie still screamed and cried, but her screams were not as loud, and she did not sob like the first week.

On the sixth week, Grace started the therapy on Suzie's arm. Looking at Suzie's tiny little arm and hand she had no idea where she would place the probes because there was no muscle tone at all, only skin and bones. Her arm was no bigger than a broom handle, and her hand the size of a small plum.

"Suzie, me girly, we're gonna try your arm today," said Grace.

"Ahh Maw. I bet that's gonna hurt real bad," Suzie whined. "K, Maw, I try to be a big girl."

"Suzie, me girly, you are a big girl ta be doin' this. Maw is proud of you even if you screams and cries," Grace reassured her.

Grace placed one probe on the front of Suzie's forearm and one probe on the upper arm and turned on the machine. Suzie did not flinch or scream. Grace thought she must not have it plugged in properly, so she unplugged it and plugged it back in and turned on the machine.

"Here we go, girly," Grace said, and placed the probes on Suzie's arm. Still no reaction. Grace was puzzled.

"Maw is the machine broke," asked Suzie. "I don't feel nothin'."

At first, Grace also thought the machine was broken but she could see small burn marks on Suzie's arm from the current.

"Let's try your leg and see ifin we can figure it out," replied Grace.

Grace applied the electrode probes to Suzie's leg and Suzie bit hard on the face cloth. A scream escaped between her clenched teeth.

"It's a workin'. Guessin' we have to turn the machine up fer your arm. Let's finish doin' your leg first," stated Grace.

Once Suzie's leg treatment was finished Grace continued the treatment on her arm. With the machine on the lowest setting, Grace gave Suzie five shocks. The only complaint from Suzie was that she felt nauseated.

"Lays down and you will be feelin' better," Grace told her.

Grace knew if Suzie was not feeling any pain in her arm that the nerves were probably damaged beyond repair. At Suzie's next medical appointment Grace would inform the doctor.

By the sixth week, Suzie was receiving five shocks per session, which was the initial recommendation from the pharmacist.

At the supper table one evening, Arthur piped up out of the blue, "So are you still a crybaby, Suzie, when you gits your shock treatment done?"

All the children laughed at his statement.

Suzie looked up at him sheepishly. Even thinking about the treatments upset her stomach. Often, she had nightmares about having shock treatments all over her body and being burnt everywhere. Grace would hear Suzie whimpering or screaming in her sleep and would rush to her side to comfort her wee girly.

Bill was furious with Arthur and the rest of the children who were amused at Suzie's anguish. He stood up and as he headed to the living room he commanded, "All of you come with me right now, except for you, Grace and Suzie."

Bill took out Suzie's medical apparatus and prepared it to be used. He set the power on the second level and called each of the children over to have a taste of what Suzie was going through. One by one, starting with Arthur, he turned the machine on and placed the probes on each child's leg. Each one of them screamed in agony and the two girls had tears running down their cheeks.

"Now, next time you think about teasing Suzie, you will think twice. I hope you learned a lesson and see what hell she is going through. Now go and finish your supper, the lot of you," stated Bill sternly.

They sheepishly returned to the kitchen table and saw Suzie with her head resting on the table, covering her left ear. She had tears in her eyes.

Grace was rubbing her back and comforting her, "It's alright, me girly."

"I'm so-so sorry Suzie, I'm so sorry, forgive me," cried out Arthur. The rest of the children also requested forgiveness and they all hugged her.

CHAPTER 16

The Engagements

At the end of September 1941, Fran announced that she and Wallace were engaged to be married. Fran was mature for seventeen, but Grace could barely believe that her eldest would soon be a wife.

The house was all a-buzz with wedding preparations. Fran wanted a stylish wedding like she had seen in the Chatelaine magazines. Grace sternly repeated that they did not have much money to spare, and the country was in a depression. With sugar, butter and meat being rationed, it would be challenging to make the cake and meal for the wedding. Fran had to settle for a small church wedding and a luncheon at home.

Although Fran was displeased, she accepted that her dream wedding was not to be. The one dream she would not give up was to have a fancy, modern wedding dress, made of white satin and lace. Her fiancé, Wallace, gave her the money for the dress materials and sewing notions.

The following month, autumn flowers were collected and dried for her bouquet. The wedding was to take place in February. Six months was long enough to plan a simple wedding. It allowed Grace time to make Fran's bridal dress and bake a few desserts that could be stored.

Fran was in a dither over every detail and just about drove Grace off the deep end.

Between Suzie's treatments, caring for her family, and helping Fran with wedding preparations, Grace was feeling very fatigued.

Meanwhile, Marg had been sneaking out of the house and seeing a man. His name was Norm, he was a miner and twenty-five years old. Marg was only fifteen years old, and she knew Bill would have a problem with the age difference. It was time to tell Grace her secret and engage her mother in telling Bill.

When Marg and Grace were alone in the kitchen, Marg approached her mother. "Maw, I has to tell you somethin'," said Marg nervously.

Grace had noticed Marg had not been herself for the past few weeks, which aroused her suspicions. "What's up, me girly?"

"I've been seein' someone. His name is Norm."

Grace thought Marg must have been dreaming since she was home all the time, except for when Grace sent her to the store in town. "When did you has time to be seein' this fella?"

Marg was silent for a few moments as she tried to concoct a story instead of telling her mother the truth. "Ah . . . darn, Maw . . . I been sneakin' out at night to see him . . . and . . . we is engaged."

Marg waited for Grace to reprimand her, but Grace just stood silently. Grace pulled a chair out from the kitchen table, sat down, and pointed at another chair, indicating for Marg to sit down.

"I'm not happy that you was sneakin' out, but at least you told me da truth. I'm not happy 'bout you bein' engaged. You're a bit too young, girly. Have you laid with him? Tell me the truth," insisted Grace, giving her a stern look.

Marg shamefully nodded.

Grace had to ask, "Are you in a family way?"

"No, Maw."

"Well, I figure you better be gettin' married before you is."

Then Marg told Grace Norm's age. Grace was not thrilled about the age difference, and she knew Bill would have a problem with it. Sensing her mother's concern, Marg quickly stated, "Maw, if you and Bill meet him, I know you'd like him. His age wouldn't be a-botherin' you."

The two discussed the best way for Norm to be introduced to Bill. They planned on raising the subject at supper time. Grace also invented a plan to get Bill and Norm alone, so they could talk and get better acquainted.

That evening at supper, Fran was going on and on about herself and Wallace and the wedding. When Fran stopped a moment to eat, Marg looked at her mother and her mother gave her the nod signal. Marg then took the opportunity to tell the family that she was seeing someone, and his name was Norm.

Before Marg said too much, Grace interrupted, "You two need to be a bringin' your beaus 'round here fer supper on Sunday. Bill and I need to meet Norm. We need to get to know Wallace a bit more too," said Grace.

Wallace and Norm came for supper that Sunday. Wallace was a tall, handsome man and he worked in the mine as a labourer. Norm was short and stocky, much like Bill. Norm had been discharged from the army and was looking for work.

During the meal everyone chattered and asked the men tons of questions. Where did they live? Did they like to fish or hunt? What was it like fighting in the war? How many family members did they have? The poor men barely got to reply or eat before another inquiry was blurted out.

Norm's nervousness was evident in his trembling hands and stuttering speech. As everyone was finishing their apple pie, Grace could not stand to see the poor guy tormented anymore. "Bill, why don't you take Norm outside fer a cigarette and have a talkin' with him? Critch, you go with 'em. Wallace and Fran, have your tea in the livin' room and take Suzie and Howie with you. Marg, Audrey, and Arthur, help me cleans up from supper."

Of course, Arthur complained that he was missing all the action and he did not like doing "woman's work." Marg was in such a fluster, she rewashed clean dishes that Audrey put on the counter to be put away. She wondered what Bill was saying to Norm and what he would think of the age difference.

While the two men were outside, Norm asked, "Bill, I reckon that you know my age and you seem to be ok that I am datin' Marg. I want to be askin' your permission to marry her."

Bill was not expecting Norm's request and he took a few seconds to reply, "Norm, you know she's young and may not be ready to get married yet."

"I realize she is young. I gotta find me a job afore we set a date. I was thinkin' we could get married next summer. That would be givin' us time to get to know each other better and plan the weddin'."

Bill nodded and said, "Well, Norm, sounds like you have a plan and a good head on your shoulders. I give you, my permission. Now you need to ask Marg."

Bill had no idea Marg had already been asked. Norm kept that secret to himself.

Thirty minutes later the two men entered the kitchen. They were laughing and going on like two old friends. Marg could not believe her eyes or ears and was relieved, to say the least. Norm gave Marg a reassuring wink and she knew all was well. Their engagement had Bill's approval.

That evening Marg and Norm announced their engagement and future wedding plans to the family. Everyone was full of congratulations and Bill announced, "We need to have an engagement party."

Grace almost fell off her chair. The last thing she needed was another item on her agenda. She felt like screaming at Bill.

Sensing her mood, Bill quickly added, "It will be a small gathering. The girls can make a few sandwiches and the men will all pitch in for a keg of beer. Grace, you just relax, and we will take care of it."

The next Friday, the party was held at the Fenton home. Bill invited a few work buddies. Fran and Wallace invited two other couples they knew. Marg invited one of her girlfriends and since Norm barely knew anyone in Antigonish, he came by himself.

Two of Bill's friends brought their fiddles, another brought his harmonica, and they played East Coast, foot-tapping, jigging music. Marg pulled several tablespoons from the kitchen drawer and Suzie and Audrey played the spoons. It was a festive time with jigging, laughing, and drinking.

Grace should have predicted that the party would go on all night, since they were Easterners, after all. Bill's friends from work had brought two kegs of beer and she knew the men would not leave until the beer kegs were empty.

The following two weeks, Fran and Wallace were busy setting up their future home. They rented a two-bedroom apartment in downtown Antigonish. Grace gave them what she could spare in dishes, cooking ware and linens. The remainder of their apartment was furnished by friends, neighbours, and purchases from the thrift store.

With most of the extra money going towards the wedding, Christmas was sparse that year. The family decided only the two youngest children would get gifts. Suzie received a doll and Howie a toy truck, both bought at the thrift store. Their stockings were stuffed with a pencil, a candy cane, and an apple. (Oranges were in short supply during the war.) Christmas supper was chicken and dumplings.

CHAPTER 17

The Wedding Day

On a windy, overcast, and frigid February 7th, 1942, the house was a whirlwind of activity, as the family prepared for the afternoon wedding. Audrey was cleaning the living room and kitchen. Critch and Arthur were shoveling the driveway and back yard walkway. Fran rearranged the serving area, the kitchen counter and table several times and made the boys move the chairs three times. With the leftover material from her wedding dress, she made bows to decorate the chairs. Fran wanted everything perfect for the reception.

The wedding was to be held in Wallace's hometown, Isaac's Harbour, but Grace had insisted the reception be held in Antigonish in the Fenton home. It was an hour's drive to Isaac's Harbour, but Grace would see that her girly had a nice reception. Besides, it was easier to have the reception in Antigonish so the bride and groom could go straight to their apartment after it was over.

At the Baptist Parsonage in Isaac's Harbour, at 00 p.1: m., with both the Fenton and Davidson families in attendance, Fran and Wallace's wedding service began. When Bill walked Fran down the aisle, Arthur played "Here Comes the Bride" on his harmonica. The bride was a vision of beauty with her hip-length, loosely curled, dark brown hair, her pale complexion and her long white satin and lace wedding dress. Her netted veil, edged in lace, framed her delicate face. Wallace had bought her six roses to carry down the aisle instead of dried flowers.

As the minister started the service, Grace had tears running down her face. Her girly was getting married, and it seemed like just yesterday she was running on the shoreline, with bare feet and sometimes a bare butt, chasing butterflies and dragonflies.

The service was short and sweet. Then the bride and groom and all the guests headed back to Antigonish.

The wedding reception and partying went on all afternoon and into the wee hours of the morning. Bill had invited a few of his friends from work to the luncheon and they, as usual, brought two kegs of beer.

There was plenty left over from the luncheon to feed the guests for supper. The newlywed couple headed to their apartment shortly afterwards. The Davidson family left at the same time and returned to Isaac's Harbour.

Grace was exhausted and wished Bill's buddies would leave. At nine that night, she told Audrey and Arthur to go to bed, then she tucked Suzie and Howie into their bed. Critch had joined the men and Grace figured he would take care of himself. As Grace was heading up the stairs to go to bed, she overheard one of Bill's friends saying that they sure were going to miss Bill.

She stopped on the steps and addressed the man, "What do you mean you're gonna miss Bill?"

CHAPTER 18

A Bit of Revenge

Grace went in the backyard to look for Bill. He was three sheets to the wind from all the beer he had consumed. Regardless, Grace needed to know why the man said that he would miss Bill. She tapped him on the shoulder. "Bill, I be needin' to have a talkin' with you."

"Gracie, my love, here you are. I was wondering where you were," he laughed.

Grace put her arm around Bill and started directing him away from the group. "Bill, I be needin 'to know why the men said they're gonna miss you. Why is they gonna miss you? What was they talkin' 'bout?"

Bill was staggering and she had trouble holding on to him. "Bill, stand still, and tell me what they mean?" Grace was growing impatient.

"Oh they . . . missss me . . . move to Truroo. I . . .job in . . . mine." Bill's inebriated speech made him hard to understand, but Grace heard "move, Truro, job, mine."

Grace was furious. "Bill McLoed! And when was you gonna to be tellin' me 'bout this?"

Bill laughed. "You're cute when you got knickers in twist, my Gracie."

Grace stormed back into the house. It was not in her nature to hit anyone, but she was so angry she wanted to smack him. Grace knew there was no reasoning with him in his present state. In the morning when he was sober, she would talk to him. "I hope he's gonna have a headache in the mornin'," she said audibly.

When Grace awoke the next morning, she was still upset with Bill. A bit of revenge was on her mind, so she took out the frying pan and started breakfast. There was an open vent that led into their bedroom just above the wood stove. The smell of bacon and eggs cooking would awaken Bill. A hangover mixed with cooking aromas was not a good combination.

"That'll gits him outta bed and runnin' to the outhouse to be pukin'," she snickered.

Once the smell of frying bacon filled the air, Grace heard Bill's feet land on the floor and run down the stairs before there was the sound of the backdoor slamming. Through the kitchen window, Grace watched as he bolted through the snow in his stockinged feet, to the outhouse. He was in such a hurry that he did not take time to shut the outhouse door. Grace had a clear view of Bill on his knees, his head over one of the outhouse holes.

"That'll learn you, you bugger," she chuckled.

Just then she heard a second set of footsteps running down the stairs and heading outside. Critch ran to the outhouse with his hands over his mouth. He saw that Bill was hanging over the first hole. Critch moved to the second hole, knelt, bent over, and started vomiting. The sight of the two of them on their knees hanging over the reeking outhouse holes made her laugh so hard, she was snorting and holding her stomach, tears running down her cheeks.

Bill and Critch had toast and tea for breakfast, while the rest of the family enjoyed the delicious meal Grace made. Before the family left the table to do their chores, Bill announced that they were moving to Truro and his job started in just one week. While he was there, he would find a place for the family to live.

Grace forgave Bill for not telling her about the move sooner. Marg was upset at the news and did not want to leave her fiancé behind so Fran agreed that Marg could stay with her and Wallace in Antigonish, until Marg was married.

Grace knew Bill was not one to waste time and would quickly find a place for them to live.

The house was in turmoil, and it was a chore to keep Howie and Suzie occupied and out of the way. Suzie wanted to help so Grace gave her the job of tending to Howie. That arrangement did not last long as, every few minutes, Suzie was yelling because Howie was pulling items out of the carefully packed boxes. After one hour running back and forth between Howie downstairs and packing boxes upstairs, she told Audrey to stop packing and take care of the youngsters.

CHAPTER 19

Truro

The following frigid snowy weekend, Bill returned with a truck and announced he had found them a home half a mile outside of Truro. He had even found employment for Critch at the mine site as a cleaner.

The sons-in-law came to the house to help pack the truck. The wind blew the snow in all directions so fiercely that at times it was difficult to see where to place the next box in the truck. They managed to get it all done by Saturday evening.

The next morning the snowfall was softer, but the wind still blew the snow every which way. Fran and Marg hugged everyone and cried as they waved goodbye to their family. The family set out on their new adventure on that blustery day. Grace hoped the stormy weather was not an indication of what their lives in Truro would be like. If it had been a clear sunny day she would have felt better. She even begged Bill to wait one more day until the weather cleared, but he had to be at work the following day.

The one-and-half-hour drive to Truro took six hours. Grace was never so glad to reach her destination as she was that day. She was a nervous wreck the entire drive and every time Bill braked, she felt like she was going to throw up. The snow drifts caused the truck to be pulled toward the ditch. The ice underneath the snow made the truck swerve. The last twenty miles, the truck was crawling along. Grace did not have to ask the children to be quiet because they were as terrified as she was, and they barely said a word. Even Tucker was quiet, hunkered down on the floor. Grace's back was killing her.

The long driveway of their new home had snow drifts and Bill knew the truck would get stuck, so they had to walk in through two feet of snow and drifts to get to the house. The boys used their feet and hands to move the snow in front of the door.

Once they were in the house, Bill hurried to start a fire in the wood stove. Grace walked around her new dwelling. It was smaller than her other home in Antigonish but seemed cozy enough, with no ugly peeling wallpaper. The greyish-blue walls looked like they had been recently painted. Grace thought there must have been a sale on that colour because it covered every wall in the house. It would have been nice if they were light yellow, but at least it looked clean, she thought. There were three bedrooms, a living room, and a kitchen with a pantry. There was an icebox in the kitchen and a root cellar under the pantry. Beside the pantry was a bathing room with a tub, a sink, and a cupboard for towels. They would still have to haul hot water from the stove but at least the sink and tub faucets ran cold water and had drains. There were several closets for storage. The living room had a small fireplace. Grace had never lived in a home with a fireplace. The back porch had a door that led to a long hall where there was another door that went to the outhouse. Grace was amazed by such convenience.

Once everyone had explored the new home, the boys and Bill started to unload the truck. The extra snow made their work twice as time-consuming. Meanwhile Grace unpacked some of the dishes so they could have supper. Grace had made corned beef and mustard sandwiches in the morning and a thermos of tea for herself and Bill. She knew there would be plenty of work to do once they arrived in Truro, and there would be no time to cook.

That night Grace told Suzie she could go to bed without her shock treatments. She made it clear that this was an exception, and they would resume her therapy the next day. Suzie was elated and welcomed the one-day reprieve.

Grace would announce when it was time for Suzie's treatments, "'Tis time, Suzie," and Suzie would cringe. Sometimes, Suzie would hide behind the sofa or under the kitchen table if she could scoot fast enough before Grace came into the room.

"Where is me girly? Where did she git too? Oh, there's me Suzie," Grace would say, playing along.

Suzie would giggle, giving away her hiding place. This hide-and-seek game brought joy to Suzie before her session, so Grace always indulged her.

Once her hiding place was discovered she made her way into the living room to once again be subject to the horrendous therapy that was supposed to help her leg and arm gain strength and function. Suzie was now able to bear the second level of shock, but Grace did not like the burns it left on Suzie's delicate skin. The burns were wider and took longer to heal.

The days in February and March were but faint memories as the family was busy settling into Truro. Arthur and Audrey were registered at the local school and started attending the week after the move. Grace was grateful that everything had been unpacked before the two children started school. Finding where things had been placed was another matter. Grace spent most of her time that week looking for items she needed.

Howie was crawling everywhere and getting into anything he could. He got into the kitchen cupboard and poured molasses on himself and the floor. Unsuccessfully, Suzie tried to clean it up with a tea towel before her mother saw it. From then on, the cupboard doors were secured with tied twine.

Suzie was starting to get around more. Critch had made her what he called, "Suzie's walking box." It was made of plywood and built like a right-angled triangle. He put small wheels on the back, and a handle on the top. Someone would hold the walking box still while she pulled herself up with her left hand. She was able to stand. Once she was standing, she would lean into it and grab her right hand and place it on the handle. Because her right leg was getting stronger, she could walk several steps. Every day Suzie practiced walking. Sometimes Grace had to tell her to take a break because she could get too tired and fall. Grace fretted that Suzie would break her functioning arm or leg.

The shock treatments continued to be a painful experience. Although Suzie's leg was showing improvement, her arm did not seem to be benefitting from the therapy. In February, Suzie began to complain her heart was pounding so hard that she thought it would come out of her chest during the therapy. She began to throw up and was pale after each treatment. Grace knew it was time to make an appointment with a doctor in Truro.

CHAPTER 20

Dislocation

Grace took Suzie to see Dr. Slaberly. Dr. Slaberly was professional and, as Grace called it, "a bit uppity."

Abruptly, Dr. Slaberly asked, "What are you here for?"

Grace started to explain to him about Suzie's shock treatments. He cut her off. "Yes, I am familiar with shock therapy for polio. So just tell me the problem."

Grace felt intimidated and had difficulty explaining what was happening with Suzie. She stuttered several times.

"Put her up on the table and I will examine her," Dr. Slaberly said in a commanding voice.

Grace helped Suzie get on the table. Suzie was squirming because she also felt uncomfortable with this man.

"Stop moving, child!" Dr. Slaberly was gruff.

He listened to Suzie's heart, checked her reflexes, and checked her left leg and arm. When he was checking her right shoulder, he was rough. Suzie flinched and started to weep uncontrollably.

Dr. Slaberly became impatient. "Stop crying right now. You are a big girl and there is no need for that."

Suzie tried to control her tears, but she was in so much pain she kept crying.

"Did you hear me? Stop being a baby. Stop crying!"

Suzie was so afraid of him that she got control of herself and was whimpering as quietly as she could.

If this obnoxious man weren't the only doctor in Truro, Grace would tell him to shove his practice where the sun doesn't shine and hightail out of there with Suzie. At this point she had no choice but to allow his brutishness.

"Mrs. McLoed, it seems the amount of shock treatments your daughter is receiving is too much for her. From what you have told me it appears to be negatively affecting her heart. That is why she is vomiting and feels her heart racing. We need to stop one of the treatments. She needs to have therapy only on one limb from now on."

"Which ones does we picks?" Grace asked timidly.

"It seems to me the arm is gaining a small degree of any therapeutic value from the shock treatments. The leg is showing progression. I ask you this, do you want her to walk, or do you want her to use her arm?"

Grace knew there was no choice. To walk was the only answer.

Dr. Slaberly also told Grace about Truro's "The Visiting Nurses Team" and that he was putting Suzie on their list. They would visit Suzie to keep an eye on her progress. Grace was not keen on the idea of nurses being involved in their business, but she was not eager to have more appointments with this doctor either. Suzie was still whimpering on the way home. "Suzie, what's da matters with you?" asked Grace.

"Maw, da doctor hurt me shoulder. I hate that doctor. He's means to me and you, Maw. He needs a good whoopin' to learn him some manners!"

"Suzie, we have to put up with him. He's the only doctor here. I'll look at your shoulder when we gets home."

When Grace touched Suzie's shoulder, Suzie yelled and started to bawl. As Grace gently removed Suzie's shirt, she saw a lump and knew her shoulder was dislocated. Grace was indignant and called Audrey to bring some wine. When Grace was younger, she saw her mother put her brother's shoulder back into place. She knew one thing for sure: she would be damned if she would take Suzie back to that doctor to do the job, since the doctor's rough handling of Suzie was the cause of the dislocation.

Audrey rushed in with the wine and a glass. "Maw, what's the matter that you want to be drinkin'?" Then she saw the buldge on the top of Suzie's right arm. "Ahhh, I see. What can I do to help?"

"Hold Suzie on your lap. Put one of your arms 'round her tummy and used your udder hand to holds her right shoulder," directed Grace. "Here, Suzie, drinks this wine."

Suzie did not argue. She drank the wine her mother offered her.

Grace took the glass away, cupped Suzie's face in her hands and said, "Suzie, you need to sit as still as you can for Maw. I'm gonna fix you all up."

Grace put one hand on the lump and another on Suzie's arm, pulled slightly and then pushed Suzie's shoulder back into place. Suzie did not scream because she passed out. The pain was too much for her little body to bear. While Suzie was still unconscious Grace tore up a pillowcase and made a sling for Suzie's arm. Once the sling was on, she wrapped strips around Suzie's body over the sling to keep her shoulder immobilized. That would not be the only time that Suzie's shoulder would dislocate. Neither would it be the last time a rough, rude doctor would be the cause.

CHAPTER 21
Unwelcome Visitors

One afternoon in the second week of April, a nurse from The Visiting Nurses Team knocked on the McLoeds' front door. When Grace opened the door there stood a woman in a black overcoat, white dress, white nurse's cap, and black boots, holding a black medical bag. "I'm here to see how your daughter Suzie is doing. Dr. Slaberly gave us her name. I am Nurse Williams."

Grace hesitated to let her in but knew if she did not, she would be severely scolded by the doctor if she had to see him again. Grace wished she would have known the nurse was visiting so she could have tidied up the place. Unfolded laundry was piled on the couch in the living room and the kitchen counters were dusted with flour and strewn with dirty baking dishes from the cookies and bread she baked that morning. The nurse wiped her boots on the braided rag rug in front of the door and followed Grace into the kitchen, where Suzie was seated at the table, colouring, and Howie was in his highchair, scribbling on paper. Grace was not impressed that the nurse did not remove her boots, because she had washed the floors that morning.

The nurse removed her overcoat, flung it over the back of a kitchen chair, sat down beside Suzie and said, "Hello, young lady. I am Nurse Williams, and I've come to see how you are doing."

"I'm doin' fine, and how are you?" Suzie looked up and was in awe of the pretty young lady with blonde hair pulled into a bun at the back of her head. She looked so clean in her starched uniform and cap.

As the nurse spoke, she opened her medical bag and pulled out a thermometer and stethoscope. "I'm fine also. I am going to take your temperature and listen to your heart first. Then I will examine your right leg and arm."

"Be a mite careful with dat arm and shoulder," stipulated Grace. "It's just gotten better from bein' dislocated."

The nurse took out a file with Suzie's name on it and glanced inside. "I don't see anything about a dislocated shoulder. Did you go to the hospital when this occurred?"

"Maw fixed it," said Suzie proudly.

The nurse's eyes widened in disbelief, and she looked at Grace. Grace knew she might be in for a lecture from the nurse, but she was not going to be bullied in her own home. "Ya, I did at that. I have seven children and I know how ta dos a thing or twos. 'Sides, 'twas the doctor who's caused it. He was a mite rough with her wee arm. You need to be very gentles with it."

Nurse Williams scribbled some notes in her file, then rolled up Suzie's pant leg and examined her leg, feeling the muscles and bones. She then proceeded to carefully examine Suzie's arm. Grace hovered over her to ensure she did not do any harm to Suzie's shoulder.

While the nurse documented her findings, Grace sliced some warm, homemade bread. Finally, the nurse put the file into her medical case and turned to Grace. "Suzie's temperature is normal. Her heart rate is much better than when she was at the doctor's office. It is no longer racing. Her leg is gaining muscle tone, but her arm is very weak and there is no muscle tone in it, nor in her shoulder. That is why her shoulder can be dislocated so easily. Have you considered having the arm removed?"

Grace couldn't believe what she was hearing. She put one hand on her hips and waved the bread knife at the nurse. "NO!" Grace hollered, "You ain't takin' me girly's arm off!"

"But Mrs. McLoed—" The nurse attempted to get her point across, but Grace interrupted her, as she continued to wave the knife.

"NO! There be no talkin' 'bout it. She's a keepin' her arm."

Nurse Williams realized there was no reasoning with this enraged mother, so she put her coat on, said her goodbyes, and let herself out.

"Maw, is she gonna take off me little arm?" Suzie's lip trembled.

Grace patted Suzie on the head. "No . . . nobody's gonna take your arm off as long as I's your Maw. Who's wants warm bread and jam?"

"Me, me!" Howie piped up. He had been unusually quiet during the nurse's visit Grace had almost forgotten he was in the room.

When Bill arrived home from work, Grace was still fuming. She told him about the nurse's visit and the horrid suggestion Nurse Williams had put forth. Bill was appalled at the nurse's proposal and completely agreed with Grace's handling of the situation.

"Bill, can they make us let them take Suzie's arm off?" Grace asked.

"No, Gracie, my dear. They can't do that. We won't let them even try such a foolish thing. Land sakes, the poor thing has enough wrong with her. She doesn't need to go around with one arm."

Grace hoped that was the end of the subject. Two weeks later, Nurse Williams dropped in again but this time she was accompanied by an older nurse.

Grace thought, *oh no, she's brought reinforcements*. She had a bad feeling about the visit but made up her mind not to let them browbeat her. If she did not agree with them, she would stand her ground.

At first the visit went smoothly. The two nurses were playful with Suzie and even took time to engage with Howie for a bit. They examined Suzie and were careful when they checked her right arm and shoulder. The older nurse took extra time examining Suzie's right arm and especially her shoulder, remarking to Nurse Williams, "Mmm . . . I see what you mean."

Grace was feeling relaxed, but when she heard this comment, she stiffened and stared at both nurses. "What are you meanin' by that?" demanded Grace.

"Mrs. McLoed, I see that your daughter's arm is very limp and floppy and that it could get caught in places and cause her shoulder to be easily dislocated. This will be a problem all her life. Dislocations of joints can cause serious health issues," explained the older nurse.

"Dr. Slaberly was informed of the shoulder dislocation that Suzie experienced, and he recommends amputation."

Grace stood up, pushed her chair back and grabbed a butcher knife off the counter. Waving the knife and walking towards the two women, she screamed. "You git outta me house now! Git, I say now! I told Nurse Williams, you ain't takin' me girly's arm off!"

Suzie slid off her chair and hid under the table. Howie started crying because he had never heard his mother scream like this. The two nurses grabbed their coats and started rushing towards the door. The older nurse insisted, "Be reasonable, Mrs. McLoed. It's for Suzie's own good."

Grace kept advancing, waving the knife, and yelling, "I told you git outta me house now! You ain't gonna ever touch me girly ag'in and nobody's cutting her arm off!"

The nurses ran out the front door and Grace returned to the kitchen and noticed they left in such a haste that they left their medical bag behind. She grabbed it and ran to the front door, threw it outside and yelled, "Don't you ever be comin' here ag'in!"

Grace hurried to the kitchen to calm her two children. Giving Howie a cookie calmed him immediately, but Suzie was still hiding under the table sobbing and shaking with snot running down her face. Grace knelt, took out her handkerchief, wiped Suzie's nose and motioned for her to come and sit on her knee. Suzie crawled up onto her mother's knee and Grace consoled her by rocking her and rubbing her back. "Suzie, you stop your frettin'. I told you nobody's gonna cut your arm off. Nobody, no sirey."

Grace was in such a rage that she did not realize what she had done until she calmed down two hours later. "I chased them with a knife. Damn, that's not the smartest things to do. Oh my, I could gits in troubles fer that," she muttered to herself as she prepared supper.

During their evening meal Bill asked Grace how her day went.

Suzie blurted out, "I'm keepin' me' arm. Maw chased afta' the nurses with the knife. Maw told them 'You ain't cutting me's girly arm off.' You shoulda see them runnin', Bill."

Bill's jaw dropped. "What in God's name did you do, Gracie?"

Grace was not proud of how she had reacted so when she explained the events of the nurses' visit, she rested her head on her hand and looked down. Then she waited for Bill to criticize the way she handled it but instead he burst out laughing. "Well, Gracie, I am sure we've seen the last of those nurses. They should have never challenged a she-bear with her cub."

The rest of the family roared with laughter, teasing Grace, and telling each other, "Don't make Maw mad or she be a chasin' you with her butcher knife."

The nursing company never did return. Grace was sure they crossed Suzie off their list. Maybe in their file they wrote, "Crazy mother. Do not visit." Bill and Grace decided that if any member of the family needed to see a doctor, they would travel to Antigonish.

Suzie had regular nightmares about doctors and nurses cutting her arm off. It took several years before these bad dreams subsided.

CHAPTER 22

Another One

One morning in July, while Grace was making breakfast and Bill was enjoying a cup of tea before leaving for work, she bent over to pick up some wood for the woodstove and gasped from a sharp pain in her back. She didn't think Bill had heard her, so she continued her meal preparations.

"Your back seems to be bothering you more these days, Gracie. Are you taking the morphine when you need it?" asked Bill. "The doctor didn't prescribe it for nothing."

Maybe now was her opportunity to let Bill in on a secret, thought Grace.

"Bill, I've not been takin' the morphine 'cause . . . well, 'cause . . ." Grace said, as she took a mug from the cupboard, wiped her hands on her apron and sat at the table beside Bill. "Pour me a cup a tea, would ya."

He obliged and poured her a cup. "Because what? Why on earth wouldn't you take it? It will be easier for you, and I hate seeing you in so much pain."

"Bill I might as well just spill it. I'm in a family way," Grace blurted out, and nervously waited for Bill's response.

Bill stared at her for about fifteen seconds and then a smile slowly crept across his lips. "Well Gracie, I know this one is mine. I am glad you did not take the morphine. I heard it is not good for pregnant women. You were smart to stay away from it. So how far along do you think you are, Gracie?"

Bill was babbling which was not in his nature. It was obvious he was thrilled at the prospect of having a baby together, which alleviated Grace's concerns about having this child.

"Gracie, I asked you how far along you think you are?" Bill repeated.

"I'm thinkin' I'm 'bout four months," she responded.

At the supper table that evening, Bill declared, "Your mother and I have some news we want to tell you."

The children stared at Bill and Grace, waiting for their announcement.

"Your mother is expecting another baby. She is having my baby," Bill proudly declared.

"Not 'nother one, Maw." Arthur was appalled.

"Maw, this is embarrassing. You're too old to be havin' anudder baby," said Audrey with dismay.

Critch snickered and said, "Well Maw, like you say, you lay you pay."

Grace was not impressed with Critch's smart-assed remark and was about to reprimand him when Suzie spoke, "I'm thinkin' it's great! I love babies. Hope it's a girly."

Bill was disappointed at the children's reactions, especially Arthur and Audrey's. "Listen, all of you. You had damn well better be happy for your mother and help her out a lot more. Do you all hear me! Now off you all go to do your chores before bed."

On August 8th, Marg and Norm unexpectedly showed up in Truro. They had been in Argyle, visiting a friend of Norm's. They stopped on their way back to Antigonish. Grace was thrilled to see them both. As she went to hug her daughter, Marg held her left hand out and displayed her wedding ring.

"What's this?" Grace was shocked as she held Marg's left hand and rubbed her finger over the gold ring.

A smiling Norm stepped forward. "We did it. We went and got ourselves married yesterday, at the justice of the peace. My friends stood up for us. I'm hopin' that you ain't upset with us, Grace," stated Norm.

Grace gave Marg a huge hug and congratulated them both. "I'm just fine. Glad you married. Come in da house and tell Bill and me all 'bout it."

Marg explained that her wedding outfit was the same one she wore at Fran's wedding, a blue long-sleeve, calf-length dress that Grace had purchased, at the thrift store and altered for Marg. Grace had used lace left over from Fran's wedding dress to trim the collar and sleeves. Marg had pulled her shoulder-length auburn hair back in a bun and tied it with blue ribbon. Her Aunt Inez's daisy porcelain necklace perfectly complemented her wild daisy bride bouquet. Norm said that she was a vision of loveliness and after the ceremony they went back to their friends' home and had a nice chicken supper.

Grace was relieved she did not have to worry about planning a wedding, especially since she was pregnant.

During the month of August Grace had felt the baby kicking and she wondered if she was further along than she presumed. Every time this wee one had a kicking episode her back would go into spasms and take her breath away.

"Wee one, could you be settling down some. You're hurtin' your Maw." She would talk to her protruding belly as she gently stroked it.

Suzie was so thrilled about the baby that she took every opportunity to pat Grace's tummy and talk to the baby. "You be a good girly and stays in that there oven 'til you're ready. One early bird Suzie is 'nough."

It seemed to Grace that summer and fall flew by. They did get the berry picking done and the garden harvested. She was able to put down many jars of preserves using honey she got from a local farmer. Sugar, meat, and butter were still being rationed since the war was still raging in Europe.

Bill had become good friends with a farmer. The farmer supplied them with odds and ends of meat, such as chicken wings, chicken necks and gizzards, pork feet and boiling ribs for soups and casseroles. Grace was accustomed to food rations by now and knew how to make satisfying meals with these farm scraps. One of the family's favourite meals was chicken-gizzard-and-potato pie.

Besides the food rations, the only other reminder of the war was the air sirens. When the sirens were blaring, everyone had to go into their homes or a nearby house or building. Blackout drapes had to be drawn across the windows and lighting in the homes had to be minimal. A second set of sirens with a different tone would go off an hour later, signaling all was clear.

Grace hated those sirens, not just because they reminded her that the war continued, but also because the shrill ear-busting noise startled her every time. She swore one day she would have a heart attack from the darn things.

CHAPTER 23

The Holiday Visit

A month before Christmas, Grace was missing her two older girls, so she wrote one letter that they could read when they were together.

Dear Fran and Marg,

Hope you all doin' well. Would be nice ifin you could come fer Christmas. Luv your maw."

They responded with a simple note: *Yup we're comin' for Christmas Maw.*

Although Grace grew weary as her pregnancy progressed, she was looking forward to seeing her grown daughters and catching up on their lives. Because Howie was such a handful and Grace was exhausted, she hoped the girls would give her a break and take care of her rambunctious toddler.

Just the thought of having her girls home during the holidays gave Grace an energy boost. She managed to bake cookies, two apple pies and a tomato soup cake for the festivities. She hid these in the root cellar so the men would not eat them. All three of them loved sweets.

In the afternoon of December twenty-fourth, Fran, Wallace, Marg, and Norm arrived. It was as cold as the dickens, but the sun was shining and there was no wind. They greeted each other with hugs, kisses, and handshakes.

Marg smiled at her mom and said with concern, "You're lookin' a mite tired, Maw, and big for bein' 'bout eight months along."

"That's 'cause I had seven afore this one. I'm also tendin' to Howie and Suzie all day. Makes a body plum tuckered out," replied Grace.

Grace turned her attention to Fran. "Fran, you lookin' mighty pretty and happy."

"I am happy, Maw," Fran leaned over and whispered in her mother's ear. "I may be in a family way. Shhh . . . Wallace don't know yet."

Grace gave Fran a big hug and whispered back, "I'll keep it our secret."

"How 'bout you men visit in the livin' room. We girls will fetch snacks," Grace suggested and gestured to the women. "We girlies will do our talkin' and have tea and biscuits in the kitchen."

Suzie and Audrey joined the ladies in the kitchen. They were not about to miss out on biscuits and a glass of milk. Critch and Arthur joined the men. Baby Howie was having his afternoon nap.

The men discussed their jobs and the latest world news. Fran and Marg told their mother about their cooking and cleaning adventures as newlyweds. They also asked a lot of questions, especially Marg. Marg had next to no cooking experience. When she lived at home with Grace and Bill, her chores centered around house cleaning. The extent of her cooking experience was occasionally making toast for breakfast and sandwiches for lunch.

Fran piped up, "Marg, you gotta tell Maw 'bout the chicken you cooked."

Marg curled her nose up and looked at Fran in disgust. "You just had to be a-bringin' that up, Fran. Well, I'm guessin' it is good fer a laugh or two . . . Maw, you see, I never saw you cook a chicken. Norm brings me home a chicken and tells me to cook it up fer supper the next day. The next day I take the chicken out of the icebox, and I was lookin' at it. It had awful guts in it and what I hoped was the neck. I took that outta the bird. I was figurin' the inside was dirty, so I got the Rinso soap out. It cleaned out that bird real good. I scrubbed it inside and out."

Fran burst out laughing even though she had heard the story several times. Grace was chuckling at this point because she could envision Marg scrubbing the bird and bubbles and suds flying everywhere.

Marg was blushing as she continued, "So I put that their bird in the oven. I let it cook for four hours. When I fetched it out of the oven it was kinda burned."

"Mores like black as the bottom of a kettle on the wood stove. That's what Norm said," interrupted Fran.

"Did you give that to Norm fer supper?" Grace asked.

"I sure did. I went to all that fussin' and botherin', and I was figurin' he could scrape the black off," declared Marg.

With tears running down their faces Fran and Grace could barely catch their breaths from laughing so hard.

Grace just had to know: "Did Norm eat it?"

Grace and Fran's laughter was contagious, and Marg started to laugh with them.

Marg struggled to gain composure as she continued, "He looked at it as if he'd never seen a chicken afore. He asked me, 'What's this?' I told him it's the chicken. He says, 'The one I brought home yesterday?' Of course, I told him. He says, 'Are you sure it's not one of them their ravens from the back woods?' Norm scraped the black off, cut himself a big piece and put it in his mouth. He starts to chew and then he runs to the sink, spits it out and rinses his mouth over and over ag'in. I told him that I works all afternoons cookin' for him and that bird was cleaned good. I used Rinso. I was mad at him fer wastin' food."

Grace raised her hand. "Stop . . . stop. I'm 'bout to pee meself. I run to the outhouse afore you finish."

Grace walked the long hallway to the outhouse with her legs crossed, holding onto the walls. Fran and Marg could hear the echo of her laughter.

When Grace came back Marg went on with her story. "Norm said that I should take a bite. I went over to the table, cut a piece of the chicken, and put it in me mouth. Oh Maw . . . I'm not sure what crap tastes like, but I bet it be tastin' like that bird. Norm told me that's the worst crap he's ever eaten. So, I asked him how many times he's eatin' crap. We both got to laughin'."

The rest of the afternoon the ladies continued to chat as they made supper. Fran and Grace teased Marg throughout the meal preparations. When Marg peeled the potatoes, Grace reminded her that she did not need to wash them in Rinso.

"I shoulda never told you that story, Maw," Marg repeatedly said as she shook her head. "I knows I will never live that one down."

And she never did.

That evening, when most of the family had gone to bed, Marg volunteered to help her mother put the children's presents under the tree. She wanted time alone with Grace.

"Maw, before we head up to beds, can we be havin' a chat," asked Marg. "Come and sit down for a bit." Marg patted the chair beside her.

Grace welcomed the short break and rest before climbing the stairs to go to bed. "What's on your mind, girly?"

"Maw, you know Norm found a job while back. Well, the company shut down and he can't find a job in Antigonish. He's gonna try and sees if Bill can git him into the mine here. Can we stay with you ifin he gets a job? It will only be for a bit."

"Marg, I have to be askin' Bill first afore I tells you yes or no. How 'bout we talk to Bill tomorrow? Now you and me needs some sleep," said a weary Grace.

The two of them headed off to bed but Grace had a hard time falling asleep even though she was bone tired. She thought it would be good to have Marg around for a while to help with the younger ones and she could help with the delivery of Grace's new baby. Then Grace would not need that miserable doctor to deliver her child. All these exciting prospects whirled around in her head, keeping her awake. She did not know if Bill would agree to the young couple moving in for a while, but Grace knew she could reason with him if he didn't.

On Christmas morning Audrey and Suzie woke up at six. They wanted to see what Santa had brought them. Audrey ran down the stairs and Suzie was close behind, going down the stairs on her bum as fast as she could. They looked under the sparsely decorated tree and saw a few presents.

Suzie started to scream with delight, "Wake up, everyone. Santa came. He came and he be leavin' us presents."

Critch sat up from his makeshift bed on the floor beside the couch and said, "Land sakes, girly, stop your hollering."

Arthur, who was sleeping on the floor not far from Critch, also sat up, rubbing his eyes. "What's happenin'?"

Grace had heard the two girls going down the stairs and was on her way downstairs to the living room when Suzie started yelling. Grace rushed to the living room. "Shhhh . . . you need to be waitin' a bit, girlies. Come and has some hot chocolate while we wait fer the others.

All the yelling and commotion the two girls made woke up the rest of the household. As the girls sipped their hot chocolate one by one, the family made their way downstairs.

Once everyone was sitting in the living room on the couch, chairs and floor, Arthur insisted he be the one to give out the presents. The gifts were wrapped with the Truro Daily Newspaper and tied with twine.

"Santa musta collected all the Truro newspapers this year to wrap all of them there presents," joked Critch.

"Now, Critch, don't spoil it for the younger ones," cautioned Bill.

When it came to Suzie's turn, Arthur handed her a long gift.

"What is it? Wow, it looks like your rifle, Bill," said Suzie, full of anticipation.

Bill snickered. "Now, Suzie, why would Santa give you a rifle?"

"To shoot Arthur when he's a mouthin' off," she snickered. Everyone laughed except Arthur.

Suzie struggled to untie the twine and Audrey tried to help.

"NO! I do it meself." Suzie pushed Audrey's hand away from her present.

Once Suzie got the twine off and unwrapped her present, she stared at the two items before her. She had no idea what they were. "What are these?" she asked.

Critch spoke up. "Why them there are walkin' crutch sticks. They're to be helpin' you walk on your own. Audrey, come here and show Suzie how to work them."

Audrey stood up, put the handles of the crutches under her arms and demonstrated how to use them. Critch had made the crutches and had Audrey practice using them prior to Christmas morning.

"Me turns, me turn," insisted Suzie.

Critch stood her up and put the crutches under her arms. Suzie had no difficulty putting the crutch on the left armpit and grabbing the handle. Critch helped her put the crutch under her right armpit and lifted her right hand and put it on the handle.

Suzie had no difficulty moving the left-side crutch and taking a small step, but she was unable to move the right-side crutch. Because she still did not have any strength in her right hand to hold it, or the strength in her right arm to move the crutch, Suzie could not maneuver it.

"Damn it, I forgot you can't be usin' that arm!" said a discouraged Critch.

It took him many evenings and hours to make the crutches. Suzie could see that Critch was upset so she told Critch to come on her right side and hold her around the waist. He was too tall to stand and reach around short Suzie's waist, so he got on his knees. Suzie told him that when she starts to step forward, he needs to pull her along on the right side. Although her instructions were not as clear as he would have liked, he got the gist. Leaning on Critch, she was able to walk several steps using the one crutch on her left side. Suzie was now able to move her right leg and bear more pressure on her foot than she had months earlier. It seemed the shock treatment and the walking box were paying off.

The family group cheered and clapped when Suzie stood still. Suzie's face lit up brighter than the Christmas tree and she looked at Critch and said, "See, Santa gave me two 'cause he knew I might be needin' a spare. You got it wrong puttin' it under me bad arm. Hey, maybe Tucker will learn to walk aside me like Critch?"

Critch smiled and agreed with her because he had a soft spot in his heart for his wee sister Suzie and Suzie adored him. There was no mistaking their close connection.

The family had a wonderful time together that Christmas, and the biggest gift was Suzie walking. The two days that followed Christmas, Critch tried to train Tucker to do just what Suzie had suggested. Suzie would pull herself up on a chair and grab the crutch. Tucker would stand behind her on her right side and push her along as she walked. After several incidents of Suzie falling, Critch and Bill designed a harness that went around Suzie's waist which connected to a harness on Tucker's body and neck. Tucker would walk a few steps ahead of Suzie on her right side. She was able to slowly walk forward. This miracle invention gave her more independence.

Marg, Norm, Grace, and Bill discussed Norm's unemployment and it was decided that Bill would see if he could get Norm a job in the mine. If Norm was hired, Marg and Norm would stay with Grace and Bill for one month and one month only. Grace was relieved and comforted by the fact that her daughter would be around when Grace had the baby.

Fran and Wallace left for Antigonish on the third day after Christmas. Fran was not thrilled with the prospect of Marg staying behind or moving to Truro. She would miss Marg.

CHAPTER 24

A Ruby New Years

On New Year's Eve the family had an early supper at around three. Grace told everyone that she thought they should eat early, then take a nap so they could stay up and bring in the new year together. The truth was Grace had an inkling that she was going to have the baby that evening. Although she thought the baby may be a bit early, she did look like she was full term.

Once supper was done everyone went off for their naps. Bill preferred to nap on the couch. With everyone out of her way, Grace got out a wash basin, some clean towels and some string and disinfected the scissors in preparation for the birth. She gathered a pile of old newspapers with the other items and went upstairs to her bedroom. She placed everything neatly on the bed-side table, except the newspapers which she unfolded and put under the blankets on the bed sheet. Then she took a clean ragged old towel and placed it on top of the newspaper. Grace double-checked the crib to make sure everything was ready for the baby.

Howie had slept in the crib until two weeks ago. Now he slept in the three-quarter size bed in the girls' room with Audrey and Suzie. He slept against the wall so he would not fall out of bed. He was so thrilled to sleep with his sisters that he adapted to his new sleeping arrangement the first night.

Grace took out a blanket, infant nighty, diaper, and safety pins from the dresser drawer and placed them inside the crib. On the dresser she put a pitcher of cold water and a glass. She'd delivered the last two babies after being in labour for a few hours, so she suspected this one would also make a quick entrance into the world.

Instead of taking a nap Grace prepared a few sandwiches and trayed some biscuits and jam for the gang to snack on in the evening.

Everyone was awake by six-thirty that night. Bill lit the fireplace in the living room to make it warm and cozy. The three older children played the card game Crazy Eights on the living room floor, while the four adults played cribbage at the kitchen table. Suzie was colouring on the floor near the fireplace while Howie did his usual wandering around. Everyone was in a festive mood, chatting, telling jokes, and teasingly accusing the winners of cheating or having a horseshoe up their butt.

Just before ten o'clock Grace turned to Marg and said nonchalantly, "Time to git the snacks out and it's time for me to be a birthin' this baby."

"Ok Maw, I will git the—" Marg turned around quickly and looked at her mother. "Maw . . . are you . . . are you?" stuttered Marg.

Grace smiled and responded, "Yes. I is."

It took a few seconds for the others in the room to catch on to what was happening.

"What, Gracie?" Bill jumped out of his chair and yelled, "Are you serious?"

"Yah, I'm havin' birthin' pains. They've been a comin' fer the last thirty minutes or so," explained Grace.

Bill took control. "Critch and Arthur, come here," he ordered. "Critch, your Maw's going to have the baby tonight. You fill up the wood box by the stove and some by the fireplace. Arthur, your Maw made snacks. You get them out of the ice box. Give the youngest some and keep an eye on them. Marg, get things ready for the birth."

Grace intervened, "I have all the stuff fer birthin' ready upstairs, Bill." Bill gave her a questioning look. "I had a gut feelin' that I'd be birthin' tonight."

"Should I go and get the doctor?" Bill asked nervously.

Grace shook her head and said, "Bill, I've birthed seven babies and I know what to do. Marg can help me. I don't want that butchering miserable doctor deliverin' our wee one."

Just then Grace grabbed her stomach and grimaced. "Ahh, that one was hurtin' some.

Bill put his arm around Grace and said, "I am taking you upstairs now. Come along with us, Marg. Your Maw's going to need you."

They headed up the stairs and Bill yelled down. "Norm, fill the kettle and put it on the stove."

Bill helped Grace change into an old night gown and helped her into bed. Marg was busy making sure they had everything they needed for the birth. Fran had always been there to help bring other babies into the world. This would be the first time Marg would deliver a baby on her own.

"I want to be here when the wee one is born, Grace. I will stay with you and Marg," Bill insisted.

Grace did not want him there the whole time because she wanted to walk around, and she knew Bill would insist on her staying in bed. His anxiousness was already making her feel nervous.

Gently she placed her hand on Bill's arm and said, "Bill, go and play cards. Marg will call you when the baby's a comin'. It's gonna be a while yet."

"Are you sure, Gracie. I could stay and hold your hand or something," said Bill as he paced.

"Sides, you don't wanna be in the room when I'm hollering from the birthin' pain. Scoot now," she demanded.

Reluctantly, Bill headed downstairs. Norm made Bill and himself a cup of tea. They played two handed cribbage even though Bill was having a hard time concentrating on the game. Every now and then they could hear Grace scream then say, "AH darn . . . that one's a hurtin'."

When the "ah darns" became more frequent, Bill tried to get up out of his chair, but Norm put a hand on his arm and said, "Not yet, old boy. Marg will be callin' you when it's time."

The New Year came in and Grace was still in labour. Everyone seemed to have forgotten about celebrating.

At five minutes past one a.m. Marg bellowed, "BILL, COME UP HERES NOW!"

Bill darted up the stairs and just as he entered the room Marg said, "The baby's head's a comin' now, Bill."

Bill did not know whether he should watch the baby being born or kneel by the bed and hold Grace's hand.

Grace had her knees bent and legs apart. Marg was sitting beside her and calmly said, "Grab me a towel, Bill."

Bill handed Marg a towel and decided he would rather kneel beside Grace and hold her hand. Grace squeezed Bill's hand and smiled.

"Oks, Maw, give a slow hard push. This young'un's gonna be here any minute," said Marg.

Marg gently cupped the baby's head while Grace pushed slowly. The baby's head came out, Grace gave another push, and the new member of the family was born.

"'Tis a girly, Maw, and Bill, and she's a good size. You must have been further along than you thought," declared Marg as she wiped the baby's face.

"Turn the baby and take the gunk out of her mouth. Then rub her gently to get her crying. If'in, she don't cry, give her a few gentle wacks on her back, Marg," instructed Grace.

Marg did as her mother instructed and the wee girl started to cry. A big sigh of relief came from all three of them.

"Now do you remember how to be cuttin' the cord?" inquired Grace.

"Ya. I sure do. Seen you and Fran do it a hundred times afore," stated Marg.

To reassure her mother, Marg told her what she was doing step by step. Marg waited until the cord stopped pulsating, then she tied one piece of the string about three inches from the baby and another string three inches from the first one. She took the scissors and cut in between the two strings. Then she wrapped up the baby, handed her to Grace and waited for the placenta to be delivered.

"Bill, she's a might pretty little girly," commented Grace, as she stared down at the sweet infant girl in her arms.

Bill kissed Grace on the forehead, looked at Grace with a huge smile on his face and said, "The prettiest wee girl I've ever seen, just like her Maw."

Bill left Grace and Marg to finish their post-birthing tasks. He ran down the stairs and announced, "It's a girl! I have a daughter."

Everyone cheered and Suzie squealed, "I knew it be a girl. Yahoo, a baby sista. Got me 'nough of them brudders."

Bill sent the children to bed. They could see the baby in the morning.

When Suzie and Audrey awoke, they went straight into Grace and Bill's bedroom to peek at the baby. Bill and Grace were asleep, so they tried to be quiet. Audrey stood over the crib staring at her baby sister.

Suzie pulled herself up at the crib to look at the sleeping baby. "She's a mite tiny. Is she 'pose to be that wee?" Suzie whispered to Audrey. "She lookin' like Bill with no hairs. Are you sure she's a girl. She lookin' like an old man."

Audrey had to cover her mouth to muffle her laughter. "It's a girl. You will see when Maw changes her diaper."

"How's come she's so red. She kinda lookin' like a tomato or that's old red ring Maw has. You know the one from her Nanny?"

"Yah, I think it's called a ruby. Fran told me that," answered Audrey. "Oh, the baby is a stirrin'. We best get outta here, afore Maw or Bill wakes up."

Grace had heard the two of them tiptoe into the room and lay listening to their conversation. She got a chuckle out of Suzie's description of her new infant sister.

That day was filled with excitement and commotion as the family absorbed the arrival of their new addition. There were many kisses on the baby's forehead and hugs for Maw. Bill could not keep his eyes off the baby, and he was reluctant to hold her because he said that he might break or drop her. The two older boys thought the baby was cute but expressed they were hoping for a boy to even the girl-to-boy ratio in the family. Suzie questioned Grace non-stop until Grace's patience wore thin. Marg could see her mother was at her wits' end with Suzie. Reluctantly, Suzie agreed to leave the baby and go outside with Marg and Audrey to build a snowman. Suzie suggested they build a snow woman and a baby snow girl instead.

At the supper table Suzie asked, "What's her name, Maw. We can't keep callin' her wee one."

"I was a thinkin' we should call her Ruby. What do you think, Bill?" said Grace as she winked at Suzie and Audrey.

Bill pursed his lips together and looked upwards in deep thought. Suzie and Audrey looked at each other in disbelief.

Audrey whispered to Suzie who was sitting beside her, "You think Maw heard us talkin' afore?"

Suzie shrugged and looked at Bill, waiting to see what he would say.

"Well, I think her name should be . . . Ruby Grace McLoed," he declared.

So it was settled: the baby of the family was named Ruby Grace McLoed.

CHAPTER 25

Sunny

Norm acquired employment at the copper mine as a miner. Norm and Marg stayed three months with Bill and Grace to save money to move into a place of their own. Marg was a big help during that time. She tended to Howie, helped Audrey with the housework and ensured Suzie's treatments were done each evening. Meal preparations and taking care of Ruby were left to Grace. She did not want Marg to know that Norm had confirmed that "Marg couldn't cook worth a lick."

Marg and Norm were expecting their first baby in the summer. Fran had miscarried her first child, so Grace had this utmost on her mind. She couldn't help but wonder if Marg would carry her baby full term. It seemed that she was hearing more and more about women miscarrying their first child.

As each month grew closer to Marg's due date, Grace felt relief. After the miscarriage, Fran was upset and cried, but within a week she told her mother that she would try for another one. Grace did not understand why she herself was grieving so deeply, since it was her daughter who had lost the baby.

One day Grace had a talk with herself: "'Nough of that. Dis is pure nonsense. 'Tis like I loss me own little one. Oh . . . I think I've been a cryin' fer me lost grandbaby." Tears streamed down her face as she realized that her grieving came from deep within her. It was as if the moment that child was conceived Grace's heart had prepared a spot for the wee one. Now that space was empty. She came to realize that no matter how many grandchildren she would have, none would fill that specific spot. Before now Grace had not known how much love a grandbaby could stir up in a soul before they were born. Grace's mother had shown very little interest or affection towards her grandchildren; therefore, Grace had no idea such emotions were possible.

In July, Marg gave birth to a baby boy and named him Marshall after her father. Grace had the privilege of delivering her first living grandchild. As the baby was being born Grace had difficulty seeing through the tears of joy flowing from her eyes. Once the baby was cleaned up, Grace went to hand him to Marg.

Marg shrugged her shoulders and said, "Not now, Maw. I's so tired."

This new mother's reaction stunned Grace since she knew how important it was for a mother and baby to bond. She would ask Marg to nurse the baby when she woke up.

"Rest a while then, me girly. You can hold him later," whispered Grace. "You worked some hard ta have this wee one."

Grace sat in the rocking chair with the little bundle. As she rocked and cuddled her grandson, she whispered to him, "Sweet wee one. I hope you grow up strong like your pa and grandpa. Welcome to this crazy family. I'm your Nan. I will be here fer you whenever you need me."

Grace rocked the baby for over an hour, just taking in his presence and letting her love flow over him.

After Marg had a few hours of sleep Grace woke her. She handed the baby to her and suggested she put the baby to her breast. Marg took the baby and did as her mother instructed. Grace was relieved. Although Marg did not appear excited to see her infant, she did not hesitate to hold him.

Later that evening, as Norm was holding his infant son, he kept referring to him as Sunny. The sunshine of his life. This nickname, Sunny, would follow Marshall all his life.

Marg was constantly at Grace's place the first few months after Sunny was born. Sunny had colic and Marg thought she would lose her mind walking the baby for hours on end. Grace would take turns walking and rocking Sunny to give Marg a break. The colic was finally resolved when Grace remembered a mixture her mother had made for Critch when he had colic. The mixture consisted of boiled dried peppermint leaves, chamomile tea and a dash of red wine. Before each feeding, Marg gave Sunny a small dropper full, which was less than a quarter of a teaspoon. Though it may have been the alcohol in the mixture that sedated Sunny, Marg was grateful for the homemade remedy. Marg was amazed at her mother's child-rearing knowledge, especially since Grace only had a grade-five education. She thought her mother was smarter than most "learned folks," as Grace called them.

Throughout those months Grace became aware that though Marg was taking care of Sunny she appeared to be emotionally detached from him. The baby's physical needs were met but Grace had not seen her cuddle, kiss, or fuss over her infant son.

CHAPTER 26

Determination

During that same summer Suzie was determined to walk before her sixth birthday. She was spurred on when Howie started walking. Suzie was perturbed that her baby brother had learned to walk before she did, so she was determined not to be outdone by him.

Audrey had told Suzie about all her adventures at school. For Suzie to attend school one day she had to walk on her own. Therefore, she developed a plan to walk on her own without a crutch or people to support her.

The place she would execute her plan was her bedroom. The bed that Audrey, Howie, and Suzie slept in was against the wall in a corner. Howie slept against the wall so he would not fall out of bed. Audrey slept beside Howie in the middle so she would wake if Howie tried to crawl out of bed. Suzie slept on the outer edge. There was a chair in the opposite corner and the door was on the wall opposite to the end of the bed, beside the dresser. Suzie knew if she moved the chair next to the bed near where she laid her head, she could use it. She also knew if she moved it Audrey would put it back in its original place.

One morning Suzie pretended to have trouble getting out of bed and purposely fell to the floor. Audrey jumped out of bed to see if she was hurt.

Suzie responded, "No, I'm ok, but it be good ifin we could move that there chair over near the bed. I could hold on to it when I git outta bed. Ifin you put the rug under it I won't get hurt ifin I fall."

Audrey moved the chair and rug, placing them where Suzie had requested. Suzie realized that the three of them left their slippers or socks by the bed when they removed them at bedtime, and she did not want these to be a hindrance to her attempts. Once again, she engaged Audrey, asking her to put the slippers and socks at the end of the bed at night. She explained to Audrey that they were in the way when she had to use the potty at night. Then Suzie also realized the chamber pot had to be moved.

Audrey rearranged the room to Suzie's liking and after doing this she added, irritated, "Anything else, your highness?"

Suzie smiled and said, "No, that be just perfect. Thanks, Audrey, you're a good sista."

That compliment touched Audrey's heart and she sweetly responded, "You're welcome. You're a good sista too."

The hall light remained on at night and the door was always slightly open so Grace could check on Ruby and Howie. This would give Suzie just enough light to accomplish her ploy.

When the three of them went to bed, Suzie would lay awake waiting for Audrey and Howie to fall asleep. She could tell when they both were asleep because Audrey's breathing changed, and Howie snored.

Since the family were early risers, they were all in bed by nine.

While Suzie waited for the evening quietness to settle over the house, she silently prayed, "God, please helps me to have the strength to be walkin' tonight. Help me not to falls and wake anyone. Amens. Oh ya, and bless me family, 'specially Maw."

Suzie had started praying one day two years ago when she overheard Grace praying for Suzie and the other children. Although Grace was not a religious person, she had been raised Baptist and felt it never hurt to send a prayer heavenward occasionally or when a family crisis occurred.

Once Suzie finished her prayer, she imagined herself walking into the house and dashing up and down the stairs. She visualized walking to school with Audrey and running in the school yard with the other children.

When the house was finally quiet, Suzie sat on the edge of the bed, stood up and put her left hand on the wall. She used her left foot to push the chair away from her, then took two steps to the chair without holding on to anything. Then she would hold on to the wall and push the chair with her foot again, before letting go of the wall and walking to the chair. When the chair was pushed against the opposite wall she turned around and repeated the process all the way back to the bed. Exhausted, content, and proud of herself, she would crawl into bed and fall fast asleep. Every night she practiced pushing the chair further away and taking more steps without support. Suzie continued this nightly ritual all summer and would even take an extra lap until she was able to walk from one end of the room to the other side. There were nights she would walk the distance several times. She did fall intermittently but it did not wake anyone in the household, nor did it deter her resolve to walk independently.

There was one incident which woke up Audrey. Suzie was halfway to the opposite wall when she fell.

Audrey, half asleep, muttered, "What are you doin'? The crap pail is over by the dresser."

Suzie quietly said, "Oh yah . . . guessin' I was too sleepy, and I forgot. Go back to sleep, Audrey."

After that incident Suzie got Audrey to move the braided rag rug to the center of the floor. She just had to remember that it was there and not trip on it. Suzie became an expert at navigating the dimly lit room.

When Suzie was downstairs, she continued to use her walking crutch because she wanted to surprise her family when she was ready. When no one was around she would put her crutch down and take several steps unsupported.

CHAPTER 27

Disappointment

In September, the weekend before Audrey's first day of school, Suzie decided it was time to let her family in on her secret.

After breakfast while the family finished their tea and milk, Suzie stated, "You all need to wait afore you go to do chores. I have sometin' to show you."

The family gave Suzie their attention, except Howie who was busy finishing his porridge.

"What's you gonna show us, girly?" her mother asked.

Suzie stood up and pushed her chair back, she turned towards the living room and said, "Watch this."

Arthur was sitting beside Suzie and handed Suzie her crutch. Suzie pushed his hand away. Critch was sitting on the other side of Suzie and braced himself to catch her.

Suzie slowly walked to the living room, which was about twenty steps away, then she turned around and walked at a normal pace back to the kitchen and sat down. She raised her hands and exclaimed, "TA DA!"

Maw and Critch had tears running down their cheeks. Bill's jaw dropped and Audrey screamed, "She's a walkin' . . . Me sista is a walkin'. Maw, 'tis a miracle!"

Arthur, being a smart aleck, said, "'Tis 'bout time!"

Critch slapped him across the back of the head.

Suzie cried and laughed at the same time when she heard and saw the family's reactions.

The family was full of questions: But how? When did she learn how to walk like that? Who taught her?

Suzie explained that she believed God had given her a plan because she prayed. She described how she got naive Audrey involved.

Audrey chuckled. "You sure did, ya rascal."

Suzie filled them in on all the details. They were all amazed at her fortitude.

"Well ain'ts you a smarty pants, girly. You remind me of your dad 'cause once he would make up his mind, there was no stoppin' him," declared Grace, who still had tears running down her cheeks.

"And her mother too," said Bill as he handed her his handkerchief.

Arthur broke the somber mood by saying, "Yup, she's just like that farmer's mule nexta us. I'm gonna call you Sue the Mule." Once again Critch smacked Arthur on the back of the head, and everyone laughed.

"Maw, now I can stop me treatments," stated Suzie.

"Not yet, me girly. We will make an appointment with Dr. McLellan in Antigonish. Let's see what he figures first," Grace replied.

Suzie was extremely disappointed. She was sure that once she walked on her own the dreadful therapy would be eliminated. She also thought she was ready to go to school, but her mother told her she had to wait one more year to make sure she was strong enough. One outcome that Suzie did not expect was that she would now be required to help with the chores in the house.

Grace had already taught Suzie how to dress. Grace managed to do this by practicing using only her left arm to dress herself. When no one was around Grace hung her right arm down, relaxed and floppy. She laid a sweater on the bed with the back of the garment facing up. She put her pretend floppy right arm in the one sleeve using her left hand to guide it and pull the sleeve up to the middle of her right arm. Then she put her left arm into the other sleeve and raised the sweater, pulling it over her head. She was pleased with herself when she figured it out. Grace also showed Suzie how to pull up her panties and pants by pulling at the sides and wiggling and reaching to the back of her pants and pulling them up. Suzie had been dressing herself since she could stand at the age of five, either holding onto an object or leaning on an object for balance.

Now that Suzie could walk and hold her balance, it was easy to teach her to sweep and mop the floor with one arm. Suzie figured out how to do dishes on her own. When drying dishes, she put the tea towel on the counter and placed a wet plate or cup on it. She grabbed her right hand and placed it on the side of the dish so it would not move, and she used her left hand to dry the dish with the sides of the tea towel sticking out from under the dish, bowl, or cup. Although Suzie's right hand had remarkably little muscle tone, it did have some weight which she used to steady light objects. She could also use her left hand to close the fingers of her right hand around an item such as a spool of thread, enabling her to carry small light objects. Because Suzie had no feeling in that hand, she would often forget she was carrying something.

Suzie took twice the time to do her chores compared to Audrey, but she did not care and was an enthusiastic and fast learner.

Suzie wanted to learn how to tend to a baby. When she asked her mother about this Grace was reluctant to show her since she was sure Suzie would never have children of her own. "Suzie, I need to tell you no man's gonna wanna marry a cripple like you, so you ain't gonna be havin' babies. I know this sounds mean but it's the truth. Best you know this now so you will understand as you growin' up." It broke Grace's heart to be so blunt with her daughter but having foolish dreams and expectations were unacceptable to Grace. In the long run she felt it was best for Suzie.

Suzie had never heard her mother refer to her as crippled before and that would not be the last time her mother would remind her of her condition. Tears started to fall from Suzie's eyes, then she stopped herself from crying. Inside she thought, *I will show her I can do anythin'*. Right there and then Suzie sent up a silent prayer, "God gives me babies. Lots of babies to fill every window in the house I lives in . . . not now, but when I'm growed up and married course."

Suzie did learn how to change Ruby's diapers and dress her despite her mother's original objections. Ruby was a squirmy little thing.

Suzie finally got tired of picking herself with the safety pins and in a gruff, almost masculine voice firmly told Ruby, "Stops movin' now ors I gonna paddle your butt."

Usually, Ruby stopped moving after a scolding. Occasionally Suzie did smack her rear end and Ruby would cry but stay still. Suzie saw her mother use this method and she was glad it worked for her also.

When Suzie was introduced to unfamiliar activities, such as peeling a banana, she became frustrated and would say to her mother, "I can't, Maw. I just can't do it!"

Finally, Grace grew weary of hearing Suzie use that expression. "There's no's such words as 'I can'ts' in your life Suzie. You mays not be doin' it like udders, but you will do it your way!"

Once her mother made that clear, Suzie never said "I can't" again. That saying was one that Suzie would not tolerate the rest of her life, from herself or others. She became determined that "if there was a will there was a way," and she would do whatever she wanted or needed to do.

CHAPTER 28

Prayer

Spring and summer passed quickly that year. The family was busy picking berries, harvesting mint leaves, taking care of their garden, pickling, and making preserves, gathering their wood supply for the winter, and enjoying time at the beach.

When fall came Suzie was sure she would be going to school with Arthur and Audrey. Once again, she was disappointed. She wanted to cry and scream and cause a fuss, but she knew that would be to no avail. Her mother would not change her mind even if Suzie threw a tantrum. Instead, she went to her room and prayed and cried in private. "God, I'm sad 'bout dis. I'm guessin' you know somethin' I don't know. Help me to be strong. Help me bad leg to git strong."

Grace assumed that Suzie had come to grips with her disability and developed a thick skin since she was not as sensitive. She had no idea that her young girl developed a faith that she would carry with her throughout her life.

Grace believed that Suzie needed one more year at home to strengthen her right leg and to try and resolve her knee issue. Suzie was sturdy on her feet when she was walking, but her right knee would frequently give out on her. Out of the blue, they would find her on the ground or on the floor on her knees. Her knees always had black and blue bruises, especially her right knee because she landed on it first.

Tucker, Suzie's canine protector, continued to stay close by her side. If she fell and could not get up, Suzie would say, "Goes fetch Maw, Tucker."

Off he went to find one of the family members. He would stand in front of them, emit a high-pitched bark, and run to where Suzie was laying. Critch referred to his bark as "The Suzie Distress Signal." They all became familiar with Tucker's barking alarm. Sometimes Tucker took off so fast that the family member was not sure which way he headed. Tucker would go straight to Suzie and lick her face and lay down beside her, waiting for the rescuer. If the person did not arrive within a few minutes Tucker was up and heading for home again. The second time he barked longer and louder, as if to say, "Didn't you hear me the first time?" Eventually he automatically sought help without instructions from Suzie.

Usually, it was Critch or Arthur who went to Suzie's aid. If her knees were cut up or she was feeling weak she would have to be carried home. Even though Suzie was small for her age, it was not easy carrying her long distances.

The strength in Suzie's leg grew more substantial as the months went by. During the winter months she did not do as much walking because of the frigid temperatures and snowy weather conditions. That winter seemed colder and stormier than usual. The winds from the north blew across the Northumberland Strait and the winds from the east blew across the Bay of Fundy. Both were equally polar in temperature. High humidity formed bone-chilling ice crystals in the air. January and February were the harshest months, when venturing outside for more than fifteen minutes, no matter how much winter clothing a person wore, meant risking frostbite. The temperature would dip to minus forty some nights. During the day it was often between minus twenty-five and thirty, not including the bitter wind chill. A person's breath could be seen and would hang in the air like thick smog.

Grace would say, "'Tis colds enough to freezes the ball offin a brass monkey" or "'Tis cold enough to freeze the titties offfin the cows."

The younger children never knew what she meant by the brass monkey, but they understood the "titties off a cow."

School was cancelled that January until further notice due to the extreme cold. Audrey and Arthur stayed home, and Grace made sure they did schoolwork each day. Suzie helped with chores and insisted that her mother let her do schoolwork too since she wanted to be prepared when she did get to go to school. Grace started by teaching Suzie her ABC's, then how to print her name and a few simple words. Having only a grade five education herself, she knew her spelling was not up to par, but she could spell simple three-letter words to get Suzie started. Audrey and Arthur took turns teaching Suzie how to read from *Mother Goose's Nursery Rhymes*, a book the children received for Christmas. This challenged Suzie since the reading level was above her abilities, but she had a good memory and began to learn the words by recognition.

Audrey and Arthur returned to school in early March. The deep freeze of winter released its fervent grasp on the land and the cool winds of spring arrived to melt the snow. Although Suzie had a pair of black galoshes, walking in the snow and slush made her knee ache and give way more easily than in the warmer weather. Suzie still made every effort to go outside and practice walking in her rubber boots. Everything she did focused her on her goal of going to school the next September.

When summer came, Critch and Arthur built a treehouse for the younger children. Howie was almost six years old and was thrilled to have a place he called his "fort." Critch brought home old, weathered wood planks salvaged from a scrap pile at the mine site. Arthur hammered out the rusty old nails, straightening them the best he could. The old horse chestnut tree in the backyard was about fifty-feet tall. Its branches were smooth and because of its age, its once pinky-grey bark was now succeeded by an armour of dark scaly plates on its trunk. The first two large branches were strong. The third branch and fourth branch were positioned at the same height on the trunk, spaced five feet apart. Critch knew this was the perfect spot to build the tree house because it would be supported by the three sturdy branches of the triangle, and he could brace the structure on these branches and the trunk. The treehouse would be about seven and a half feet off the ground, not too high for young Howie.

Each evening, after Critch returned from work and had his supper, he and Arthur worked on the tree house. The project was completed in a few weeks, just in time for the scorching hot summer weather. The tree house was shaded by the branches and a cool breeze blew through the two windows which were roughly framed and covered with old, rusted screening. It was a welcoming refuge from the heat. The door slanted slightly to the right, as did the whole treehouse. To keep the mosquitoes out, Critch and Arthur stuffed newspapers in the cracks where the boards were warped and left gaps. When it rained the roof leaked in several places, but it all ran down to the right corner. Critch used Bill's hand drill to make a hole in that corner for drainage. Grace found two cheap old chairs at the thrift store, an end table, and a well-worn braided rag rug. These were her contributions to the project.

When Critch and Arthur finished their project, they invited the family to see the results of their hard work.

"Well, it looks . . . mmm . . . looks better than the outhouse," said Bill who was trying not to laugh.

Critch and Arthur could not help but laugh at Bill's description. They knew it looked shabby. "Well, it's sturdy. May not be the nicest lookin' buts it'll be there for a hundred year!" declared Critch.

Grace spoke up, "I think it's great. Goods job, me boys."

Howie was dumbfounded by what he thought was a magnificent treehouse that belonged to him.

Arthur asked, "Well, Howie, what do ya think 'bout your treehouse? Speak up, boy . . . Does the cat have your tongue?"

Howie finally broke his silence and said, "It's wonderful . . . I love it!"

"Can I go into the treehouse too?" Suzie asked.

"Ifen you can get up there you can," Arthur said teasingly.

He knew she would never be able to climb a tree with one arm, but he forgot that to Suzie this meant a challenge, and one she was determined she would figure out.

The next day, after Suzie did her chores, she and Tucker headed to the tree house. Arthur was there showing Howie how to hang on to the low-hanging smaller branches to climb up onto the sturdier branches to get into to the tree house. Arthur held Howie up on his first attempt. Coming down was easier. He just had to step down and then hang onto a branch and swing down to the ground.

Suzie and Tucker sat silently on the grass several feet away from the tree taking in every movement and the instructions Arthur gave Howie. After three attempts, Howie was up and down the tree like a monkey.

Once Arthur headed to the house, Suzie walked over to the horse chestnut tree, leaned on it, and then glanced around the yard to make sure no one else was around.

Suzie commanded Tucker to lay down and stay at the base of the tree. She tucked her limp right hand into her pants to keep it out of her way, then she grabbed and pulled on one of the branches in front of her. She bit into it just above her hand. While hanging on to the branch with her teeth, she moved her hand a few inches above her mouth. Hand over mouth she climbed and reached the first branch.

Once she reached the underside of the first branch, she wrapped her left arm several inches down the branch, put her feet against the trunk and took the few steps that got her to the top of the branch. Tucker started to whine. He was uneasy watching Suzie hanging from a tree by one arm with her legs wrapped around the branch.

"Shush, Tucker. I'm fine. Just be quiet and lay down," Suzie firmly commanded. Tucker slowly circled the tree a few times then reluctantly obeyed.

"Darns, now what am I gonna do?" she asked herself. "Can't just hang here like a monkey."

Suzie rested a moment. Then she realized if she moved her arm slowly down the branch, she could wrap her left leg around the trunk, use a notch on the trunk as a foothold and swing her right leg over. She used her left foot to feel along the trunk for the notch she knew was there.

"Hopin' this works," she whispered to herself.

On the first attempt she did not swing her leg high enough.

Suzie looked down at her right leg and said, "Come on, bad leg, you can do this."

Taking a deep breath she tried again, got her leg over the branch and was able to pull herself up into a sitting position, straddling the branch. Leaning against the trunk, she grabbed her left leg and brought it over, so she was sitting with both legs dangling. She grabbed another branch and pulled herself up on her feet. Suzie assessed the distance she needed to climb to get to the next branch. It was only a few feet higher. She was sure she could reach it by using the closest hanging branch, holding it with her teeth and hand, and walking her feet up the trunk. That is exactly what she did. When she stood on the second branch, the third branch was within her reach, so she pulled herself up and landed on the boards in front of the tree house door. Howie was startled as he watched Suzie drag herself along the rough wooden floor into the tree house.

"How the heck did you gits up here?" he yelled at her.

Suzie was out of breath and motioned to him to give her a minute. Then she sat up and proudly told him, "I climbed."

Howie was in awe of his big sister's accomplishment and told her that she would have to teach him how to climb that way.

Suzie was unaware that Grace and Arthur had been watching her the entire time from the kitchen window. Arthur wanted to stop Suzie, but Grace insisted he leave her be.

Without taking her eyes off the window she stated, "Ifin she falls, Tucker will come for us. Ifin she gits up the trees . . . well good for her. I'm sure ifin she git herself up there she will git herself down."

Getting down from the tree was much easier than climbing up, to Suzie's relief.

That summer Suzie became skilled at climbing trees her way, by twisting, turning, and using her stronger limbs and her teeth. It would be her saving grace one day.

CHAPTER 29

Visiting

In August, Bill, Grace, Audrey, Suzie, Howie, and Ruby all piled into the car and headed to Antigonish. Suzie had an appointment with Dr. McLellan and Bill decided it would be a good time for a visit with Fran, Wallace, and their daughter. Grace had not had the opportunity to visit Fran since she gave birth to her first child almost two years prior. Baby Audrey (named after her aunt) had not met her grandmother Grace, Bill, or any of her aunts and uncles.

Providing for the large family had been expensive and Bill worked as much overtime as he could to make ends meet. He had some money saved and he felt this was the time to use some of it.

Audrey was thrilled that Fran had named the baby after her. Marg, on the other hand, was insulted. She expected Fran to name the baby after her, since they had always had a close relationship. In fact, Marg was so infuriated she decided she would never speak to Fran again.

Fran and Wallace moved to a bigger home right after their baby was born. Fran furnished it with up-to-date pieces and new curtains. It was modern and looked expensive. Grace was shocked when she walked into Fran's new dwelling.

"How can you's afford this?" she let slip out.

Fran looked at her mother and said, "We are doing well, Maw. Doesn't it look divine?"

Grace was not sure what divine meant but she realized that her daughter talked differently, acted strange and looked unfamiliar. Her clothing was much too revealing for Grace's liking. Fran's makeup reminded her of the hooker's makeup she had seen on women hanging around downtown Antigonish. Fran had also dyed her hair jet black. It had grown so much that it now reached her waist. She was losing her Nova Scotia twang when she spoke. This was not the Fran Grace knew and raised; she was acting uppity. Grace was worried but Fran was a woman, and she was not going to interfere in Fran and Wallace's affairs.

Toddler Audrey had dark brown curly hair and reminded Grace of Fran when she was that age. She ran up to Grace, hugged her legs and then went straight over to three-year-old Ruby, grabbed her hand, and led her into a playroom. The room was decorated for a princess. It had a miniature table, two chairs, a couch and lounge chair, a huge pink, blue and white wool carpet, and many of the newest toys. Ruby was in awe, but it did not take long before the two children were playing together.

Aunt Audrey, who was now thirteen, spent time getting to know her namesake. She kept an eye on the two little ones while the adults visited. Suzie and Howie spent most of their waking hours at the shoreline. Suzie sat on the beach digging in the sand, looking for smooth and frosty sea glass and unbroken seashells. The tide would wash them ashore and the second or third wave would cover them with sand. Sometimes she would just sit there with her feet in the water, taking deep breaths of the salty sea air. Howie looked for clams, hoping they would have a clambake if he found enough. Bill and Wallace spent a lot of time outside drinking beer, smoking, and talking about the war, work, and local news. Bill noticed that Wallace drank a lot and was drunk every evening of their visit.

On the third day of their visit, Grace, Bill, and Suzie went to see Dr. McLellan. Dr. McLellan was surprised to see them after two years and he was astonished that Suzie was walking.

"I must be honest; I did not think that Suzie would ever walk this well. As a matter of fact, I thought if she did walk, she would have required leg braces. I see your arm did not do as well," declared Dr. McLellan.

"No, me arm is still the same, but I do walk and can run!" said Suzie.

Grace explained to Dr. McLellan that Suzie was doing well with her walking but her right knee would give out on occasion and because of this she was not able to go to school yet.

"Well, let me see what we can do about that, Suzie. First, get up on the examination table and let me look at your arm, knee, and leg. I would like to examine your right arm as well," instructed Dr. McLellan.

Immediately Grace informed the doctor about Suzie's shoulder and her previous dislocation. She directed the doctor to be careful.

"I will . . . and you say you were the one who put it back into the socket . . . mmm. That is quite an incredible procedure for a mother to do," said Dr. McLellan.

As he examined Suzie's shoulder he said, "Well done! Her shoulder is in place. But I can see why you are concerned. It can easily be dislocated because there is no muscle tone to hold it in place."

When Dr. McLellan was finished his examination, he informed Suzie, "You need a knee brace."

Suzie began to protest, but the doctor interrupted her, "Suzie, it would not be a full leg brace. It is just to keep your knee from giving out. It is made of material and elastic and has steel rods in the side of it to support your knee."

Grace saw the defiant look on Suzie's face and firmly said, "Listen, girly, do you want to be goin' to school. Ifin you do, you will wear the knee brace or stay home."

Suzie wanted to go to school more than anything, just like other children did. Suzie knew the knee brace would single her out, but she also knew she would be staying home if she did not wear one.

Suzie reluctantly agreed, "Ok, I'll wear it."

Dr. McLellan told them they could purchase a knee brace at Sobey's Groceteria, and the pharmacist would make sure she got one that fit.

Suzie started to wear the knee brace that very day. She found it hot and cumbersome and let her mother know she was not happy about wearing it.

On the fourth day of their visit, the family left to head back to Truro. Bill had tired of Wallace's drinking and his ranting and raving. Grace was also glad to be heading home. Fran's high and mighty attitude was getting on Grace's nerves. If she heard Fran bragging for another day, she was sure she would lose control and tell her off. Grace bit her tongue so many times during the past few days that she was sure it was calloused. Suzie wanted to go home and see if this new brace made any difference. She could not wear it on the beach because it would get full of sand and irritate her skin. Audrey missed her friends and was glad they stayed only four days. Howie did not mind one way or another. Ruby cried because she had to leave her playmate toddler Audrey behind. She cried and whined for about fifteen minutes until Suzie started to sing "Twinkle, Twinkle Little Star," At which point Ruby became distracted and sang along with Suzie.

Grace was amazed that Bill tolerated Ruby carrying on like she did and didn't reprimand her. When one of the other children cried and whined like Ruby did, Bill scolded them. That was not the only difference she had noticed in Bill since Ruby was born. He was hard on Arthur and Howie. He criticized them a great deal. Grace knew Bill never had a close relationship with Howie and had always been impatient with him, but he seemed worse the past three years. On the other hand, Bill had always been fair with Arthur. Bill had previously engaged Arthur in special woodworking projects. However, Bill had not involved Arthur in any projects for at least three years. When Arthur asked Bill if he could help, Bill would say that he would rather do it himself. Bill's actions towards her other children concerned Grace, yet she felt like she owed Bill so much and was afraid if she caused a fuss he would leave.

When the two boys complained, Grace would always respond, "You need to mind Bill. He's the man of the family." And so, feeling picked on and frustrated, the boys began avoiding Bill as much as possible.

Once they were home, Suzie discovered that Dr. McLellan was right: her knee no longer gave out with the support of the brace. In those few weeks before school, the bruising and cuts on her knees healed. Although she thought the brace looked hideous, Suzie appreciated no longer falling.

CHAPTER 30

Off to School

Suzie woke up at five on the morning of September eighth. She was wound up as tight as a clock, though she had tossed and turned most of the night. She jumped out of bed and almost fell flat on her face. In her excitement she forgot she had to be careful when she put both feet on the floor. The day had finally arrived when she would attend her first day of school.

Suzie didn't want to wake Audrey by getting dressed in the room. In the living room, she turned on a lamp and got dressed in her blue-and-white-flower-print short-sleeved dress. It was a hand-me-down from Audrey. Because of Suzie's petite size and stature, her mother had to alter it. Suzie looked down at her black leather lace-up shoes. Regardless of how much she polished them, they still looked well-worn. Shrugging her shoulders, she sat on the couch, waiting for the rest of the family to awaken.

Two hours later Grace found Suzie curled up on the couch fast asleep and dressed for school. Grace smiled because she knew Suzie must have been up before the birds since she was so excited for her first day of school.

The smell of pancakes woke Suzie. The rest of the family were already seated at the table. After breakfast Suzie and Audrey did their last-minute preparations for school: washing their faces and brushing their teeth and hair.

Arthur had left fifteen minutes earlier. Grace suspected he was meeting up with a girl to walk to school. The two sisters grabbed their bagged lunches, kissed their mother goodbye and headed out the back door.

"Suzie, wait, didn't you forget somethin'," Grace yelled after Suzie. "Where's your brace?"

"Oh ya," Suzie said, disappointed.

She hoped her mother would not notice and that she could attend her first day of school without the brace. Making a good first impression on her new classmates was important. Suzie reluctantly put on her brace, while Grace stood over her to make sure it was put on properly.

That first day of school was a warm sunny day with slight wisps of clouds in the sky. The cool breeze from the Bay of Fundy made the temperature exactly right, not too hot, and not too cool. It was a perfect day for the first day of school.

Suzie was walking so fast that Audrey told her, "Good grief, girly, we ain't goin' to a race. Slow down. I'm outta breath!"

"I don't want to be late," declared Suzie.

Audrey explained they would be there in plenty of time and if they kept up the fast pace, they would be tuckered out before their classes started.

When Suzie and Audrey walked into the school yard Suzie stopped and stared at the large two-story red brick building. There were so many big windows that ran along the first floor and the second floor. She knew the building was big, but she had no idea it was so huge. Suzie was in awe because the school was almost the size of the hospital in Antigonish. Suzie stood there, taking in the scene, and appreciating her surroundings. She looked at the five steps and the railings leading to the front entrance. She knew she could maneuver up the steps with her knee brace if she held on to the railing on the left. There were groups of children playing with balls, running around, and standing against the wall. It was just like Suzie had imagined.

Audrey thought Suzie was walking just behind her when she realized she was far behind. She ran back and nudged her. "Come on!"

As they approached the entrance, there was a crowd of ten girls, laughing and talking, but as soon as they saw Suzie, they stopped. They started to talk in low voices and hushed whispers. Suzie knew they were talking about her and her knee brace.

As Suzie got closer, she could hear one girl saying, "That's Audrey's crippled sister. Look at her tiny skinny arm; it's awful. She should not be here. She doesn't belong here." Some of the other girls agreed with her.

This was not the reception Suzie had hoped for. She had envisioned her schoolmates being curious about her brace, Suzie answering their questions and then off they would go and play. Tears welled up in Suzie's eyes.

Audrey put her arm around her and said, "Never ya mind them. That buncha girls are mean. There are udders who are much nicer."

Audrey guided Suzie over to one of the teachers on the walkway, heading towards the front door. "Mrs. Vernon, this is me sista, Suzie. It's her first time at school."

Audrey was sure this teacher would make Suzie feel welcomed and be kind to her.

"Oh my . . . well . . . Suzie, you wait here just a few minutes, will you, please," Mrs. Vernon said, nervously. Then she hurried into the building.

Audrey found the teacher's reaction disconcerting. A moment later, the teacher and the principal emerged from the front door as though they were on a serious mission and headed straight for Suzie, which drew attention to her and made the other children stare.

The principal stood in front of Suzie and gruffly said, "The bell is going to ring in a few moments. Audrey, you go into the school with the other children. Suzie, you will follow me."

Audrey wanted to protest but she did not know what to say. She was perplexed and feeling anxious for Suzie. As a stunned Suzie looked at Audrey for an explanation, the bell rang.

The principal motioned to Audrey and said, "Go on, Audrey, get to your classroom. Suzie, come with me now!"

The principal led her to the back of the building, and he pointed to the fire escape. "This is where you will enter the school. You might scare the other children because you are a cripple. Your class is on the second floor."

Suzie could not believe what she was hearing. She had to climb twelve metal stairs to get to the second floor. With tears running down her face she looked at the principal.

He was not moved by her tears and commanded, "Go on now. I will meet you at the door and take you to your class." The principal left her at the bottom of the stairs and walked around to the front of the school. He headed up to the second floor to wait for Suzie.

Suzie felt so deflated. Not only were there a lot of stairs to climb with her knee brace, but now she did not have Audrey to carry her lunch bag. Suzie almost turned around and went home but she remembered what her mother had said: "There is no such thing as can't."

Suzie took a few deep breaths and said to herself, "I'm gonna do it. I'm gonna do it."

Her deep-seated courage welled up inside her. Putting her lunch bag between her teeth, she climbed the first step. She did this by putting her left leg up first then her right leg, while holding on to the railing.

She kept repeating, "I'm gonna do it." Halfway, Suzie was tired and sweating. She stopped to catch her breath. Then she climbed the remainder of the steps.

When she got to the top the principal was there with the door open. "Hurry up, girl. You're late for class."

CHAPTER 31

Disillusions

Suzie followed the principal into the grade one classroom where the teacher and nineteen children were in the process of roll call. Since Suzie was small and short for her age, she fit in with these students who were two years younger. No one knew she was soon to be eight years old.

The national anthem and "God Save the Queen" had been sung. Suzie wanted to be a part of the opening ceremonies. Arthur had taught her the songs. The disappointments were adding up and she had barely started her day. The class stopped what they were doing and stared at Suzie. The principal introduced Suzie to her teacher, Mrs. McFlin, and left the room.

The teacher gave Suzie a repulsed look and, instead of welcoming her, she reprimanded her, "You are late. In my class you must be on time from now on. There is a desk at the back of the room. You can sit there."

The children continued to stare and watch Suzie as she awkwardly made her way between a few desks to her spot. Suzie looked like a drowned cat from perspiring, and her knee brace was drenched and had slipped down to her ankle. She sat down and fixed her brace. The teacher finished her roll call but did not call Suzie's name. Suzie wanted to remind her that she was there, but she was feeling faint and rejected already. She did not want to give the teacher something else to yell at her for.

The teacher started her lesson with the ABCs. Mrs. McFlin printed the first five letters of the alphabet on the board. She instructed the children to take out their tablets and pencils and practice printing letters. Suzie watched as the other children opened their desks and took out their tablets and pencils. They were able to hold their desktops open with one hand and grab their supplies with their other hand. When she opened her desk, she used her head to keep the desk top open while retrieving her pencil and paper writing tablet. Then she moved her head and the desk top slammed shut, drawing attention to her. The teacher did not say anything but issued a loud tongue smack of disapproval. Suzie started to print the letters and was beginning to relax a bit when she got a smack on her left hand with a wooden pointer from the teacher.

"Ouch!" Suzie screamed, not only because it hurt like the dickens, but she was startled, and she had not noticed the teacher standing beside her. The teacher had a frown on her face. "You will not use your left hand. All children must use their right hand to write."

With silent tears on her face, Suzie grabbed her right hand with her aching left hand and held it up. "I don't use dis hand. It doesn't work."

The children sitting close by gasped when they saw Suzie's hand. Most of the students had not paid attention to her visible disability when she first entered the room since they had been staring at her knee brace down around her ankle.

An uncompassionate Mrs. McFlin stared at Suzie's hand and replied, "You don't belong in this school. You should be in an institution. While you are here you will use your right hand. Do you hear me, young lady!"

Humiliated and belittled, Suzie was beside herself so she got up and started toward the door as quickly as she could, banging into a few desks on the way. The teacher did not try to stop her. Out the back door and down the stairs she went. She had trouble navigating the stairs because her eyes were flooding with tears. Despite her blurred vision, she made it to the ground and headed home.

Grace was in the yard hanging clothes on the clothesline when she heard a sobbing Suzie coming down the driveway. Grace ran to her, and Suzie held her mother around the waist and bawled even harder until she was hyperventilating. The morning's fiasco and all Suzie's disillusions flowed out through her streaming tears.

Grace knelt and hugged Suzie and rubbed her back as she whispered, "It's ok now, me girly. It's ok. Maw is here."

When Suzie calmed down a bit, Grace took her by the hand and led her into the kitchen. Suzie sat on a kitchen chair and laid her head on the table like a defeated puppy. Grace got Suzie a glass of milk and some cookies.

"Maw, it was awful. I'm never goin' back there agin."

Grace took her handkerchief from her apron and wiped Suzie tears. "Now, girly, dry your tears and tell me what you're doin' here? What's happened?"

Through tears, pauses and momentary hysterics, Suzie told her mother everything that had transpired. As she listened, Grace had trouble controlling her devastated and enraged emotions. Grace did expect that the other students would be ignorant and mean but she never thought the principal and teachers would be so cruel and disrespectful. Though Grace had prepared Suzie for some of the comments she might get from the other students, she could not have prepared her for what happened that morning.

"Maw, and that's not all. I left me lunch bag there." Suzie was overwhelmed and started to weep again.

Grace almost burst out laughing because Suzie's abandoned lunch was the least of her worries. "Hush now, me girly. No use frettin' over your lunch. Go warsh up and you can help Maw for the rest of the day."

Grace managed to keep Suzie occupied for the afternoon, though Grace noticed her crying intermittently. When Audrey got home from school, she told Grace what had happened with the teacher and principal and the gossip she overheard from the other children about Suzie.

That evening when Bill came home from work, Grace updated him on the wretched verbal and physical assaults Suzie endured at school. He was livid and wanted to knock a few heads off. He had to calm down before he took his seat at the supper table with the rest of the family. Everyone avoided talking about school.

Once again Suzie was plagued with nightmares. She dreamt that the children were all laughing at her, and the teachers were yelling, and a man came and took her away to an unfamiliar big wooden building, where people with missing legs and arms were screaming and crying. Suzie woke up in a sweat, screaming. Neither her nor the rest of the family got much sleep that night.

CHAPTER 32

Angry Maw

When Suzie woke up the next morning it was ten o'clock. Marg was in the kitchen.

Suzie sat down at the kitchen table and rubbed her eyes to make sure she wasn't seeing things. Marg usually visited in the afternoon or evening.

"Marg, what're you doin' here?"

Marg placed a plate of toast and jam in front of Suzie. "Maw asked me to come over and stay with you and Ruby. Maw's gone to school to have a chat with them folks."

Suzie trembled at the mention of school and quickly changed the subject. "Where's Sunny and Ruby?"

"In the livin' room playin'. You eat up, then you can join them ifin you like."

Two hours prior, Grace put her best dress on, did her hair up and headed to the school. Although she was exhausted from lack of sleep, her indignation energized her. All the way to the school she mulled over the horror the principal and teachers had put her wee Suzie through and the nightmare-filled night.

When she got to the school, she marched into the principal's office, bypassing the secretary, swung open the door and announced, "I'm Suzie Fenton's mudder and you got some explainin' to do. No. I got some talkin' to do!" Grace slammed the door behind her.

Grace did not mince her words and verbally went up one side of him then down the other. She raked him and the teachers involved over the coals for their ignorance, cruelty, and callousness, giving him no time to excuse their behavior. In no uncertain terms, she made him aware that Suzie would be attending school and she would not be put in an institution because there was nothing wrong with her mind. She also asserted that they would be kinder to Suzie and treat her fairly like the other children. Grace demanded that they allow Suzie to use her left hand to write since that was the only hand she could use. At the end of her rant, Grace told the principal if he did not follow her requests, she would tell the newspaper and radio about the treatment her daughter received and hire a lawyer to sue the school.

Several times the principal attempted to interrupt Grace, but she stopped him every time. There was no excuse for treating a young girl with such malice. Before Grace left the office that day, she had the principal's apology and assurance that he and the teachers would apologize to Suzie, and she would receive better treatment when she returned to school.

Grace's threat to call the newspaper and a lawyer provoked fear in the principal. Even if some of the readers would think that Suzie did not belong at school, there were many who would believe she did. The principal knew the bad publicity could lead to his dismissal as well as that of the teachers involved. Grace could not afford to hire a lawyer, nor did she intend to go to the newspaper, but that was what came to her mind at the time.

Suzie was waiting on the steps when Grace arrived home. "Maw, you been to school?"

Grace sat beside her, put her arm around Suzie and said, "Yah and you're a goin' back tamorrow."

Suzie began to object, but Grace put her pointer finger on Suzie's lips to silence her. "Girly, I had a long talk with the principal and things are gonna be different fer you. No more mean stuff is goin' to happen. The teachers and principal are a mite sorry fer what they done."

That was not quite the truth, but Grace wanted to provide reassurance for Suzie. "They will tell you that tamorrow. I can't do anythin' 'bout what the udder kids do. You will have to be learnin' to ignore them 'cause you gonna have people sayin' mean things most of your life, 'cause you are a cripple."

The next day Suzie unenthusiastically went off to school. The teachers and principal apologized to Suzie. The school staff treated her better, but the other students continued their share of mocking and teasing. Suzie learned to ignore them the best she could but occasionally it would get to her, and she would sneak off on her own to hide her tears.

That year Suzie did extremely well in school, receiving A's in all her academic subjects. She developed friendships with two schoolmates in her class. Although they were teased for hanging around the "crippled girl," they did not seem to mind, and they would stick up for Suzie when other students taunted her. These two classmates were twins, Tommy and Julie, and they knew what it was like to be teased. Their family was extremely poor, so Tommy and Julie wore tattered clothing and their lunches often consisted of one slice of bread and an apple. Suzie told her mother about her new playmates, so Grace often added extra in Suzie's lunch to share. Tommy was a tough little gaffer and did not put up with any guff. A few times he beat up a classmate when he was defending his sister or Suzie. He seemed to always be in trouble, but Suzie thought he was the bravest boy she had ever met. Though her school year had a rocky start, she ended up enjoying most of her time at school.

CHAPTER 33

Summer Break

On the first day of summer break, Grace announced that Suzie no longer needed shock treatments. Suzie was stunned but thrilled and did not understand why the horrendous therapy was ending. Not that she wanted to continue them, but she had resigned herself to the fact that she would have to have shock treatment for the rest of her life.

Suzie was baffled and wanted to make sure she was not hearing things. "Maw, are you sayin' I really don't have to have me treatments anymore? Are you sayin' that they are done forever? Maw, are you sure? Maw, tell me you ain't foolin'."

Grace laughed at her bewildered daughter. "Yah girly, I'm sure. I didn't want to tell you afore 'cause I knew you would git too anxious. At your appointment with Dr. McLellan last summer, he said that ifin you keep doin' well, there was no need to keep doin' the treatments. He told me's to give it one more year, 'til next summer, and then stop them. So here we are and its next summer."

Suzie cheered and laughed as tears of relief flooded her eyes. She hugged her mother and Audrey. Then she grabbed Audrey and danced around the kitchen. The day had come when she was free, free of the repulsive and excruciating therapy. Suzie was on cloud nine.

"Me prayers were answered and now I'm free. After five long years I'm free! Yippee!" shrieked Suzie. Then she stopped and looked at her mother. "What about the brace?"

Grace shook her head and replied, "Suzie, don't push it. You still must be a wearing the brace."

Regardless, Suzie laughed and carried on as if she had just found out she was a princess.

When the school year ended, so did Arthur's education. He was sixteen and he would join Critch and Bill working at the mine and bringing home a paycheck to help support the family. Critch had been working in the mechanics shop since he was eighteen. Bill continued his career as an electrician. Arthur was hired as a cleaner on surface. His job was to clean the offices, the men's changeroom, the bathrooms, and to be an errand boy for the office staff. Arthur was delighted to be out of school; he did not excel academically. He would miss his friends, but schoolwork was something he wouldn't miss.

Marg struggled with her maternal duties. She just did not have good mothering instincts. Norm was worried because Marg would often forget to feed Sunny lunch and she habitually left him unattended while she ran errands. Leaving a four-year-old on his own was irresponsible. Norm scolded Marg over these issues but to no avail.

Norm was at his wits' end, and he expressed his concerns to Grace. Grace spoke to Marg, but Marg saw no harm in Sunny staying by himself. "I do leave a sandwich and milk on the table fer him. I lock the doors and he have a potty in the living room. Maw, he's just fine. He's not a baby no more," Marg said indifferently.

Grace did not know why this daughter so lacked common sense since she had tried to set a good example. Obviously, Marg did not inherit her mother's good judgement.

Norm and Grace realized talking to Marg about this problem was like talking to a brick wall. So, Bill and Grace decided that for Sunny's safety, Marg would bring him to Grace and Bill's home every morning, while Norm was working. In the beginning of this arrangement, Marg spent the day with Sunny at her mother's place. After two weeks, Marg would just drop Sunny off and collect him at around four in the afternoon.

When Grace questioned Marg on her whereabouts, Marg would answer, "Just around. I keep busy." Then she would change the subject.

Grace knew for the sake of her grandson she must have him over at her house as much as possible. Raising another child was not in her plans, but she felt she had no choice in the matter. Sunny needed some good strong mothering. He had already developed some nasty habits such as peeing and spitting on the floor and hitting others. His table manners were atrocious because he had not been taught how to use eating utensils. He ate with his hands and chewed with his mouth wide open as food fell on the table and floor. Ruby was amused by some of his antics and Grace had to nip these behaviours in the bud before Ruby mimicked them. It did not take him long to learn that his nan meant business and that he would have to be a little gentleman at her house. Sunny was bullheaded; a firm hand and an occasional paddling were required to set him straight.

Sunny idolized Howie and followed him everywhere except up to the tree house because he could not yet climb the tree. Howie did not have the patience to deal with a hyper, pestering four-year-old, so he would climb into the tree house before Sunny arrived in the morning. When Howie was not successful at disappearing early, Grace would ask him to keep Sunny busy while she did her chores.

One day late in August when the weather was warm but not hot, and the sky was overcast, Sunny was getting on Howie's nerves so badly that he thought he could not stand the thought of putting up with Sunny for another day. Howie had been thinking of a scheme all summer and this was the perfect day to execute it. He told Sunny they were going to play cops and robbers and appointed Sunny as the robber. Being the bad guy appealed to Sunny's devious nature. Howie was the cop. Since Sunny was the bad guy Howie tied him to the tree so he would not hurt anybody. Sunny agreed and laughed because he had never been tied to a tree and thought it would be fun.

"Come here by the tree house," instructed Howie. "You stand behind the tree so no one can see you. Stand still while I tie you up good and tight."

Howie had a heavy fifty-foot twine rope, which he wrapped around Sunny a few times first. Then he pushed Howie back against the tree trunk and proceeded to wrap the rope around the tree and Sunny. Sunny was wrapped in rope from his feet to his shoulders. Howie tied the end of the rope as loosely as he could and asked Sunny to try to escape. Sunny wiggled and jiggled, attempting to slacken the rope. He could not get himself free. Howie was pleased that his hostage was not going to escape. Then he realized if Sunny started yelling, Grace would come running, insist that Sunny be untied, and give Howie a paddling for his devious plot. Keeping Sunny quiet was a vital part of the plan. Howie ran into the house and looked to see if Grace was in the kitchen. It was all clear; his mother was nowhere to be seen. He snuck a small apple from the bowl on the counter, put it in his pocket and ran back to Sunny.

He showed Sunny the apple as he shined it on his shirt. "See, Sunny, I git you an apple. Now open your mouth as wide as you can."

Sunny obliged and Howie put the apple in Sunny's mouth as far as he could shove it and told Sunny to bite down on it.

"Can you chew or spit the apple out?" Howie asked Sunny.

Sunny made several attempts but was unable to bite or spit the apple out. Sunny shook his head.

Howie had one more inquiry for his prisoner: "Can you scream with the apple in your mouth?"

Howie tried to scream and all that was heard was a muffled "ah."

"Good, me cop job is done. You're gonna stay there fer a bit while I go in me treehouse or, I should say, me cop station," Howie said with a smirk.

Sunny looked like a stuffed pig ready to be roasted. He looked at Howie and shrugged his shoulders since he was clueless to the prank Howie had just pulled on him. As Howie climbed up to the tree house, he burst out laughing and was quite pleased with himself.

Howie was reading *Huckleberry Finn* and was anxious to continue from where he had stopped reading last evening. He laid down on the floor, picked up his book and once again got lost in Huckleberry Finn's world. Howie did not realize that he had been in the treehouse for two and a half hours until he heard Grace calling out the kitchen window to the two boys, telling them to come in for lunch.

"Ah shit, I didn't check on Sunny!" Scrambling to his feet, Howie quickly made his way down to the base of the tree.

Howie went behind the tree and there was Sunny with his head hanging down and flopped over to one side and his eyes closed. For a moment Howie thought he had killed the young boy. He rushed to Sunny in a panic. Howie licked his middle finger and put it under Sunny's nose to feel his breath. Howie heaved a huge sigh of relief as he realized Sunny was sleeping. Howie walked nonchalantly back to the house and into the kitchen.

He asked his mother, "Can Sunny and me have our sandwich outside? We're havin' fun and we would like to stay outside."

Howie had never expressed having fun with Sunny before and Grace did not want to ruin a good thing, so she agreed. She put their sandwiches, two apples and two mugs of milk on a cookie sheet for Howie to carry outside.

When Howie returned to the tree, Sunny was still asleep. Howie sat on the ground in front of Sunny and ate his own sandwich and apple and drank his milk. He also drank half of Sunny's milk. He left the cookie tray on the ground and climbed back into the tree house to continue reading his book. Once more Howie became consumed in the adventure he was reading. At two o'clock in the afternoon, he heard Audrey from the base of the tree calling him and Sunny.

Howie jumped up and answered her, "We're in here, Audrey!"

Audrey looked down at the cookie sheet and saw a dried-up sandwich, an empty plate, an uneaten apple, an apple core, half a cup of milk and an empty cup.

"What the heck?" Audrey exclaimed.

She heard a soft moaning noise from behind the tree. When Audrey investigated, she found a flustered Sunny tied to the tree with an apple stuffed in his mouth. She could not help but giggle at the sight. He did remind her of a stuffed pig her mother had cooked a few years ago.

"Howie, you gits yourself down here now!" Audrey commanded.

Howie reluctantly dragged himself away from his book and slowly climbed down the tree. "I know. I have to untie him," he conceded.

Audrey was amused by the situation. Sunny was a royal pain in the butt. He constantly pulled her hair and got into her belongings. His non-stop silly talking usually gave her a headache. Audrey guessed that Howie needed some peace and quiet.

"Yah, you better untie him," Audrey agreed.

"Are you goin' to be tellin' Maw on me?" asked Howie.

Audrey shook her head and said, "Nah but sure as shootin' Sunny will. Although, I bet he deserved it, the little bugger."

Howie walked up to Sunny, held his pointer finger out and shook it at Sunny and said forcefully, "You're not gonna tell anybody I tied you up. Ifin you do, I'm gonna . . . I'm gonna get a screwdriver and unscrew your belly button 'til your butt falls off. Has you ever seen a kid with no butt? It's a scary sight. Do you hear me!"

Audrey had to put her hand over her mouth and go around the other side of the tree to keep herself from laughing hysterically.

She could hear Howie giving Sunny further instructions: "When you're untied you gonna sit down and eat a sandwich and an apple . . . not da one in your mouth but one over there on the cookie tray. You're also gonna drink the rest of the milk in the cup. No screamin', no cryin', just eatin'."

Sunny nodded, sheepishly. He would have agreed to standing on his head in manure at that point. He just wanted to be untied and the apple taken out of his mouth.

As Howie slowly untied Sunny, he kept reminding Sunny of the conditions of his release. When Sunny was completely untied, he grabbed the apple out of his mouth and threw it on the ground. He stretched his arms out in front of him. The glare Sunny gave Howie gave Howie the creeps. Sunny sat and gobbled down the sandwich and milk.

Sunny never did tell on Howie. Often when Howie was around Sunny, Sunny would put one hand on his belly button and the other hand on his rear end. He wasn't taking any chances that his Uncle Howie would go through with his threat.

One day Howie would regret the stunt he pulled on Sunny. It turned out that Sunny had a good long memory.

CHAPTER 34

Up the Apple Tree

Autumn was quickly upon them. The leaves began to turn magnificent hues of reds, oranges, and yellows. The delicious apples in the county were ripe. The ocean breeze changed its direction and blew mainly from the northeast and northwest, infusing the air with a fresh salty fragrance. Suzie loved the smell of the salty cool air. To her it smelled like an expensive perfume.

That autumn was special because World War II came to an end. Japan had finally surrendered. The war left many families mourning for their loved ones who were lost in battle. Grace's brother, Hector, lost his life when his ship was bombed. Bill lost several cousins. Not one family went without a loss over those six years of combat. On September 2nd, 1945, when news broke that the war was over, towns and cities all over Canada and many other countries piled into the streets to celebrate. Families and friends threw parties to mark the end to the horror and to welcome new beginnings. Grace and her family were no exception. Grace and Bill decided they would host a party for their friends. Bill took care of the beverages and Grace the food. Of course, homemade apple desserts were on the menu since apples were so plentiful at the time. Grace asked Howie and Suzie to gather apples for her.

One activity that Howie and Suzie enjoyed was picking up the apples that had fallen from the trees outside the fence at a neighbouring farm. The apples were often bruised but Grace transformed them into tasty applesauce, apple jelly and apple pies. Her apple pies 'were to die for' as Bill repeatedly said.

Suzie and Howie would fill the old wooden bushel basket that had been used to gather apples for years. Once it was full the two of them would carry it together, each holding a handle. It was awkward and heavy when it was full. They often had to carry it about ten feet and stop for a rest. They did not mind because as a reward for picking and bringing home the apples, they got to be the first to taste the goodies that Grace made.

Howie and Suzie set out to gather apples with Tucker following close behind them. Howie carried the empty old wooden bushel basket. Suzie carried a bag lunch that their mother had packed for them. They took their time gathering the apples to choose the best ones. Howie and Suzie searched for apples that had few bruises and no wormholes. Tucker was busy eating apples and chasing flies.

On that day, Howie thought they should move down the road to Old Farmer Fred's place. Howie claimed the apples there were in much better shape than the apples they had been harvesting.

"I'm not sure we should be goin' there, Howie. You know the mean mare is in that there field," said an uncomfortable Suzie.

Howie used his skills of persuasion: "Suzie, it's gonna take us way less time ifin we pick at Old Fred's place. The apples there are much nicer, hardly a bruise on them. I heard they are the best apples in all of Nova Scotia. Can you imagine how good Maw's pies and jellies would be a tastin' with those apples? I can just taste them now . . . mmmm." Howie smacked his lips as if he had truly just eaten some of the imaginary goodies. He rubbed his stomach and repeatedly made a "Mmmmmmmm" sound.

Howie's antics made Suzie laugh so he hammed it up even more and begged her until she gave in. They walked half a mile down the road to Old Fred's farm. They both went close to the fence to see if the miserable old grey horse was anywhere in sight. They did not see her, so they started looking for apples. The grass was taller, and it was not as easy to spot the hidden fruit. By moving the grass aside with their hands, they were able to find and gather half a basket of apples.

Suzie announced it was time to eat their lunch. As Suzie and Howie ate, they chatted about the family, especially Sunny. Howie shared his story about the time he had tied Sunny to the horse chestnut tree. Suzie laughed so hard she started to choke on her sandwich.

"Stop, Howie. I'm chokin'. Stop makin' me laugh," chuckled Suzie.

When Howie and Suzie finished their lunch, Suzie got busy searching for apples in the deep grass. Howie walked down the road along the fence, looking for the old cantankerous mare. The mare had a reputation for charging and biting people. A few of Howie's friends had their rear ends bitten by this beast.

Grace had previously warned Howie and Suzie to stay out of the fenced-in field that held the old mare. Besides, they had no business being in the farmer's fields for any reason.

The gossip around town was that Old Farmer Fred had made the mare mean by mistreating her. He trained the horse to guard the apple field. The other rumor was that the horse was a demon horse. The minute anyone besides Old Farmer Fred was in her sight or in smelling range, the mare charged at them full speed. People said she had stomped two men to death and maimed a woman. Some said that the horse killed Old Farmer Fred's wife. Farmer Fred and his wife used to fight all the time, so he did not have the horse put down when the mare bit her and stomped her to death.

Others said the horse was over one hundred years old and would never die.

Howie did not see the mare anywhere. He was sure the horse was in the barn. That meant they could climb the fence and get some good apples out of the tree. Howie returned to where Suzie was picking. He grabbed the basket and walked a few hundred feet down the road where there was an apple tree close to the fence. Howie put the basket down and looked up at the tree branches that reached over the fence. Then he found a sturdy tree limb he could stand on and throw apples down. He placed the basket right under the branch.

Suzie looked up and noticed the basket was gone. "What da," she exclaimed.

"Over here, Suzie. Come on over here. I has the basket," Howie shouted and waved his arm so she could see exactly where he was.

Together Suzie and Tucker walked down the road and when she was standing in front of Howie she asked, "What are you doin' over here? There are plenty of apples where we was."

"Now, Suzie, before you say 'no' just be hearin' what I gonna say," insisted Howard.

Suzie thought, *what is he gonna come out with now? What hair-brained scheme is he's going to ask me to be involved in?*

Howie told her his idea, explaining that he had walked up and down the fence and the mare was not around. He assumed that the horse was in the barn or had finally died. Therefore, they could climb over the fence and climb the tree. They could pick the apples and throw them in the basket right below the branch.

"Is you crazy or somethin'. What if the old mean mare is hidin' somewhere?" inquired Suzie in a whisper as she nervously glanced around.

"Suzie, she ain't a mouse that can hide in the grass fer Pete's sakes. She is a big old gray mare. Ifin she was in the field we could see her. The grass ain't that high." Howie kicked an apple in the grass. "Ifin you was a boy you'd do it. Girls are such fraidy cats. They can't do nothin' that takes nerve!"

"Hey! I can do anythin' a boy can do. I ain't no fraidy cat fer sure. You better never tell me I can't." With that declaration Suzie squeezed herself between the first and second rails of the fence into the field.

Howie was larger and had to climb over the wooden fence. He was over it lick-it split before Suzie changed her mind. Tucker tried to follow Suzie, but she ordered him, "Sit and stay there, Tucker!"

Both stood a few feet back from the tree, figuring out how they were going to climb it. They were discussing their options when Tucker started to bark loudly and incisively. Suzie was about to yell at Tucker to stop his barking when she and Arthur heard snorting in the distance behind them. Howie and Suzie turned around and saw the old mean gray mare. The mare was about one hundred feet away. The horse had her ears back, the whites of her eyes and teeth were showing, and her tail was swinging violently. She began to bob her head up and down and was pounding her front hoofs on the ground. Suzie and Howie knew what was coming next. They both rushed to the tree. Howie was up the tree within seconds. Suzie was struggling to get up because there were no branches hanging down for her to get her teeth on. The mare was already in a full gallop heading towards her. Howie reached down and grabbed Suzie's left arm and yanked as hard as he could just as the horse reached Suzie. Howie managed to pull her up onto the branch but not before the mare took a bite out of her britches. This was one time Suzie was thankful for old worn-out clothes. The material in her pants was so thin that when the mare bit into them and Howie pulled Suzie, they ripped.

The mare shook her head and released the piece of material in her mouth then reared up on her two hind legs and pawed at the tree with her hoofs. Then she dropped back down on all four legs and pounded the ground with her front hoofs. The mare repeated the up-and-down pattern several times with her hoofs. They were just out of reach from the ferocious beast, so they climbed up one more branch. Tucker was now howling and running back and forth along the outside of the fence. This spurred the mare on.

Suzie hollered down at him, "TUCKER! STOP IT! BE QUIET, SIT DOWN, AND STAY! TUCKER, SIT AND SHUTS UP!"

Tucker always obeyed Suzie's commands but this time he knew she was in danger. Though he stopped barking, he whined quietly as he looked sadly up at Suzie and Howie in the tree.

Shaking and out of breath, Howie said, "Holy shit, that was a close call." As he wiped the sweat off his brow with his sleeve he looked over at his sister.

Suzie's heart was beating so fast it felt like it did when she had started shock treatments on her arm years ago. She was trembling all over. Shaking her fist at Howie and crying, she yelled out, "You stupid, stupid ass! You almost gots us killed. What was I thinkin' to do what you say. I know better. I knew we'd be in a pickle if we come in the field with that monster mare. We gonna git a good lickin' fer this fer sure."

Then they both grew quiet to calm themselves down. After fifteen minutes the mare finally walked away from the tree but stayed nearby. She was keeping her eyes on the two intruders.

Suzie said, "So, smarty pants, what are we gonna do now?"

Howard blushed and dropped his head in embarrassment. "I don't know. We're in a mess, we are. That darn mare is still over there. I'm guessin' we have to wait till she leaves."

It took thirty minutes for Suzie's heart to stop racing. Howie was so exhausted from the ordeal that he leaned against the tree trunk and took a nap. Suzie kept a watchful eye on him because she was worried, he might slip off the branch. Although, she thought if he did, he would get what was coming to him. She wanted to throttle Howie for getting them in such a jam. Then Suzie started internally reprimanding herself. She knew better than to listen to Howie. She was older than him, only by a year, but still older.

When Howie woke up, they tried to remain quiet, hoping the mare would leave. When they spoke, it seemed to rile the horse up and it would look up at them and stare. Dusk was falling, and they had no idea how long they were in the tree.

Taking matters into hand, Suzie yelled down at Tucker, "Tucker, go get Maw, go get Maw."

Howie realized he had to renounce any of his plans to escape their dilemma. Sending Tucker to get Maw was probably the only way they were going to get out of the tree and to safety.

It was pitch black out and Tucker had not come back.

"Gosh, Suzie. Doesn't Tucker usually come back right away?" asked Howie, feeling on edge.

"Ya he usually does. I'm gettin' worried and wonderin' what's happened to him," whispered Suzie anxiously.

As Howie reached out and took Suzie's hand he whispered, "Guessin' Maw is goin' to be a mite worried 'cause we're not home yet. She don't know where we are 'cause we're usually up the road. I sure got us in a heap of a mess, Suzie. I'm sorry!"

Both had no idea if the mare was still around, but they knew they had to just stay put. They could not risk an encounter with the beast in the pitch black of the night.

Hours went by and it grew a bit cool, and it started to drizzle. The two sat in the tree holding each other to try to stay warm. They both wondered if anyone was going to come to their rescue.

CHAPTER 35
The Rescue

Tucker did his duty and raced back to the house. No one was outside in the yard, so Tucker went to the back door and barked piercingly. Grace recognized Tucker's emergency call and rushed to open the back door where Tucker stood in front of her and continued to bark. Grace immediately grabbed his collar before he fled. It was hard enough to keep track of Tucker when he took off in the direction of where Suzie was in the daylight, let alone in the dark.

Grace brought Tucker into the house and tied a rope to his collar. "Good boy, Tucker. Sit there fer a minute and NO BARKING!" commanded Grace as she put on her jacket.

The whole household had heard Tucker's S.O.S. bark. Critch was the first to rush into the kitchen.

"Critch, come with me. I suspect Suzie and Howie has gotten demselfs in a fix. They shoulda been home hours ago," said a concerned Grace.

The rest of the family came running from all directions in the house.

"What's happenin'?" asked Arthur.

Grace responded, "Critch and I are goin' to look for Suzie and Howie. The rest of you can stay here and go back to what you was doin'. Bill, I'll be back soon."

Critch put his coat on, grabbed a flashlight and stepped outside with Grace. Grace handed him the rope that Tucker was tied to.

"Tucker, take us to Suzie and Howie," instructed Critch.

As soon as Critch gave this command Tucker was raring to go. He bolted so fast that he jerked the rope and threw Critch off balance.

"Stop, Tucker. Slow and easy, boy," said Critch, as he steadied himself and shortened the rope, leaving little slack. Tucker slowed down but he kept pulling on the rope, attempting to run.

As they arrived at the spot where Howie and Suzie usually picked apples, Grace called their names. There was no answer. When they shone the flashlight near the fence, they saw the impressions in the long grass of where the two children had walked and where Tucker had laid down. A trail in the grass led down the road. Grace, Critch, and Tucker followed the trail down the road.

Critch stopped and said, "Maw . . . stop. I think I hear them a talkin' ahead. Tucker, sit and no barkin'!"

Grace stopped and tilted her head and ear in the direction Critch had indicated. Sure enough, she could hear the faint chattering of the missing children.

"Turn the flashlight off, Critch. I will keep Tucker here. You go ahead and see what the two of them is doin'. Don't let them know you're there. Come back and tell me where they are," instructed Grace.

Quietly Critch crept down the road and when he discovered where the voices were coming from, he reported back to Grace. "Maw, they are in the tree in Old Farmer Fred's field, and I heard the mean old mare snortin'."

Grace shook her head and said, "Of all the tomfoolery that they could do! I've told them over and over agin not to go in that there field."

Grace stood there a few minutes thinking. She had in mind to teach Howie and Suzie a good lesson. Since it was a mild night, the rain had stopped and the children were wearing coats, Grace decided she would leave them in the tree overnight. Critch agreed to stay near the tree throughout the night in case they needed help. He kept the flashlight off to keep his presence undetected. Tucker led Grace back home in the dark. Tucker kept trying to head back to Suzie and Howie, but Grace kept telling him, "No, home, Tucker."

When Grace got home, she made sure Tucker stayed in the house. She instructed everyone to not let Tucker outside, even though they may find him whining at the door. Grace knew the minute Tucker got the chance he would be hightailing it to Suzie. She told Bill about finding Suzie and Howie up in the tree in Old Farmer Fred's orchard and that they would be spending the night there.

Bill laughed. "Well, that will teach them. I bet they will never go in a farmer's field again."

Throughout the night Suzie and Howie attempted to take turns sleeping. They knew if they both fell asleep one or both could fall out of the tree. Suzie tried to take her turn first, but although her eyes were closed, she could hear everything around her. She heard coyotes howling, an owl hooting and, every once in a while, something below them was moving in the grass. The coyotes and owl did not bother her but the unknown critter in the grass below caused her alarm.

Suzie opened her eyes and nudged Howie. "Do you hear that? There's a somethin' in the grass over there by the fence."

Howie whispered, "I know. I've been tryin' to figure out what it is. Maybe it's just a skunk or coon? Ifin it's a coon I hope it don't try and climb this tree. You know coons has rabies and if we got bit, we'd have rabies and go mad. We'd be foaming at the mouth and Maw would have to tie us up like a dog or put us in a cage."

Of course, it was Critch making the sounds they were hearing. When Critch heard them talking, he moved his legs around to make the rustling noise more intense. He was getting a kick out of scaring them. At one point he found a few stones and threw them at the tree trunk.

"Holy Christ! What was that? Is the coon shooting sometin' at us?" a startled Howie yelled.

Right away Suzie shushed him. "Shhh, not so loud. You goin' have the mean old mare comin' over here. And stop your swearin'. Maw would be worshin' your mouth out with soap ifin she heard you. Asides, coons don't chuck things."

Howie was not in a mood to be chastised by his sister. "You're really bossy, do you know that?" he retorted. "You thinkin' you know everythin'. You ain't my maw, so stop tellin' me what to do and not to do."

"Well you sure needed tellin' what to do today or we wouldn't be up a tree in the dark . . . tired, hungry and cold," cried Suzie.

"Now you're goin' to be a crybaby. You know I was just buggin' you," Howie said, trying to stop Suzie from crying. He put one arm around her and pulled her close to his side. "Try and sleep a bit, girly. I'll watch for the coon and mare."

Because Suzie was exhausted, she did fall asleep. Howie was worried her snoring would draw attention to them. It really did not matter because they were high enough in the tree that the miserable mare could not harm them. The other animal appeared to have left.

Critch was beginning to feel sorry for them, but he knew his mother wanted them to get the full impact of what they had done, so he stayed in the grass and kept quiet. He decided he might as well sleep since the two in the tree were not in any imminent danger.

The rest of the evening Suzie slept. Howie kept himself awake for a few hours by whispering his recollection of the Huckleberry Finn story to himself. When the first ray of sunlight shone on Suzie's face, she woke up and found Howie asleep, leaning to one side. She tugged on his shirt to pull him upright. He was in a deep sleep because this motion did not even wake him. She gently touched his arm and said, "Howie, it's mornin'."

Howie yawned and started to stretch. Suddenly he realized where he was. He almost lost his balance and fell off the branch.

Critch heard the two of them talking and stood up. "Hey, you two brats. What are you doin' up that tree?" he snickered.

"Critch! Critch, you come fer us," squealed Suzie.

"I'm gonna help you down. The old mean mare went to the barn so it's a good time to git yourselves outta there."

Critch climbed the fence and helped Suzie down first, then Howie followed quickly behind her. Suzie went through the two fence railings like she did before, and Howie and Critch climbed over the fence.

Critch could not help but notice that Suzie had a big hole in her pants. "What happened? Did the mare take a chunk outta your pants?"

Timidly she nodded her head.

Critch burst out laughing. "You're just damn lucky he didn't bit your arse off."

When Critch got control of himself, he picked up the basket that was only half full of apples and they headed home.

"Is Tucker at home? He never comed back!" asked a worried Suzie.

Critch told her that Tucker had come to get help and he led them to where they were stranded.

Howie was annoyed when he heard this story. "And you fringin' left us in the tree all night. We were cold, hungry, and worried."

Critch responded with a grin, "More like you was scared shitless. Did you learn a lesson?"

"Sure, to never listen to Howie and his stupidity!" exclaimed Suzie.

Howie responded with a smack to her arm and said, "You went along with me. You wanted those nice apples as much as I did."

Before they could continue their bickering, Critch put a stop to it. "Enough of that. We best get home. Maw will be watin' fer you two."

Howie and Suzie entered the kitchen looking sheepish. Grace was making breakfast. She did not even look up, but just asked, "You two hungry? If you is, go and git worshed up."

They quickly washed up. Suzie also changed her pants and hid the torn pair under the bed.

Grace never asked them where they had been all night. She did not bring up the subject, nor did anyone else in the family. Howie and Suzie thought it was strange, but they were pleased that they did not have to revisit the embarrassing episode. Grace did make sure the two of them stayed awake all day by giving them extra chores. By the evening they were both exhausted and went to bed on their own right after supper. Grace knew the experience was enough for them and she was sure they had learned their lesson.

Family life, regular routines, school, and work kept the family busy over the next couple of years. Suzie's knee was doing better, and she did not have to wear her knee brace constantly. Ruby adored her big sister Suzie and spent as much time with her as Suzie would allow.

Marg gave birth to another son, Danny. He and Sunny were seven years apart in age. Grace refused to become mother and grandmother to two of Marg's children. Grace insisted that Marg stay home with Danny. Marg protested but her mother was adamant. Sunny continued to be a regular visitor at Grace's place. When Sunny started school, he would go to Grace's house afterwards until his mother picked him up. Sometimes Marg did not show up until six o'clock. Sunny did not seem to mind spending most of his waking hours with his nan. He enjoyed having supper with the crew. Marg had still not learned how to cook, and Sunny would say that his mom even burnt water. He had calmed down a bit and was not as much of a nuisance. Grace helped curb some of the wild side in him. Norm continued to work as a miner and had become accustomed to Sunny being gone most of the time. He barely knew his own son.

The family had lived eight years in Truro and Grace enjoyed the sense of belonging and familiarity. It had been a good place to raise her three younger children.

Audrey ended her schooling at sixteen years old like the rest of her siblings. Critch, Arthur, and Bill continued to work at the mine. When Arthur turned eighteen, he took a position as an underground miner. Grace was not thrilled to know her young son was working deep in the ground. She knew it was a dangerous job and she often worried about him. There had been many miners' deaths over the previous few years in Nova Scotia. The thought of those men's fates sent chills down her spine. Each morning when the four men in the family went to work in the mine, she would pray that God would keep them safe and bring them home.

Fran had one more child, Ralph, who was now six years old. Audrey, her daughter, had just turned seven. Grace saw them once a year in the summer when Fran came to visit. Fran and Wallace continued to appear to be rich folks. Grace could not figure out how they had so much money when Wallace was between jobs most of the time. When the topic was raised, Fran was evasive. Fran had lightened up on the makeup and Grace had to admit her daughter did look elegant, like a movie star.

Just before Suzie's thirteenth birthday, Bill announced he had taken a new job. Grace was not too pleased. She had hoped she would live out her life in Truro. Little did Grace know that the move they were about to make would bring many changes into her life and her family's. Some changes would be beneficial; others would cause internal turmoil.

CHAPTER 36

Off to Quebec

The family packed up once again but this time they were moving out of Grace's beloved Nova Scotia to Duparquet, Quebec. The gold mine industry in Quebec was flourishing; the mining industry in Nova Scotia was slowing down, and Bill wanted to secure a better future for the family.

When Marg heard that her mother was moving, she was distraught. She had never lived away from her mother for more than a few months. Raising her children without Grace was too much for Marg to even imagine. Therefore, she insisted that Norm go with Bill to seek employment in Duparquet.

Bill and Norm went to Quebec to apply for jobs and find accommodations for their families, while Grace and the children packed up all their belongings. Critch and Arthur planned on moving with the family. They kept their jobs until Bill returned with a report on the job market and accommodations in Quebec.

Bill made a phone call home to let Grace know he had been hired by the Beattie and Dorchester Mining Company, as an electrician. Norm acquired a job with the same company, as a miner. Bill told Grace to let Critch and Arthur know that the mine was still hiring, and they should give their notices to their employer and move with the family. Housing was difficult to find in the booming small mining community, but Bill was able to find a main-floor apartment with three bedrooms. Norm had not found a place for his family. He would stay at the hotel and keep searching. He would contact Marg as soon as he did find accommodations. She wanted to move at the same time as her mother, but this time no amount of crying or complaining could change the situation.

When Bill returned to Truro, he described Duparquet as a small town that was growing fast because of the many gold mines in the area. It had two corner stores, a hotel, a grocery store, a dress shop, and a pharmacy. There were two doctors in town, one for the miners and one for the public. The mining company had contracted for twenty houses to be built in the small town. Numerous homes had been turned into apartments by their owners. A town hall held dances and other community activities. There were two schools, one for the Anglophone students and one for the French Catholic students. Most people spoke French, but there were several miners and their families from the east coast and Ontario who spoke English. He was told that Lac Duparquet had nice beaches and good fishing. Bill said he did not find it as cold since they did not have the ocean winds from every direction like in Truro. His portrayal of the town of Duparquet sounded wonderful. The children were excited for the new adventures that awaited them in Quebec.

Early the next morning the sun was shining, but the frigid temperature still lingered in Truro. Critch, Arthur, and Howie finished loading the truck then left for Duparquet. Bill, Grace, Audrey, Suzie, Ruby, and Tucker piled into the car about one hour later. Bill had a heck of a time starting the frozen car. It was so cold that the tires were square and for the first thirty miles it felt like they were riding in an old horse-drawn wagon . . . *clunk, clunk, clunk*. The car heater barely kept the front windshield clear of frost. The back windows were frosted over and the two shivering children sitting beside them could see their breaths and cuddled up to one another. Tucker lay shivering on the floor by the back seat.

Grace wanted to slap Bill silly. She could not understand why he always had a hankering to move in the winter. It was so hard on everyone, especially her. This kind of weather always made her back ache in the worst way, and she would have to take a morphine pill to make it through the day's drive. She grabbed her purse from the floor and searched in what she called the 'abyss.' Finally, after much rummaging, taking out tissues, lipstick, pencils, hair pins and her wallet, she found her bottle of pills. She opened it and to her dismay there were only two pills left. It would take them two days to travel from Truro to Duparquet if they had no delays. She would run out of pills and the thought of it made her heart race. She was sweating and panicking. To try to calm herself down she took one pill and silently did deep breathing.

After forty minutes she began to relax. The pain in her back was easing. Grace knew the pill would not take all the pain away because she had upped her dosage to two pills over the past six months since one pill was not effective anymore.

The trip was long and exhausting. When Bill stopped for gas, everyone made a run for the restrooms and Tucker had to be taken out to do his business. Grace had packed enough food for several meals.

That evening around nine o'clock, Bill pulled into a motel just before Quebec City. It was not a classy place by any means. The paint on the walls was chipping, the floor looked like it could use a good scrubbing, and there was a film of dust on the bedside tables. The common bathroom was filthy, with rings around the toilet and sink. When Grace rolled back the bedspread, she saw brown, stained dirty sheets. Grace was worried the children would catch some dreadful disease and insisted they all sleep on top of the covers in their clothes. At least the room had two double beds and it was heated. This motel also allowed pets. Grace had not even thought about what to do with Tucker when they stopped overnight. He would have frozen to death if he were left in the car. The girls slept in one bed and Bill and Grace in the other.

The next day was a repeat of the day before. They only stopped to fuel the car, run to the restroom, and take Tucker out to do his business. It was still bitterly cold, and the ride was just as uncomfortable.

The children knew better than to complain because Bill did not have patience on this trip. Suzie had complained at the beginning of the trip that she was cold. Bill angrily yelled at her, "Stop complaining or you're walking the rest of the way!" After his outburst the children whispered when they talked, and they did not talk much.

Grace was not pleased with Bill's display of anger because she too was cold. When she thought about it, he had been less and less lenient with the children over the past year. He was becoming a grumpy old man. Keeping the children quiet when Bill was around put a lot of pressure on Grace. She also began keeping things from him that she knew would upset him. Grace and Bill's personal relationship seemed to be alright, but she was not sure about that either. With that last thought Grace pulled out her purse and took her last morphine pill.

They arrived in Duparquet at eleven o'clock that night. The children were all huddled together, fast asleep.

Critch, Arthur, and Howie were at the apartment. They had arrived early that morning, unloaded the truck, set up the beds and unpacked the kitchen supplies and dishes. Critch even picked up a few groceries so Grace would not have to go shopping for a few days.

Grace's three sons came out of the apartment to greet them as soon as they saw the lights from the car pull into the driveway. As soon as the back door of the car was open Tucker bolted out to go pee. Critch carried Ruby into the house and put her in her bed. Suzie just wanted to know where she was going to sleep so she could get into her bed and warm up. Audrey, although tired, wanted to stay up and have a hot cup of tea to warm herself up. Tucker ran in the house ahead of Grace and found a warm radiator to lay beside. Bill, exhausted from driving, said his goodnights, and headed straight to bed. Grace, Audrey and the three brothers stayed up, had a cup of tea, and talked about their trips.

While they were chatting, Critch pulled a bottle of whiskey out and poured himself half a glass. Critch had grown partial to whiskey; he usually had some stashed away somewhere.

"Maw, do you want some to warm your innards?" asked Crtich.

Grace nodded. "Sure, could use some warmin' up. Sure, give me a few mouthfuls."

That night Grace slept like a log. When she awoke the next day, she was disoriented. She had such a deep sleep that she was groggy.

The other family members were already up, and Audrey had made breakfast.

When Grace went into the kitchen, she said, "Well I'm thinkin I should be a-sleepin' in more often!"

After breakfast Grace walked around the apartment and was pleased with her new home. They had indoor plumbing with hot water, a washroom with a toilet, an electric stove, and an electric fridge. These were luxuries she had never dreamed she would have. She was nervous about the stove because she had heard that it could give you cancer. That is what the older folks back in Truro would say.

When she expressed her concern to Bill, he laughed. "Good grief, woman, that's just a bunch of malarkeys."

Grace was still unsure about the new kitchen fandangles, but she knew she would have to get used to them.

CHAPTER 37

Not Again

According to Bill the apartment upstairs was vacant, and Grace wondered why Norm had not rented it. Bill did not want to tell her that rumours were that it was haunted, and Norm was extremely superstitious. Just the idea of moving into a place that could be haunted freaked him out.

The family had been in their apartment a few days when Grace heard water running. She checked the sink in the kitchen and in the bathroom and the taps were not on.

Bill was out getting groceries. When he came home Grace told him about the running water noise she was hearing. He stopped what he was doing and listened. He said, "I think it's coming from upstairs. I bet some kids from the neighbourhood were up there and turned the taps on. I'll go and check."

Bill went outside, climbed up the back stairs and found the apartment was unlocked. He went into the bathroom and sure enough the tap was on. He turned it off and went back downstairs. The next morning at breakfast they heard water running again. Bill jumped up and ran outside, thinking he'd catch the scallywags who had gone into the apartment and turned the tap on. No one was coming down the stairs. He thought the intruders sure were swift at getting out of the apartment but must be within earshot.

Bill yelled, "I know you were in the apartment upstairs and turned the tap on and you damn well better not do it again."

Bill went up the stairs, into the apartment and turned the taps off. He went downstairs and got his toolbox out and found a lock with a key which he installed on the door upstairs.

When he came down, he confidently said to Grace, "That'll fix the buggers. I'll put the key to the lock in the kitchen cupboard."

At supper time they heard running water again. Bill jumped up from the table and looked in the cupboard. The key was still there. He took the key and headed back up the stairs to the apartment. The lock was still on the door and had not been removed or tampered with.

Bill unlocked the door and went into the bathroom. The tap was running once again. As he looked in every room there was no evidence that anyone had been there.

Bill scratched his head and realized two things. The first was he had to stop renting places that were cheap and that no one else would rent. The second thing was that maybe once again some kind of spirit was involved.

"Damn it . . . maybe there is a loose tap and when the trucks went by it turned on. But I'm sure I closed that tap and made sure it was secure," mumbled Bill to himself. "Well, I guess I am going to do what I think I should do. I remember my father doing this at one point." Then aloud, Bill commanded firmly, "In God's name, leave here immediately."

He blushed as he said it, although no one was upstairs with him. The tap immediately turned off and he felt a breeze on his face. He decided he would tell no one about his encounter. The family had enough fearful memories about the ghost lady in Antigonish. In that moment he made a vow that he would always find out the history of any place before renting or buying.

When Bill went downstairs, he told Grace he figured out the problem and gave her the explanation of the tap being loose and when the big mining trucks went by the tap would turn on.

"Oh really," Grace said. She did not believe a word he said but she was not going to call him a liar.

When Norm came over for supper one evening, Bill told him the apartment upstairs was still empty. Norm started to object, but Bill interrupted, telling him the same story he told Grace about the tap.

Norm laughed in relief. "You're a kiddin'. This whole-time people thought the place was haunted and it was just a loose tap. Well, I guess I better be a checkin' into rentin' it then."

Norm moved his family to Duparquet one week later.

CHAPTER 38

A Special Christmas Present

Christmas was upon them before they realized it. Grace was so busy with the moving and unpacking, the holiday had hardly crossed her mind. A few days before Christmas she went out to look for presents for Suzie, Howie, Ruby, and her grandsons, Sunny and Danny. The older children did not need to have gifts as much as the younger ones. Grace had discovered a second-hand store on the main street right beside the hotel. She went into the store and was greeted by a pleasant woman about Grace's age.

"Bonjour, Madame. Joyeux Noël. Puis-je vous aider?" said the woman.

It was the first time Grace had heard anyone speak what she assumed was French. Grace was mesmerized and charmed by the flow of the words and the woman's voice, but she could not understand one word.

The woman looked concerned and put her hand on Grace's shoulder. "Ça va, Madame?"

Grace snapped out of her daze and told the woman, "Sorry, I don't be a speakin' French."

The woman smiled at her and, in broken English, said, "I speak little bit English. Can I help you?"

Grace told her she was looking for Christmas presents for her children and two grandsons. Between hand gestures and pointing to objects, the two women were able to communicate.

Grace was pleased with her purchases. When she got home, she asked Audrey to wrap the children's gifts. There had been no time to purchase Christmas wrapping paper, so newspaper and string once again were used. Critch and Arthur cut down a small white pine outside of town and brought it home for the family to decorate. Critch filled a big, galvanized pail with water to use as a tree stand. The tree was so bushy and full that its lowest branches held the tree sturdy in the bucket. Grace thought it was the prettiest tree they ever had.

Somehow during the move their Christmas tree decorations were lost. Grace and Bill's search of the apartment and the shed was not successful. Grace was disheartened because in the lost Christmas box were a few wooden ornaments that her father made for her when she was a young girl. The day before Christmas Audrey popped popcorn for the children to string. Suzie cut out paper snowflakes from a writing tablet. Marg had a box of buttons and she tied loops of thread to them to hang as ornaments on the tree. A cardboard star covered with aluminum foil was placed on the top of the tree.

While the girls were busy decorating the tree, Grace was in the kitchen with Howie and Sunny who volunteered to help Grace make sugar cookies. Grace knew why they were so anxious to help; they wanted to have a few cookies from the first batch. The boys helped roll the dough and cut the cookies. Some of the baked cookies would be strung and hung on the tree. Bill came home with candy canes and he and Ruby hung them on the tree. When the family put the last touches on the Christmas tree, they all stood back and admired it. All except Marg who kept rearranging the decorations to her liking.

A serious and concerned Sunny pulled at Grace's apron and told her he had to talk to her alone. Grace and Sunny went into the only room in the apartment that was not occupied to have their secret conversation.

"Nan, there is no chimney here. How's Santa going to be comin' down it ifin it ain't there? Maybe we should be a leavin' a window unlocked for him. We need to put cookies out fer Santa also. I'm thinkin' Danny and me should be a stayin' here tonight. You know that Santa may get confused ifin we are in our apartment. He won't know where to put ours presents," babbled Sunny.

Grace smiled at her oldest grandson and was thrilled to see the innocence in his eyes and excitement on his face. Life would pass all too quickly, and these would fade but for now she was taking in these precious moments.

Sunny waited for Grace to answer him and since she didn't, he cupped her face in his hands and looked her in the eyes and said, "Nan, I'm a talkin' to you! Can Danny and me stay here tonight?"

"Yes, you can," Grace said gently and kissed her grandson.

In return he gave her a long hard hug and then ran off to tell Danny and Ruby that they were staying overnight. Grace got a good chuckle out of their reasoning and agreed that they could lay blankets on the floor in the girls' room and sleep there.

Sunny, Danny, and Ruby went to bed early. They were so excited about Santa coming that they gulped down their supper, changed into their pajamas and went straight to bed. Of course, they didn't go right to sleep. The rest of the family could hear giggling coming from the bedroom for over an hour.

The presents were placed under the tree and Bill filled the stockings. Bill put an orange, a candy cane, and a pencil in each stocking. This had become a family tradition since the first Christmas that he spent with the family.

The next morning the children were up at five o'clock and screaming that Santa had come. The sleepy adults dragged themselves out of bed and headed to the living room. While Grace made tea and coffee, the children emptied their stockings and ate their oranges. Bill gave the presents out and each child had their turn opening their gifts. Ruby got a diary bound with a rose fabric and a pair of mittens. Sunny and Howie each got a Swiss Army knife and a toque. Danny got a metal toy truck and mittens. Suzie unwrapped a pair of black leather lace-up shoes with half-inch heels. She was a bit confused since her shoes were still in good shape, but she did not want to appear ungrateful, so she thanked Grace and Bill. The other two presents had her stumped. Suzie stared down at the two metal objects in her hands.

They were shaped like the toe area of a shoe sole, each with six small holes evenly spaced along the edges.

"They are . . . are . . . lovely, Maw." Suzie hesitated because she had no clue what they were.

"Yah they are me girly. You don't know what they is, do you?" snickered Grace.

Suzie confessed that she was baffled. The rest of the family, except Audrey, were also mystified. They all tried to guess what the strange objects were and had a good time joking and laughing over the answers.

Finally, Suzie couldn't wait any longer. "Maw, fer Pete's sakes, what is they?"

"My dear girly, they is taps. They go on the bottom of your new shoes. Those shoes is called tap shoes. When you dance you can hear the tappin' noise on the floor. They give tap lessons at the community hall fer any girls or boys who's a wanna to learn. It's a big thing that the French girls your age enjoys. Since you love to be a jiggin' around the house, I was thinkin' it be a good gift."

Suzie was delighted and wanted to put on her shoes right away. Critch offered to nail the taps to the soles of the tap shoes. With her new tap shoes Suzie did a jig in each room of the house. Suzie realized if she wanted to learn how to tap dance, she had to wear her knee brace. While she was jigging her knee gave out and she ended up on her knees right in front of Arthur.

Arthur, although older now, was still Arthur. "I know I are lookin' and actin' like a king of this castle, but since you're me sista, you don't have to kneel before me."

Suzie reached out and smacked his arm. "You're more like the king of the shitter."

"Damn, girly, your arm is strong. That bloody well hurt." He winced and rubbed his arm.

CHAPTER 39
Friendship

Suzie took tap-dancing lessons at the community hall on Monday evenings. She developed a close friendship with another fourteen year old girl, who also took lessons. Glenda and Suzie spent a lot of time together and over half of that time they practiced tap dancing. The teacher was so impressed with Suzie and Glenda's tap-dancing routines that she recommended them as entertainers to the local hotel owner. At first Grace and Bill did not think a thirteen-year-old should be dancing in a hotel bar. Suzie pleaded and begged.

"Suzie, ifin we say you can, remember people will talk 'bout you bein the 'cripple girl.' They will notice your arm. Is you strong 'nough to be a handlin' that?" Grace wanted to prepare Suzie.

"Yah, Maw, long as they don't pity me. I really hate when people pity me," Suzie angrily declared.

Bill spoke up: "Suzie, we will agree to you doing this if your mom, me, or one of your older brothers is there when you dance."

Grace and Suzie thought that was a fair compromise.

Suzie and Glenda were accompanied by a fiddle player, and they tap danced to their hearts' delight. They were one of three acts that the hotel patrons enjoyed on Friday and Saturday evenings. Occasionally, Suzie would overhear a member of the audience referring to her as the "poor cripple girl."

After her act, Suzie would walk up to them and proudly announce, "I'm just fine . . . Nothin' poor 'bout me!"

When Suzie's tap-dancing days were over, she kept her precious taps safely tucked away in her jewellery box until the day she died.

CHAPTER 40

The Scare

On April 24th, 1947, tragedy struck the mining communities in Quebec. In the town of Malartic, two hours from Duparquet, at the East Malartic Mine, a fire broke out underground and twelve miners perished. The mining towns in Quebec were in mourning and Grace was horrified. Grace had been drinking daily to ease her back pain. Morphine was no longer available since the medical profession had realized its addictive nature, so it was used only for severe medical conditions. With the mining tragedy and Grace's trepidation for her family, her alcohol consumption increased. The family knew she was taking a drink occasionally, but they had no idea to what extent.

Her posture now was in a hunchback position. Some of the children in town called her "The Humpback of Notre Dame." The family, especially the children, found this cruel and wounding. Howie and Sunny often got into scraps with other boys who ridiculed her.

Grace found it demoralizing. At one time she was a good-looking woman, but the years of pain and struggles had taken a toll on her body and aged her. All the anguish and toils she had endured through her life caught up with her. She was an emotionally, mentally, and physically exhausted woman, but she continued to tend to her family.

Suzie, Howie, and Ruby attended the small English-speaking school. It was a two-room schoolhouse. Grades one to four were in one room and grades five to eight were in the other room. Their two teachers were a young husband and wife from Ontario. The children found them strict, but fair. This couple were modern in their thinking and field trips were often planned.

The mine had buses that ran from the town to the mine for their employees. During the day when the buses were not running the school was able to use one. At the end of the school year, the students all piled on the bus and headed to the beach for a picnic. That sunny warm day was perfect for swimming, games, and scavenger hunts. Suzie was often the last to board the bus. She just found it easier if all the other students went ahead of her. This day the bus was full. When she got on the bus there was only one seat left, which was at the back of the bus. A young man from the eighth grade who was sitting at the front of the bus got up and headed to the empty seat in the back. Suzie was horrified and knew she had to sit in the seat that he left open for her because she did not want to appear ungrateful. She thanked him and sat down, but at the same time she was suspicious of his actions.

The girl beside her leaned over and whispered, "You know what this means? I'm glad I'm not you!"

All the way back to the school Suzie was beside herself and wondered how she was going to tell her mother about the incident. Suzie was in tears by the time the bus arrived at the school. Without saying a word to any of her friends or waiting for Howie, Ruby, and Sunny, she ran home.

When she got home, she went straight to her room and tried to figure out what she was going to do. Suzie decided she had no other choice but to tell her mother the predicament she was in. Howie and Ruby had arrived home and were in the kitchen filling Grace in on the activities of their awesome day.

Ruby turned to Suzie. "How come you didn't wait for us? Howie and I turned around and you were gone."

"Never you mind. I have to be a talkin' to Maw. So, you two scoot and put your stuff away," responded Suzie.

"Ahh, we want to know what's happenin'." Howie was a nosey one and wanted to know all the family happenings.

"Scoot, you two. Off you go so Suzie and I can be havin' a chat," instructed Grace.

They left reluctantly but did as their mother told them.

Suzie sat beside her mom at the kitchen table. "Maw . . . oh Maw . . ." Her voice was shaky, and tears were running down her face.

Grace held Suzie's hand. "Suzie, whatever it is, it can't be that bad. Come on, girly, tell Maw what's botherin' you."

"Oh, Maw, I been so careful, and it wasn't my fault. The boy offered and what was I to do. He was nice and kind. Oh, Maw!" Suzie took her hand away from her mother's hand and covered her face.

"Land sakes, girly, what are you talkin' 'bout?" Grace was growing extremely concerned.

"I'm in a family way!" Suzie blurted out.

Grace's eyes got huge; her heart started pounding in her chest and her mouth got dry. She rose from the table, took the whiskey from the cupboard, and poured herself a glass. Suzie's eyes followed her mother and she wished she could have a few sips of the golden liquid to calm her own nerves.

Grace's thoughts were whirling around: *Suzie is thirteen and a half and too damn young to be having a baby. She just started menstruating five months ago. Maybe I gave her too much freedom.*

Grace sat back down and gathered the courage to ask, "Suzie, who is the boy?"

"I don't know. He is in grade eight, Maw."

"Good grief . . . grade eight. You're both too young to be beddin' down together! Where did dis happen?"

Suzie was confused by her mother's remark about "beddin' down." She did not even know what her mother meant so she answered the question as to where: "In the bus!"

Grace could not believe that her Suzie did such a thing on the bus. "In front of the udder students?"

Grace thought she was going to be sick. How could her sweet little Suzie be a hussy? How did she miss this side of her character?

"Yes, Maw, in front of the other students. I tried, Maw . . . tried to get meself to the back of the bus. I really did," Suzie defended herself.

"In the front of the bus! Oh my God, Suzie. How could you? Did you lose your mind? What possessed you to do such a thing?" demanded Grace.

Suzie was full of shame. She was pale and her body felt numb. There were no more tears left. Of all the struggles she had in her life this was not one she would have ever imagined.

Grace took another big gulp of whiskey before she asked, "When did this happen?"

"Today on the way home from the beach." Suzie hung her head as she answered.

Grace was puzzled. "Suzie, ifin it only happened today, why do you think you're pregnant?"

"Well, Maw, you and everyone knows ifin you sit in the same seat a boy was just sitting in, you get pregnant," Suzie replied unwaveringly.

Grace smiled and asked Suzie to repeat what she had just said. Then she took a deep breath to keep from roaring with laughter. "Suzie, are you a-tellin' me that all you did was sit in a seat a boy gave up for you?"

"Yes, Maw. Isn't that bad enough?" Suzie was growing impatient with her mother's lack of understanding.

Grace burst out in hysterical laughter, holding her stomach, tears running down her face. She pounded her fist on the table and could not stop howling. Grace was overwhelmed by a combination of total relief and amusement at Suzie's misinformed belief about pregnancies.

Suzie was frustrated with her mother. "Glad you're a thinkin' it's funny that I'm pregnant. Maw, stop it."

Suzie stood up to walk away in indignation, but Grace, still laughing, grabbed her arm to stop her. Between bouts of laughter, Grace told Suzie, "Stay here. I'm not laughin' at you bein' pregnant, 'cause you're not, girly. Believin' me, you're not pregnant."

After about five minutes Grace got her laughter under control and explained to Suzie that a girl does not get pregnant by sitting in a seat that a boy had just sat in. Suzie was shocked. All the girls at school in her grade believed this. Shelly's mother had told Shelly and Shelly had shared the misinformation with the other girls in the class.

"Suzie, dear child, you sit in chairs that your brother and Bill have sat in many times and you and Audrey ain't ever been pregnant," rationalized Grace. "Time I be tellin' you all 'bout baby stuff."

Grace explained the "birds and bees" to Suzie. Suzie was shocked but thankful her mother brought clarity to the topic. Grace and Suzie would laugh at this memory for many years afterwards.

CHAPTER 41

Froggy

Just outside of town along the Duparquet River, Suzie found a quiet place; a rock that overlooked the river. From there she could see several islands, including the island where the Pikkogan Indian Reserve was located. She loved to watch the boats coming and going from the island; it reminded her of her cherished Nova Scotia. This place was her haven when she needed quiet and space away from the busy apartment.

One Saturday in June, when Suzie was fifteen, she met a young indigenous man while she was sitting on this rock, deep in thought. The young man ventured up the rock and sat a few feet behind her. He coughed and she just about jumped out of her skin.

"Good grief, you should have told me that you was behind me!" She reprimanded the stranger.

"Sorry!" he said, grinning. "I did not mean to scare you. My name is Fred, but people call me Froggy." He moved closer and sat beside Suzie.

"Hi, my name is Susan, but people call me Suzie. Why do they call you Froggy?"

"Well, my Kookum, my grandmother, said that when I was little, I loved to jump. One day she called me a frog. My older sisters and brothers thought it was cute, so they called me Froggy and it stuck! I am used to it now and sometimes when people call me Fred, I am not sure who they are talking to."

They both laughed. For hours they sat and chatted. Suzie liked Froggy and found him interesting. They agreed to meet at the rock the following Saturday.

Although Froggy was four years older than Suzie, they developed a deep friendship. He would talk about his family and their customs and Suzie would share information about her family and their customs. Suzie discovered that Froggy's family had lived in Quebec for many generations. He grew up on the reserve and he was employed by the same mine her brothers worked at. By the end of the summer, Froggy and Suzie had fallen in love. Suzie was head over heels for this polite and good-looking young man.

Sue and Ruby sitting on the rock where Froggy and Sue met.

Grace knew something was up because Suzie was singing a lot more than usual. When people spoke to her, they often had to repeat themselves because she was daydreaming. Although Suzie generally had an easy-going nature, now she was so mellow even her brothers' teasing did not affect her.

Bill heard rumours at the mine that Suzie had taken up with an indigenous man. As soon as he got home, he spoke to Grace. He insisted that she get to the bottom of the situation and that, if it was true, it had to stop. "No stepdaughter of mine is going to marry an Indian," Bill declared harshly.

Grace took Suzie aside and asked her if she was involved with an indigenous man. Suzie told her that she was and explained how they met and how they had fallen in love. Froggy had proposed to her, but she had not answered him. She wanted time to think. Froggy understood this response because he knew if they married their lives would be totally altered. Cross-cultural marriages were unthinkable in their day. Froggy made it clear that he not only loved and adored Suzie, but that he would protect and cherish her. No matter what it took he would find a way for them to be together and be happy.

"When was you gonna to tell me 'bout this Indian?" Grace asked angrily.

"When the time was right. I knew you would not approve of him, but if you got to know him, Maw, you would see he's a good man," declared Suzie.

Shaking her head, Grace made her opinions clear: "No, child, it makes no never mind ifin he's a good man or not. He's an Indian and you is white. Ifin you married do you know your children would have the one half of their body brown and the other half white. They would look like freaks. Sometin' like a skunk. No, child, this is not goin' to be happenin'. You're goin' to end it the next time you meet up with him. Do you's hear me!"

Suzie started to argue but Grace stopped her and told her that no amount of crying or discussing would change her mind. Bill and Grace would not permit this to occur and since she was fifteen, she had no legal right to marry without their permission. Grace warned

Suzie if she was thinking about running off with Froggy, Bill would get the mounted police involved and it would become an ugly situation.

Suzie was devastated and she knew Froggy would be also. She dreaded telling him about the situation since she was not even sure she would have said yes to his proposal but now she had no choice. She loved Froggy, yet she was not sure if she loved him in a sisterly way or as a girlfriend should. Now she would never know the answer to that question.

At Froggy and Suzie's next rendezvous, Suzie filled Froggy in on the discussion she had with her mother and told him that she could not marry him. Froggy was shattered and begged her to reconsider. Suzie made it clear that they could never be married or see each other again. Froggy left running with tears running down his face. Suzie sat on the rock sobbing and watched as Froggy got in his motorboat and drove away. He did not dock at the reserve island but pulled up to a small island further down the river.

For the next two weeks Suzie was in a daze. Her heart was broken, and she sank into a depression. She had no appetite, and sleep would only come in the wee hours of the morning; her body felt like lead, and she had no energy. Concentrating on schoolwork was impossible. Grace pulled her out of school. Suzie was indifferent about missing school. When Grace heard the news about Froggy, she was reluctant to tell her daughter.

Froggy went missing and his family and friends launched a search that continued for two weeks. Froggy was found dead by his brothers on the island where Suzie had seen him take the boat. His family was not aware of the relationship between Froggy and Suzie; therefore, she was never approached or questioned. Unbeknown to Suzie, Froggy had tuberculosis and was staying on the island with no food, in the cold, without his medicine. The situation he placed himself in killed him and she knew that was his intent. There were rumours going around that he had hung or shot himself, but Grace kept those gruesome details to herself.

Depression overtook Suzie as she struggled to come to grips with the loss of Froggy and the guilt she felt.

One day when she was sitting on the rock, her sanctuary, she had a long talk with God. "I don't understand this, Lord. Froggy was a good man and I'm a-feelin' so horrible about his dying. I don't know what to do. My heart is aching so much. Please help me!"

Suzie sat quietly for a while and then the song "There Will Be Peace in the Valley" came to her mind. She started to sing it. She sang it several times as peace flowed over her. A calmness entered her mind and body. Suzie thanked the Lord and went home.

Whenever Suzie felt anxious, she would sing the song again. This song became a theme song throughout Suzie's life. It was a source of deep calm and peace whenever her life felt chaotic.

CHAPTER 42

Esther

After Suzie and Glenda's dance performance at the bar, they would sit and have a ginger ale. It was there that Suzie met Esther. Esther reminded her of her sister Fran because she was well dressed, wore makeup and high heels. Her long dark brown hair was perfectly styled, not a hair out of place.

Suzie and Esther realized they were kindred spirits. They had a lot in common, except for Esther's career. Esther was a lady of the night. Suzie was a bit astonished by this fact at first, but she enjoyed their friendship, so she chose to overlook it.

In the evening after Suzie and Glenda finished their act at the hotel, Suzie would visit Esther in her two-room apartment upstairs in the hotel. The old hotel and its apartments were shabby. The floor tiles were cracked, and one wall had a punched-out hole in it. The little kitchenette was furnished with a small chrome table and two chrome chairs with cracked red plastic seats. There was a sink and a hot plate on the counter. Esther kept her dishes under the sink in a two-shelf cupboard. Paint peeled from the windowsill of the kitchenette's small window. The bedroom was dark and dingy and had a door that led to the hall where the communal bathroom was located.

Suzie and Esther would socialize until a knock came at the door. Suzie knew that was Esther's next client, so she made a quick escape into the hallway through the bedroom. As soon as she heard Esther's main apartment door close, she made a fast exit from the hotel.

Their friendship continued for several months until a friend of Bill's saw Suzie leaving Esther's room. Bill's friend did not hesitate to inform him of her whereabouts. Everyone in town knew that Esther was a call girl.

When Bill got home from work, he slammed his dirty steel lunch pail down on the kitchen counter, startling Grace, Suzie, and Ruby who were preparing supper.

"Ruby, you need to leave and go to your room. I have business to discuss with your maw and Suzie," Bill angrily commanded.

Ruby knew by the sound of her father's voice and the look on his face that she needed to vacate the kitchen immediately. Ruby rushed to her room.

"Suzie, tell me what the hell you were doing in Esther's apartment last night?" Bill glared at Suzie.

Grace was flabbergasted. "You mean Esther at the hotel? Esther, the one who people say is a prostitute?"

Bill was not in the mood for questions and impatiently answered, "Yes, that's the one. Suzie, I'm waiting for an answer, and it better be damn good."

Now both Grace and Bill were glaring at Suzie.

Suzie gulped. "Just visitin' Esther. She and I are friends. That is all. I don't stay when her men friends visit. I leave right away. Honestly, I leave."

Bill slammed his fist on the table and shouted, "I don't give a shit if you leave or not . . . You are not going there again. Girl, have you no senses? First, it was the Indian, now it's Esther. People in town think you are a whore because you are hanging around with one and were seen leaving her apartment. You have ruined your reputation and ours. Damn it! Suzie, if you were younger, I'd give you a good whopping."

Suzie was in tears and knew there was no reasoning with Bill.

Shaking her head, Grace asked, "What are we gonna be doin' with you, Suzie? Your heart is a mite bigger than your brain. You're gonna end up in all kinds of trouble ifin you don't learn to use your common sense."

The room grew silent for several minutes, which seemed like forever. It gave them all time to gain some composure.

In a calmer and gentler voice, Grace said, "You're goin' to go to Senneterre and stay with Fran and Wallace. You need to leave town and get away from Esther."

CHAPTER 43

Living with Fran

Fran and Wallace had moved that year to Senneterre, Quebec, two hours east from Duparquet. Wallace was struggling to keep a job in Nova Scotia. Fran suggested they move closer to her family, but she preferred they live in a different town. Wallace found employment in the lumber mill in Senneterre. The town was larger than Duparquet, which suited Fran just fine.

Grace phoned Fran that evening, and the decision was made that Suzie would live with Fran and Wallace. She would help Fran with housework and care for Fran's three children, Audrey, Ralph and Gloria.

Tucker watched as Suzie packed her clothes. He looked as sad as she felt. Tucker's doggy instincts told him something was amiss. Occasionally, he whined. Suzie sat on the floor beside him, put her arm around him and lay her head on his neck.

"Oh, my Tucker, my friend, I'm going to miss you so much. What will I do without you? You take care of my baby sista, Ruby, will yah please." For about an hour she held on to him and cried. Suzie felt humiliated even though she believed she had not done anything wrong.

Suzie hated leaving her baby sister behind. They loved joking and laughing over their own foolishness. When they did dishes together, they spent more time blowing bubbles at each other and laughing than cleaning, and they ended up having to wash the floor afterwards. The two of them went for walks and talked for hours. They had slept together in the same bed since Ruby was two. She could not imagine getting into bed without Ruby beside her.

When they drove up to her sister's place, Fran was there to greet them. Bill and Grace went into the house for a cup of tea and to ensure that Suzie got settled in. Fran and Wallace had a nice modern apartment. It had all the latest appliances. It had three bedrooms: one for Fran and Wallace, one for Ralph, and one for the girls. Suzie would be sleeping in the same bed as her nieces, Audrey, and Gloria. Gloria was five years old and was not toilet trained yet. Fran claimed this was due to her disabilities. Gloria's mental development was like that of a two-year-old.

Ralph was eight and he was not thrilled that Suzie was there. Fran had told him that Suzie was there to babysit him. Ralph felt he was too old for a babysitter. Audrey was almost ten years old, and she was excited that her aunt had come to stay with them. She talked non-stop while Suzie hung her clothes in the closet. Suzie had to kick a pile of dirty clothes out of her way to get into the closet. Once her belongings were put away, she joined the adults in the kitchen.

Suzie sat in silence and glanced around, taking in her new surroundings. The counter was full of dirty dishes, encrusted with days-old food. The kitchen floor was sticky and dirty. Suzie knew she would have a lot of chores to keep her mind off her troubles.

Grace got up to leave and turned to give Suzie a hug. "Girly, stay out of trouble. I know you're thinkin' this ain't fair but it's fer your own good. I love ya."

Bill did not say a word to Suzie. He was still upset and would be for some time.

Fran had a list of chores she expected Suzie to do in exchange for her room and board. Suzie started doing the mounds of dirty dishes before making supper. Then, before she could rest, she had to get the children ready for bed. Suzie was exhausted not only from the chores, but also from the emotional turmoil.

Suzie was not there to help Fran. She was there to do all the work and take care of the children. In the beginning, she was kept so busy that she didn't have time to dwell on her situation, but as time passed and winter came, she yearned for friendship and time on her own.

Since Fran showed very little interest in teaching Gloria personal skills, Gloria's training was left to Suzie. She taught Gloria how to get dressed, bathe with assistance, and use cutlery.

Taking advantage of Suzie's help, Fran and Wallace often went out in the evening and came home with friends who were drunk and shady. The men would make sexual advances at Suzie, which scared and disgusted her. As soon as her evening chores were completed, she hurried to bed before Fran and Wallace came home. She wedged knives between the top of the door and the doorframe to bar Wallace's friends from entering the bedroom.

One evening, one of the men pushed on the door so hard that he broke one of the knives. Suzie was terrified and jumped out of bed. She leaned up against the door. In a firm voice she said, "Go away. I have a sharp knife in here and I will be a usin' it!"

All she heard on the other side of the door was a male's heinous laugh! That night she did not sleep until she heard the kitchen door slam, and the place was quiet. This indicated that all the men had left, and Fran and Wallace were in bed. The next day she rearranged the furniture in the bedroom and put the dresser near the door so she could use it as a barricade when she went to bed.

Suzie hated living at Fran's, and that winter she wondered if she would be stuck there forever. She was unhappy, but she dared not complain when her mother phoned to check on her. If Bill got wind of her complaining, he would be angrier than he already was.

When spring came Suzie was happy to get outside, even if only in the backyard or taking Gloria for a walk.

That summer, Ralph heard that Senneterre's men's baseball team was playing the RCAF (Royal Canadian Air Force) team from the base. He asked Suzie if they could go to the game. Suzie jumped at the chance for a change of scenery, even if she had to take the three children along.

Half the town came out to watch the baseball game. Audrey and Ralph ran off to sit with their friends. The bleachers were full of excited Senneterre and RCAF fans. Suzie could not find a spot for her and Gloria to sit down. She stood beside the bleachers with Gloria who kept sitting on the muddy ground. At first, Suzie tried to encourage Gloria to stand beside her and hold her hand. Gloria kept dropping down and Suzie almost ended up on the ground with her. Finally, Suzie just let her go. The fans cheered, booed, and chatted amongst themselves. At the end of the first inning, a young man with dark hair approached Suzie. He was wearing a pair of military green pants, a white t-shirt, and RCAF dog tags on a chain around his neck.

"Hi, I have two extra seats available over there," he explained, pointing to the other end of the bleacher. "I saw you standing here and thought you and your little girl would like to sit down?"

Suzie laughed. "She's my niece, not my wee girl."

Suzie was not sure it would be wise to accept the man's offer, but she was tired of standing.

Holding out his right hand, he said, "My name is Jack." Immediately, he noticed her withered right hand and offered her his left hand instead.

Suzie shook his hand. "I'm Susan. Nice to meet you. I sure could sit fer a spell."

Suzie was unaware that those moments were the catalyst that would change her life.

CHAPTER 44

Stood Up

Jack was captivated by Suzie's petite stature, her kindness with Gloria, her Nova Scotian accent, and her good looks. They chatted during the game and Jack asked Suzie to meet him at the next baseball game the following week. Suzie thought he was not only good-looking but kind. He was originally from the Toronto area, so he was a city man. He was five years older than her. He worked at the RCAF Senneterre base as a Leading Air Craftsman and lived in the barracks.

The evening of their date Suzie ensured supper was made in advance and her chores were all done. She picked out her best dress and shoes. At six o'clock she headed to the baseball diamond with the three children.

When she arrived, she looked for Jack, but he was not there yet. When the game started, he still was not there. Innings six, seven, eight and nine went by. The game was over, and Jack had not shown up. He had stood Suzie up on their first date. She wondered whether he'd been in an accident, if he had to work overtime, or if he was just playing her along.

Suzie was disappointed and peeved and told herself she was better off if he was so unreliable. For the next few days, Suzie continued her mundane tasks, but she could not get Jack off her mind. Annoyed with herself, she was determined to forget him.

A few days later Jack made a surprise appearance at Fran's house. When he knocked, Suzie opened the door, and when she saw it was him, she tried to shut the door on him, but he blocked it with his foot.

"I know I have no right to come around to see you, but I just had to come and explain. I am sorry I did not show up for our date. I . . . I . . . oh hell, I was broke and could not even buy you an ice cream cone. I should have sent a message with one of the other guys. I was an idiot."

Suzie interrupted, "Yes, you're an idiot. I waited fer you. You shoulda sent a message. I was so mad at you and at the same time I was worried something had happened to you."

"I am so, so, so sorry. Please give me another chance. Could we go out tomorrow evening for a meal?" begged Jack.

Suzie looked at his pleading big blue eyes. "If I say yes, are you sure you will be a-keepin' our date? Do you have the money to pay for the meal?"

Grinning from ear to ear, Jack said, "I promise I will show up, and yes, I have the money to pay for the meal,"

"Ok, one more chance, Jack. Pick me up at six p.m. and don't be late."

Suzie saw Jack skip as he walked towards the road. As she closed the door, she looked out the window and saw him throw his hat up in the air to express his delight.

The next day, Suzie once again prepared supper early and had all her evening chores done. She was just finishing the dishes when Jack arrived. Fran answered the door and was surprised that an Air Force man was calling to see Suzie. Suzie had not told Fran about Jack. She seldom told Fran anything.

"I'll be right there, Jack!" yelled Suzie from the kitchen. Suzie put the last clean dish away and ran to the bedroom to brush her hair, put on lipstick, and put on her sweater. She did not want Fran to be alone with Jack for more than a few minutes, nor did she want Fran to try to persuade her to stay home.

There stood Jack in his dark blue uniform, blue shirt, and black tie. He wore his wedged uniform cap. He looked very official and handsome. Suzie wore her dark blue dress, accessorized with a white belt to show off her thin figure. She wore her black heels and her white three-quarter-sleeve sweater. Jack thought she looked gorgeous.

Fran asked, "Where do you think you're going? What about the children and bedtime?"

Suzie opened the door and motioned for Jack to go outside first. Then she looked at Fran and said, "I'm goin' out and will be back when I get back. You can put your own kids to bed this evening."

Suzie immediately closed the door behind her before Fran had an opportunity to say another word.

Jack and Suzie went to the only restaurant in town. They sat there until it closed, then took a walk around town. They shared stories about how they came to live in Senneterre, except Suzie left the part about Esther out of her story. Instead, she said Bill and her mother thought she needed to get away because of Froggy's death. Jack was compassionate and listened intently to her story.

At 11 p.m. Jack drove Suzie back to Fran's place, and they sat on the front steps. Jack hated for the evening to end, but he knew he had to get up early to be on time for work. Suzie did not want it to end either. They made plans to meet in the coming week when Jack could get away from the base. Jack said goodnight to Suzie, leaned over, gave her a kiss and quickly retreated to his car before she could object.

When Suzie went into the house, Fran was waiting for her. "You should have told me about this man. Where did you meet him and what do you know about him? Remember you are barely seventeen."

Suzie knew she had to tell Fran something or Fran would call their mother and Bill. "Fran, you were seventeen when you married Wallace. You dated him when you was sixteen. I remember that you knew nothin' 'bout him when you first met. You were taken with him. I guess I am taking after my older sister. Jack is an Air Force man, so we know he has a good job, and he is respectable," rationalized Suzie.

If she wanted to continue to see Jack, she had to win Fran over. Before long the two were at the kitchen table talking about Fran and her dating experiences. Suzie knew if she made the situation more about Fran, then she had a better chance of Fran being on her side. If Fran was on her side, then Maw and Bill were more likely to approve of Jack.

Fran told Suzie she would allow her to date Jack if she made sure her chores were done and it did not interfere with any of the other work required of her, like babysitting. Suzie agreed to Fran's requests.

Fran allowed Jack to visit Suzie at the house. If Suzie had a date and Fran wanted to go out, she would tell Suzie to invite Jack over for the evening. Jack usually stayed until Fran and Wallace came home and the men who came home with Wallace had left. Sometimes it was early morning before he got back to the barracks.

While she was dating Jack, she asked her family and friends to call her Sue, since she was now a young woman. So, Sue it was.

When Fran spoke to Grace on the phone, she told Grace about Sue's boyfriend, Jack. Fran spoke highly of him, so Grace was not concerned, but she would reserve her impressions about him until she met him in person.

CHAPTER 45

Precious Last Moments

At the beginning of December, Sue spoke to Ruby on the phone, who mentioned to Sue that Tucker was not well, and he slept most of the time. When he stood up to go outside, his walking was laborious. He only ate if Ruby held food in her hand. Sue felt she had to go home and see Tucker before it was too late. Fran was unhappy that Sue was leaving for a weekend, but Sue was determined to go home to say goodbye to her long-time childhood companion. Nothing and nobody were going to keep her from spending time with Tucker. Jack offered to drive her because he knew how much Tucker meant to Sue. Jack also thought it was high time he met Sue's mother and Bill.

It was storming the day Jack and Sue set out for Duparquet, but it was not as cold as a usual winter day. The snow did not deter Jack. He had driven in huge blizzards and glacial temperatures when he was stationed in Frobisher Bay. Winters in Quebec seemed mild to Jack compared to the arctic climate he had endured the year he was stationed in the Northwest Territories.

All the way to Duparquet, all Sue could think about was Tucker and all the times he had been her rescuer. She thought about how he helped her to walk and was by her side when she recovered from her shock therapy. He was there when she cried and laughed. She knew he was old for a dog. His whiskers and some of the hair on his muzzle had turned white over the past four years. He slowed down and took longer rests after they went for walks. As Sue sat in silence, reminiscing about her dearest doggy friend, tears rolled down her cheeks. Jack reached over and caressed her hand. Words were not needed.

When Jack and Sue arrived at the apartment in Duparquet, Grace, Bill and Ruby were in the kitchen waiting for them. Ruby ran to the door and threw her arms around Sue.

"You're home! I missed you so much, Suzie!" Ruby exclaimed and held onto Sue for an unusually long time.

Grace noticed that Sue's colour was better and her disposition appeared much happier than when she had left her at Fran's in Senneterre. Sue introduced them to Jack, and Grace invited them to have tea and biscuits. Bill did say hi to Sue and asked how she was doing, but Sue could tell he was apathetic. She shrugged it off because she was more concerned about Tucker than what Bill thought about her.

Sue just wanted to be with her faithful companion. "Maw, I'll have tea after I see Tucker. Jack, have a seat and chat with Maw and Bill a bit. Ruby, where is he?"

Ruby led her into the living room and pointed to where Tucker lay on a grey wool blanket. His eyes were closed. Ruby left the room to give Sue time with her old friend. Sue knelt beside Tucker and patted and rubbed his head and spoke gently to him. Tucker opened his eyes immediately and his tail slowly wagged, thumping on the floor. His big brown eyes looked tired but happy to see her.

In her Nova Scotian twang, familiar to Tucker's ears, she gently said, "Oh, dear Tucker, you're not lookin' so good me boy. I gots here as quick as I could. My dear friend, I'm here now. I sure was a missin' you."

Sue bent down and put her head on his neck, like she used to do. When she wrapped her arm around him, Tucker relaxed and closed his eyes. Sue stayed by his side and whispered the memories they had shared.

Grace watched the heart-wrenching scene, tears welling up in her eyes. She suspected that Tucker was waiting for Sue to come home before he left this earth. Tucker had missed Sue. The first month that Sue was gone Tucker would go to her bed, lie down, and whine and bark softly. He appeared to be in mourning and calling out to his friend. He hardly ate that first month and Grace thought he was going to die, but he perked up a bit for a month, then started to deteriorate again.

An hour passed before Sue returned to the kitchen and apologized to Jack. He told her that no apology was necessary since he was getting to know her folks and they were getting to know him.

After supper Sue introduced Jack to Tucker. Jack sat down beside Sue and Tucker and patted his head and told Tucker, "Hey, old boy. I will take good care of Sue for you."

The next day Tucker stood up to go outside and Sue let him out. He did his business, then ran towards Sue as if he wanted to play. "What? Tucker, you don't really want to play, or do you?" Suzie laughed and played, running back and forth as he chased her.

After five minutes, an exhausted Tucker walked slowly to the back door. Sue let him in, and he went back to his blanket and lay down. Sue brought Tucker a handful of meat scraps that Grace provided. Tucker ate a few pieces and lapped up some water from a bowl that Sue held for him. Then he flopped down and closed his eyes.

Once again, Sue wrapped her arms around him and with tears flowing down her cheeks, she said, "I love you, dear friend. No dog has ever been sweeter, kinder and more lovin' than you. You poor tired old guy. Rest now, Tucker, rest."

Tucker died peacefully that day in the comfort and safety of Sue's arms. He had waited to say goodbye to his best friend, Sue.

CHAPTER 46

Absent Parents

Jack and Sue spent that Christmas at Fran and Wallace's home. Of course, Fran had a wonderful bushy Christmas tree, decorated with new store-bought glass ornaments, tinsel garland, lights, angel hair and a lit-up star. It looked like a tree in a magazine or a department store display. Sue and the children wanted to help decorate it, but Fran wanted it to look perfect, so she did it herself and would not let the children partake in the festive tradition. Sue and Jack involved the children in making popcorn chain garlands, cutting out paper snowflakes, making shortbread and sugar cookies. Christmas supper was to be turkey with all the fixings, which Sue was expected to cook.

Sue found it difficult to celebrate this holiday because she was still consumed by the loss of Tucker.

Jack stayed over on Christmas Eve. He slept on the couch and was woken by three excited children. Sue had never seen so many gifts under a Christmas tree in her life. The children each received eight gifts and their stockings were stuffed to the top of the cuffs. Sue could not help but think that the children were being spoiled and they would be far better off having their parents' attentions and time instead of toys.

Jack was acting strange. He was jittery and pacing while the children were opening their presents. Sue wondered what in the world was wrong with him. Usually, he was easygoing. She decided that she would have a chat with him later to learn the source of his anxiety.

After all the gifts were opened and Fran and Wallace were helping the children put together some of their new toys, Jack reached into the tree and pulled out a small black velvet box.

"Look, there is still a gift left. It is for you, Sue," said Jack and he winked at her.

Fran and Wallace stopped what they were doing. They told the children to hush and watch what Jack was going to do. Fran was sure she knew what the black velvet box held. Jack handed Sue the box.

"Jack, you know we weren't supposed ta get each other anything," Sue stated, holding the box out to Jack.

Jack gently pushed her hand back. "Just open it, sweetie," he insisted.

Sue opened the box. Nestled in the black velvet interior was a delicate gold and white diamond ring. Sue's eyes filled with tears, and she stared at him in disbelief.

Jack got down on one knee. "Sue Fenton, will you marry me. Will you be my wife?"

Sue was in such shock that she did not answer right away. She looked back and forth at Jack and then the ring several times. Although she only did this for a minute or so it felt like hours to Jack. He started to sweat as he waited for her answer.

Fran broke the silence. "Well, girly, are you going to answer the poor fellow or are you going to keep him on his knees all day?"

Fran's voice snapped Sue out of her stupor. "Yes . . . yes, I will marry you, Jack Wixson. Yes, I will be your wife!" squealed Sue.

After he placed the ring on her left-hand ring finger, he picked Sue up, swung her around and yelled, "She said yes! She said yes." He kissed her long and hard and it took her breath away.

Fran, Wallace, and the children hooted, hollered, and clapped. Although Fran would miss having her sister around, she was happy for her. Sue was surprised when Fran gave her a big heartfelt hug.

"So little Suzie is going to get married. Maw will be so surprised. Why don't you call her?" suggested Fran.

Usually, Sue had to plead with Fran to call home. Such generosity and affectionate displays from her oldest sister had become foreign to

Sue. She had not seen this side of Fran since their childhood. Worried that Fran might change her mind, Sue called her mother immediately. Although Grace acted surprised and happy about the engagement, she knew Jack was going to propose. When the young couple were in Duparquet a few weeks prior, Jack had asked Grace and Bill for permission to marry Sue.

The first week of January, on a Thursday, Fran and Wallace informed Sue that they were going away for two days and would return on the weekend. When Sue asked where they were going, they did not reply. Sue was concerned because there was very little food in the cupboards and the fridge. She knew she could stretch what was there for a couple of days. Sue had learned the art of making a meal out of close to nothing from her mother. She had enough oatmeal to make porridge for two days. There were three cans of peas, a bottle of milk, a loaf of bread, margarine, three potatoes, some flour, half a pound of lard, and two cooked chicken legs, left over from supper the night before. Fran usually did groceries on Thursdays, but that Thursday she left without doing them.

Sue made soup from the chicken legs, potatoes, and a can of peas. She baked soda biscuits to go with the soup. She ate little to ensure that the children had enough.

Jack came over on Friday and stayed the night, sleeping on the couch. He was furious at Fran and Wallace for leaving Sue in such a predicament with the meagre amount of food in the house. He told Sue that he was going to give them a piece of his mind when they returned. Sue begged him not to do that because she hated confrontations and Fran and Wallace would take it out on her. Until she was married, she just wanted to get through living in these dreadful circumstances.

On Saturday, Sue expected Fran and Wallace to return home. Every time she heard a car outside, she ran to the window to see if it was them, and each time she was disappointed. Sue was getting worried and wondered where they were. The children kept asking when their parents would be returning. They did not return that Saturday. At breakfast on Sunday Sue served the children toast and peas. For lunch the children had the last of the biscuits and soup. At supper Sue made creamed peas on toast.

Jack had to return to the barracks Sunday evening. He was concerned and did not want to leave. They both kept hoping Fran and Wallace would return that evening. Jack was not only furious; he was thoroughly disgusted with the pair of them for their lack of responsibility and parental concern. Jack left for the barracks early that day. He knew if Fran and Wallace returned on Sunday while he was there, he would lose his composure and give them a good verbal blast.

Fran and Wallace did not return on Sunday. On Monday evening Jack returned to see Sue and brought five bags of groceries with him. Sue was grateful and so were the children. Since there was nothing Sue could pack in a bag for lunches, the two older children were kept home from school. The children were restless and whiny because they wanted to see their parents. For two weeks Sue held the fort at her sister's home and Jack made sure Sue and the children had food. At one point, Jack wanted Sue to call the Child Welfare Office, but she insisted that they should just wait a bit longer. Besides, she knew her family would be angry with her if Fran's children went into foster care.

On the Thursday of the second week Fran and Wallace finally arrived home. They acted as if the length of their absence was appropriate, and they were flippant about the fact that they left Sue and the children with scarcely a thing to eat.

Jack had phoned every night to make sure she was ok and to find out if the two absent parents had returned. Sue finally was able to answer, "Yes, they came in this afternoon, and they acted as if they did nothing wrong."

Jack was beyond furious and said, "What the hell is wrong with those two. Pack your bags and things. I am taking you home to Duparquet. I will pick you up tomorrow right after I finish work around five. Be ready, because if I go into the house and see those two, I am liable to lose my cool!"

As Sue packed her bags, Fran wanted to know why she was leaving. Using every threat and tactic at her disposal, Fran tried to coerce her sister to stay. She reminded Sue that Bill was still furious with her and did not want her back in his house and the townspeople still thought she was a prostitute like her friend.

It took every bit of self-restraint for Sue to keep her cool and her thoughts to herself. Arguing with Fran would be a waste of her time and they both would say things they would regret. Sue did not want to tell Fran the real reason she was leaving, because Fran would involve Wallace and the two of them would bully her. Besides, confrontations made Sue feel sick to her stomach. Instead, Sue told Fran she was going home to plan her wedding and Maw was expecting her, even though she wasn't.

The children hugged her and cried before she left. Fran and Wallace were in the kitchen and did not say goodbye nor did they thank Sue for all her work and the help she had been to them.

Jack pulled up in his car at five o'clock on the dot. He kissed Sue and put her suitcase and bag in the back seat.

"Maw doesn't know we are coming. I hope she is ok with it," Sue remarked.

"Yes, she does know, Sue. I phoned her last night and told her what happened, and she said, 'Bring me girly home, Jack.'"

Sue put her hand on her fiancé's arm and thanked him. Those five months at Fran's had worn her out. She was so relieved that she would never have to go back and stay there again. Her nightmare was over. Sue was incredibly angry and hurt by her sister for taking advantage of her. Sue would carry this resentment and hurt with her for years.

CHAPTER 47

Sorrow and Joy

As they drove into Grace and Bill's yard at seven o'clock that evening, Fran's warning that Bill would be furious with her flowed back into Sue's mind. Sue looked at her mom and asked, "Is Bill ok that I'm come home?"

Grace nodded. "Yes, he is, girly, so you can relax. He's not happy 'bout what Fran and Wallace done, leavin' for days and no food fer the young'uns or you. But Bill does like your Jack and figures you did well."

"I tell you, Grace, you don't know the half of it," said Jack, who was quickly interrupted by Sue.

Sue grabbed his arm and led him into the kitchen. Cheerfully she said, "All is well now. I'm home and 'tis time to plan our wedding."

Jack and Sue wanted to get married in April, but the priest was not available. The earliest date they could get married was Saturday, May 1st.

Sue had decided she wanted to convert to Catholicism. She needed to take lessons from the priest and attend masses before she could be baptized. Jack was raised Catholic, and she wanted their children to be raised in one religion. It did not matter to Sue what denomination she was, as long as God was honoured, and she could build her faith there.

The first weekend in February, Jack flew home to Toronto on a cargo carrier. Because of his flight arrangements, Sue was not able to go with him.

When Jack got out of the cab in front of his old family home, he stood there for a while. He had not been home since joining the Air Force six years prior. Jack's father died when he was ten years old. He felt like he was transported back in time and for a moment he was that ten-year-old boy who watched his father die of a heart attack on the ice in Maple Leaf Gardens. Tears welled up in his eyes. He felt foolish so he quickly went into the house. Auntie Annie was the first to greet him. "Who are you?" she asked.

"It is Jack, Auntie Annie, Rita's son," he replied.

"Oh my . . . are you sure. Jack is just a wee boy?" Annie looked at him doubtfully.

"It's ok, Annie. It is my boy. Jack, welcome home, son. So good to see you!" exclaimed Rita as she embraced her son. "Come and sit. Let's have a cup of coffee and chat."

Over coffee Jack told his mother he was engaged to be married on May 1st. Rita listened intently to her son's enthusiastic description of Sue.

When he was finished Rita carefully chose her words: "Son, I have some concerns. Are you sure you know what you're getting into by marrying a crippled girl? She may not be able to do the housework, cooking or maybe even have children. I am afraid you will be in for a life of hardship and heart ache."

Jack felt like a deflated balloon. He thought his mother would be more understanding and tolerant because of her sister Annie, who was developmentally challenged. Rita had taught Annie to be as self-sufficient as she could be. Annie was able to do housework, cooking, laundry, and dress and feed herself, but she could not be left alone. Her reasoning skills and memory were lacking, and her mental age was around six years old.

Jack told his mother that Sue could do housework, cooking and other chores. He explained how she had taken care of Fran's home and children. Rita was not convinced.

When the family came over the next day for supper, Jack announced his engagement. His sisters, Georgina, and Peggy, and two brothers,

Wayne, and Peter, asked a lot of questions. Everyone but Peter agreed with Rita that Jack should not marry Sue, the crippled girl.

Jack was disheartened by his family's reaction to his engagement. He told them, regardless of what they thought, he was going to marry Sue. "Wait 'til you meet her, and you see how wonderful she is! Then you will know I made the right choice."

When Jack got back to the base in Senneterre he called Sue. She was anxious to hear his voice and to know how his family visit went. Jack lied and said the family was happy for them. None of them would be able to attend because of their financial situation. None of them could afford the trip and accommodations.

On the evening of April 30th, Jack arrived in Duparquet. He wore his clean blue uniform and hat draped across his arm. In his hand was a bouquet of daisies for Sue and on his face a smile like a Cheshire cat.

The women of the house were busy with last minute preparations. Sue and Jack would be married at seven o'clock in the morning. It was the only slot available at the church. After the ceremony they would go back to the house for a wedding breakfast.

On the morning of their wedding, May 1st, 1954, Norm, Critch, and Sunny thought they would play a joke on Sue and Jack. The pranksters told Jack he needed to be at the church early. They said they would drive him, and Sue would come afterwards with Bill and Grace. Jack wanted to walk but Norm said that he had an errand to do after the service, so he had to take the car anyway.

The four of them loaded into Norm's car, Jack sitting in the back. They drove in the direction of the church and sailed right by it.

"What the hell? Where are we going? We just passed the church!" shouted a flustered Jack.

"Oh, we're taking you on the scenic route!" snickered Critch.

The other two men laughed. "Yes, well, Jack, if you really wanna marry me Aunt Sue, you will have to be a provin' it," Sunny piped up.

"Come on, guys. Sue will be horrified if I am late. Don't do this to her or to me. Come on, you guys," begged Jack.

They drove about five miles out of town and told Jack to get out. Jack knew they would pull him out of the car if he did not get out voluntarily. There stood Jack on the side of the road, a good distance from the church and his wedding in thirty minutes. The men drove off, yelling out the window, "Run, Jack . . . Run, Jack!" They hooted, laughed, and beeped the horn.

That is exactly what Jack did. He wanted to pulverize those asses. Jack was in a panic. Adrenaline kicked in and he started to run. He had stood Suzie up once before and he had no intentions of standing her up for their wedding.

In the meantime, Sue laid out her aqua-green wedding suit with a white pattern, knee-length white knitted shawl, and nylons on the bed. Her outfit was a skirt and top, which her mother and Bill had paid for. Sue chose an outfit that was practical and could be worn again.

Sue looked beautiful in her suit, black high heel shoes and her long wavy auburn hair. The daisies Jack brought were her bouquet. The colour emphasized her gorgeous light blue eyes, although they did not need to be enhanced that day. Sue's eyes were shining with delight. A small amount of pink lipstick completed her look.

As Sue walked into the kitchen, Ruby exclaimed, "You look wonderful, and a mite pretty."

"You certainly do, me girly," added Grace. "I have to admit I never did a-thinkin' I would be seein' you git married."

"I know, Maw. You told me many a time no man would marry a cripple."

Grace blushed with embarrassment. "I'm a guessin' I was wrong, for sure."

Sue looked out the window to check on the weather. The sun was shining with a few clouds in the sky. She could see the new spring leaves on the trees gently waving in the breeze. Since it was May, there was still a chill in the early morning air. Sue was glad she would be wearing her warm shawl.

"I heard the guys leave earlier. Jack must be gettin' antsy. It is quarter to seven. He is a stickler for being on time," Sue calmly said as she picked up her black clutch purse and the white daisy bouquet. "I'm guessin' it's time to be a-goin' to the church."

Bill was behind Sue, wearing his best suit. "You look nice, Bill," Sue remarked sheepishly. She was still not sure how to act around Bill since the Esther incident last autumn. He remained aloof with Sue, but occasionally he let his guard down. Today was one of those days. "Thank you, bride-to-be. Are you ready for me to walk you down the aisle?" Bill asked as he held his arm out for Sue to hold.

Marg and Danny had come down from their apartment and were waiting outside. Sue and Bill walked out the door and down the street to the church, Paroisse St-Albert Le Grand. Grace and Ruby followed behind them. As Sue and Bill approached the church, Sue saw Norm and Sunny sitting on the steps. She thought that was strange. They should have been inside with Jack. The two of them were laughing and carrying on. Sue was not impressed with their behaviour in front of the church. The wedding was a happy event, but she hoped the guys would be on their best behaviour. They could be a rowdy bunch.

Sue stopped in front of Norm and said, "I'm guessin' my Jack is inside the church?"

Norm did not answer her. Instead, he turned to look at Sunny and they both burst out laughing.

Grace walked up beside Sue and saw what was going on. "You two had better not have pulled any shenanigans. WHERE IS JACK?" demanded Grace.

Sunny blurted out between laughs, "Maybe he stood you up like on your first date, Aunt Suzie." Sue was not impressed. She was furious and was about to give them a piece of her mind when Bill opened the door from the inside of the church. "Jack's in here and waiting for you, Sue. The priest said we better get on with it. He has another wedding at eight o'clock," Bill yelled out the door.

The men had no intentions of making Jack run to the church, but they just wanted to tease him and get him going. After five minutes they drove back and picked him up. Jack had a few choice words to say to all three of them.

The men and Grace, Ruby and Danny went into the church and took their seats. The rest of the family and their children were in attendance. Jack stood at the front of the church with his best man,

Critch. Marg, the maid of honour, went down the aisle ahead of Sue and Bill. The church organist played "Here Comes the Bride" as Bill walked Sue down the aisle.

Sue could not help but admire her husband-to-be. He looked distinguished and handsome in his uniform. Jack could not keep his eyes off his sweet, beautiful Sue.

The ceremony was short and sweet, just the way Sue and Jack wanted it. As Mr. and Mrs. Jack Wixson stood on the steps outside the church, the family showered them with rice. Sue had asked them not to throw rice because she thought it was a waste of good food. Sue's sisters ignored her request because in their minds that was a tradition that had to be carried out. Throwing rice brought good fortune and prosperity to the bride and groom. If this ritual was not performed, they believed the couple would have bad luck in their married life.

The wedding breakfast consisted of stewed strawberries, homemade applesauce, pancakes, biscuits, bacon, orange juice, tea, and coffee. Sue was surprised to see a wedding cake on the table. The neighbour, Mrs. Thompson, had made it. Mrs. Thompson said every bride must have a cake. When breakfast was over and the cake was cut, Mrs. Thompson wrapped a small piece of cake in wax paper and reminded Sue that she must put it under her pillow that night for this would ensure blessings in their married lives. Sue knew Mrs. Thompson had that tradition mixed up. Pieces of wedding cake were given to single women to put under their pillows, so they would dream about their future husbands.

Jack and Sue's wedding

CHAPTER 48

The Wedding Night

By ten o'clock that morning, Sue, and Jack loaded the car with her belongings and the leftover cake. They said their goodbyes and headed down the road to their apartment in Senneterre.

Jack had rented a one-bedroom apartment for them. While Sue was in Duparquet, Jack went to the second-hand store and purchased a few items to furnish the apartment. He bought a bed, a table and two chairs, a hot plate, and a ratty but clean couch. Their scant collection of kitchenware included two of everything: plates, cups, glasses, forks, spoons, and knives. Sue had also picked up one cooking pot and one paring knife. This would be her first home with Jack, and she knew she loved it.

On the way to Senneterre, they talked about the past two days. Jack filled Sue in on the escapade that Norm, Critch, and Sunny had pulled off before the wedding.

Sue gasped, "Those idiots. We wouldn't have gotten married if you were late. The priest warned us that if you were late the wedding would be postponed."

Jack smiled. "Yes, but I wasn't, and they did not carry it out. For a while I thought they weren't going to come back and get me! I must confess I was in a panic."

Sue snuggled up beside her husband. She was so happy and so in love. Sue did not remember ever being this happy and content.

When Jack and Sue got to their apartment in Duparquet, Jack swept Sue up in his arms and carried her across the threshold. She felt like she was in a dream.

They were in their own apartment only a few minutes when Jack revealed a secret that he had been keeping from Sue. Jack put his arms around Sue and gave her a big kiss and said, "Sue, my love. I did not want to tell you this and ruin our wedding day, but I must go back to the base right away. I am AWOL (absent without leave). My superiors wouldn't give me time off for our wedding, so I took it anyway. Nothing was going to keep me from marrying you!"

"Oh, Jack, what kind of trouble are you gonna be in for going AWOL?"

Jack sighed and scratched his head. "I could be brought up on charges and spend time in the Air Force clink or be discharged."

Sue had tears in her eyes and hugged him tightly. "Sweetie, I don't want you to go but I know you have to."

"I wish I could stay here with you my love, but I had better go and face the music. If I am unable to come back this evening, I will get one of the guys from the base to come and let you know." He gave Sue one last kiss and hug and headed out the door. Sue was extremely disappointed and sat at the kitchen table for a while thinking about the events of the day.

"Ok, Sue, you are not going to have a pity party. Instead, you will tidy up and get things ready for supper and pray that Jack will be ok and come home this evening," she said to herself.

Sue put her clothes away and unpacked the other items she had brought with her. She took a long leisurely bath and reminisced about her wonderful wedding and the breakfast celebration.

At five o'clock Jack had not returned. She was hungry and thought she should get some supper ready. Sue looked around for food and remembered that they were supposed to do grocery shopping that afternoon. All that she had was a can of Irish Stew and left-over wedding cake.

Sue set the can of stew on the table and went searching for a can opener. They had no can opener. Sue was good at improvising, so she grabbed the paring knife and took off one shoe. Sue put the knife and shoe on the table. She sat on the chair sideways and braced the can between her knees. She lifted her right arm with her left hand and wedged her elbow between two wooden rungs of the back of the chair. Sue opened her right hand and wrapped her fingers around the knife handle and placed the tip of the knife on the lid of the can near the edge. Using her left hand, she pounded on the butt of the knife with her shoe. It took several tries before the lid was punctured. The knife kept slipping. Sue moved the knife over and repeated the procedure until the can was opened enough for her to bend the lid back and pour the stew out. She cut her hand and rushed to the washroom, washed her hand, and wrapped a wad of toilet paper around it.

"Darn it. I's had to go and cut myself on me wedding day," said Sue. Then she wept. It was not the cut on her hand that made her cry; it was not that deep. The disappointment she felt from Jack's absence flooded over her, regardless of how positive she tried to be and how busy she kept herself. After a good cry, she poured the stew into their only pot. At that moment Sue was reminded of an expression her mother used to say: "We don't have a pot to piss in." Sue had to laugh because at least they had one pot to piss in if they needed it.

Sue put the stew on the hot plate and found a candle in one of the drawers. She set the table and sat down to wait for Jack.

At seven, Jack walked through the door. Sue jumped up, ran to him, and held him tightly. "Oh, thank God you're back, Jack. I was so worried!"

"I'm here now, Sue, my love. Let's eat and I will tell you what happened at the base."

The newly married couple sat down to eat their first married meal, which consisted of Irish stew, wedding cake and glasses of water by candlelight.

Jack told her that when he reported back to the base that afternoon, Sergeant Ship was livid and told him that he was in big trouble. Jack was resigned to the fact he was going to be disciplined. Sergeant Ship asked him if he really had gotten married that morning. Jack had the marriage certificate with him and showed the sergeant. The sergeant took the certificate and told Jack to go to the barracks and wait for him there. Jack went to the barracks and packed up his belongings. Some of his buddies stopped in to chat with him. They were shocked that he was not granted leave for his wedding day. Jack looked down at his watch and it was five o'clock in the evening. Jack wondered if the sergeant had forgotten him. At five-thirty, Sergeant Ship appeared at the barracks.

Sergeant Ship pointed at Jack and commanded, "You come with me!"

Jack obediently followed the sergeant; they were heading towards the mess hall. Jack was confused. When Jack walked into the mess hall there was a crowd of men standing around. It was Jack's entire squadron. They all yelled, "Congratulations!"

Jack was stunned and more than a little relieved. Never in a million years did he expect his sergeant to be so lenient, let alone celebrate his marriage.

Jack was served supper and a few free drinks. By six-thirty Jack announced that he had to leave and get back to his new bride. The men tried to persuade him to stay for a few more drinks, but Jack slipped out of the mess hall, claiming he had to use the facilities. Jack gathered his belongings from the barracks and headed home to Sue.

Sue was grateful for the turn of events and that evening they spent their first night as a married couple in bliss.

PART 2

Sue and Jack's Life

CHAPTER 49

The Transfer

At the beginning of October, Jack received his transfer to RCAF Station Grostenquin, France. He was to arrive on January 24th, 1955. Sue was thrilled because she had never travelled further than Nova Scotia and Quebec.

The Air Force would take care of their passports and travel arrangements. Jack and Sue were booked on a passenger ship out of Halifax on January 3rd, 1955. Their journey to the Port of Le Havre, France, would take ten to twelve days. From the port, they would travel by vehicle to 2 Wings Base, RCAF Station Grostenquin.

Jack had to have a physical. The few personal possessions they had needed to be packed.

Jack was given two weeks' leave to visit with family before moving to France. In the middle of December, the young couple set out on a cold wintery day for Durparquet, where Sue's family had gathered at Grace and Bill's apartment. They had all come to hear about the exciting transfer overseas and wish Jack and Sue the best.

When Sue removed her jacket, Grace, Audrey, Marg, and Ruby squealed, "Oh my God, you're pregnant, Suzie." Sue smiled and everyone rushed to hug and congratulate her. The women retired to the kitchen, which was customary. They chatted about babies, pregnancies, and France. The men went to the living room and had a few drinks and smokes and discussed the Cold War and Jack's transfer to France.

Ruby was excited for her sister but also unhappy. She knew her sister would be across the ocean and that terrified her. If anything happened, then Sue could not be reached.

Sue reassured Ruby. "We can write. If an emergency occurs, the base can be notified to tell us. Maw and Bill will have a number to call. Besides, Ruby, we will only be gone for five years."

"Five years," moaned Ruby. "That's forever, Suzie. I will miss you sooo much, and I won't get to see this wee one 'til she is five?"

"She?" questioned Sue and laughed. Of course, Ruby was hoping she would have a niece.

Bill talked about moving to Kirkland Lake, Ontario come summer. Grace rolled her eyes and said, "Here's we's go agin. The gypsy family."

When she said, "the gypsy family," she was including everyone, except Fran and Wallace, who would stay in Senneterre. The "whole fam-damily," as her mother would say, were moving to Northern Ontario, to another mining community.

The week-long visit flew by and was wonderful. Sue was thrilled to see everyone and catch up on their news from the past few months.

When the couple left to head to Toronto, Grace was crying. "I's will miss you, my girly. Make sure you's sees a doctor when you's get to France." Grace hugged Sue for over a minute and gently kissed her on her cheek. The rest of the family bid their farewells and the women shed their tears.

Sue cried silently all the way to Toronto. Jack and Sue arrived at Jack's mother's place at three in the afternoon. Aunt Annie was napping on the couch. Jack's mother, Rita, had just prepared a pot of coffee and was about to sit down and take a break from her housework when Sue and Jack came through the door.

Rita hugged her son and greeted her new daughter-in-law. "My, you sure are a sweet tiny thing, aren't you?'

Sue laughed. "That's what everyone says. Nice to meet you, Mrs. Wixson."

There was something about Sue's petite stature, her outgoing personality, and the love that she showed towards Jack that Rita could not deny. Rita noticed she was pregnant but did not say a word. It was up to her son or Sue to mention the upcoming baby.

Rita watched Sue like a hawk. She wanted to see how a crippled girl could function. Rita tested her and thought Sue was unaware. Sue knew what Rita was doing and it made her nervous, but she understood that Rita was concerned for her son. Jack had no idea what his mother was up to. He thought Rita was just trying to make Sue feel at home.

Rita asked Sue if she would make some cookies for them. Sue mixed a batch of her mother's oatmeal cookies and put them in the oven. She and Rita talked while they baked. When the time was up, Sue opened the oven door and knew they had burnt on the bottom. Not a good way to impress the mother-in-law, Sue thought. "Darn, I's sorry, Rita. I timed them the same as at home. I don't know why they burnt."

Rita laughed. "Sue, I forgot to tell you my oven is hotter than most. I must cook things at a lower temperature than recipes call for. Besides, Sue . . . I love burnt cookies. I mean it. I really do prefer my cookies burnt on the bottom."

They laughed and had burnt cookies with coffee. Sue was not fussy about burnt cookies either. This incident cinched the close relationship between Sue and her mother-in-law. Years later, whenever Sue and Rita visited with each other, Rita would always ask Sue to make cookies and burn a few for her.

Jack joined his brothers and their hockey teams in a few games at Maple Leaf Gardens. His sister came over and spent time getting to know Sue and becoming reacquainted with her brother. Aunt Annie was so funny: she thought Sue was a precious porcelain doll that had come to life. She wanted Sue to wear a huge red ribbon in her hair like she did and put bright red lipstick on. Rita told Sue that she did not have to give in to Annie's requests, but Sue knew how important it was to Aunt Annie, so she consented. Sue really did look like a doll with the huge bright red ribbon in her hair.

It was wonderful spending their first Christmas as a married couple with Jack's family. The food, the laughter, the chatter, the games, and the jolliness of the holidays were all present. Sue was pleased with the visit and knew Jack's family accepted her and welcomed her. It was not until years later that Sue discovered the family's concerns over Jack marrying a crippled girl. She was glad she was not privy to that information when she first met them because she would have been extremely self-conscious.

They returned to Senneterre a few days before the three-day trip to Halifax to board the ship. Sue did the last-minute packing and Jack made sure all the trip details were finalized.

CHAPTER 50
France

They almost missed boarding their ship because of a snowstorm. It was a good thing Jack knew how to drive in a blizzard. The ship they were boarding had come in four hours behind schedule. That was to Sue and Jack's advantage.

As the ship pulled out of the Halifax harbour, Sue looked back at her beloved Nova Scotia. No matter where she lived in the world, Nova Scotia would always run deep in her blood and memories. Her emotions were mixed. On the one hand she was excited for the new adventures that awaited them in France; on the other, she would have liked to have her first child in Canada, where her family was. Jack and Sue's first three months in France would bring times of heartbreak and test their faith.

The trip was a rough one. The turbulences were dreadful. The boat swayed with the unpredictable waves and ocean water gushed over the deck. It felt like the boat was being directed by nature. The storms did not seem to faze Sue, it must have been the Nova Scotian blood that ran through her veins, but poor Jack spent much of his time below deck in the cabin, puking his guts out. At times he had a green tinge to his face. Sue said that he gave a new definition to the term seasickness.

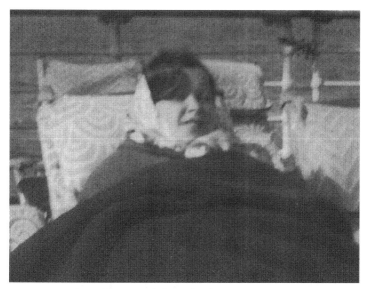

Sue relaxing on deck on the ship going to France

Sue enjoyed the journey and met other couples who were also on their way to 2 Wings Base. Sue's welcoming and pleasant disposition made it easy for her to make friends. The group began to believe that she did not have a husband since Jack never ventured out of the cabin.

When they reached the port in France, on a Friday, Jack looked like he had been put through the wringer. A bus was waiting to take the Air Force personnel bound for 2 Wings Base to Grostenquin. As they boarded the bus, some of Sue's newly acquired friends teased Jack mercilessly. He usually would not have minded the jokes and would have been right on top of reciprocating, but the trip's effects were still lingering. The thought of a five-and-a-half-hour bus trip did not make Jack feel any better.

Sue wanted to etch this trip in her mind, taking in the rolling hills, the tall trees and forests, and the lower flatlands. The landscape reminded her of Nova Scotia. Jack could have done without the rolling hills.

When they arrived at the base, they were driven to headquarters and there they signed in and received directions to their private marital quarter (PMQ) on base. The four-story brick building consisted of ninety-two apartments, each with a balcony and large picture window facing the parking area.

Jack and Sue's apartment was on the fourth floor. Their quarters had been freshly painted white. Each apartment was fully furnished, except for kitchen utensils, pots and pans and dishes. Their personal items had been unpacked for them. There were two bedrooms, a living room, a washroom, a kitchen, and a dining area. There were laundry facilities on each floor.

Sue went in search of one of her newly treasured possessions: the cradle Jack had made for the baby before they left Senneterre. It was painted white and decorated with pink and blue teddy bear decals. She could envision her sweet little baby sleeping in it.

They had the weekend to get settled before Jack had to report for duty. Jack was part of the 423 squadron that was sent to France during the Cold War. He was a communication technician. Although this was an exciting time for the couple, it was also a scary time to be in Europe. The United States and the Soviet Union were in a political battle over nuclear weapons. The American and Canadian radar bases were set up to track all Soviet activities. Jack and Sue were informed that if war did break out, they would be immediately sent to the fallout shelter, an underground refuge with concrete walls and steel doors. It was designed to protect them from nuclear radiation if the Soviet Union bombed the base. When the warning sirens were blasted, they were to follow the procedures.

There were unscheduled practice drills. Sue was in the laundry room the first time she heard the sirens. It was so loud she could hardly hear herself think.

The woman who was with her had lived on the base for two years and was experienced in the procedure. She tapped Sue on the back and said, "We must leave now! Follow me."

They were joined by other women and their children as they descended the four flights of stairs to go outside. Buses were waiting to take them to the Fallout Shelters. Once they arrived at the shelter's location, they got off the bus and lined up outside. The residents of the base did not know if it was just a drill or a real threat of bombing until they arrived at the shelter. When the drill was over the women and children boarded the bus and headed back to the PMQs. Sue found the practice surreal. Although Jack had told Sue about the purpose of his posting before they left Canada, it was not real until she attended an information meeting for the wives.

CHAPTER 51

Great Sorrow

In early March everything was ready for Sue's first baby to arrive. She had brought some baby clothes and blankets that Marg hàd given her. The neighbours in the building had also provided her with baby supplies. Since they were not permitted to hang pictures or repaint any rooms in the apartments, Sue decorated the nursery with a few stuffed animals on the dresser and a handmade quilt on the rocking chair. An animal print rug was laid beside the crib. Sue would keep the cradle in her room until the baby outgrew it.

That same week Jack had a run-in with Prime Minister Diefenbaker's aide and the Prime Minister. When the Prime Minister landed at the base, his aide went straight to the communications office. He demanded to know about the base's communication system. Jack provided him with all the information he required and informed him about the specialized security system put in place for the Prime Minister. At that point the aide started to bark orders at Jack about the changes he wanted done immediately to accommodate the Prime Minister. Jack tried to explain to him that these changes were not necessary because the system was advanced and covered his concerns. The aide continued to loudly argue with Jack.

Prime Minister Diefenbaker walked in just as Jack lost his cool and yelled back at the aide, "You don't know what the *hell* you're talking about. Get the hell out of my office now, and you too!" Jack pointed to the Prime Minister.

The Prime Minister and his aide both went beet-red in the face. They glared at Jack and then left. Jack knew he was "up shit's creek without a paddle." He had just told off not only the aide, but also the Prime Minister. He had no respect for the Prime Minister to start with, but he had crossed a line that no enlisted man should cross. Jack was brought up on charges. He was given a few days off without pay and then met with his superior officer. He asked Jack to tell him the whole story. Jack did just that without a shred of regret in his tone of voice or his words. His superior officer burst out laughing. It turned out he, like Jack, had no use for the Prime Minister or his aide. Jack dodged a bullet that time, and a court martial.

Sue's due date for the baby came and went. She thought the baby was just taking his/her time. It was still continually active inside of her. By the middle of April, Sue had an appointment with the military doctor at the 2 Wings Hospital. She explained that she was one month overdue. As the doctor took her vitals, he saw the movement coming from her stomach. She was quite large because of her short stature and the baby movements looked exaggerated. When he listened for a baby heartbeat his facial expression turned grim.

"Wait right here, Mrs. Wixson. I will be right back."

Sue did not like the look on his face or the concern in his voice. It made her feel sick to her stomach.

The doctor returned with a nurse, and he asked her to listen for the fetal heartbeat.

The nurse placed the cold fetoscope on Sue's abdomen. She moved it around until she looked at the doctor and gravely stated, "I see what you mean."

Sue could not stand it any longer. With tears in her eyes, she blurted out, "What does that mean? What's wrong?"

The doctor put a hand on Sue's shoulder and told her that they needed to take a few x-rays and that once they were completed, he would talk with her. Sue was escorted by the nurse to the x-ray department. The nurse handed the technician Sue's chart and told her this had to be done stat. The technician reviewed the chart and looked at Sue sorrowfully. By that point Sue was dazed and followed the technician's instructions like a robot. The nurse stood by, waiting for Sue to complete the tests. She suspected Sue was in a state of shock and put her arm around her as they walked back to the doctor's office in silence. The nurse took Sue to an examination room, sat her down and brought her a strong cup of sweet tea. She also put a blanket on Sue, who was shivering.

An hour later the doctor and the nurse entered the examination room. The doctor pulled his chair close in front of Sue and sat down. The nurse stood slightly behind Sue with her arm on Sue's shoulder.

"Mrs. Wixson, who told you that you were pregnant?" he calmly asked.

Sue said that no one had to tell her she was pregnant; her periods had stopped, and she gained weight. She also felt the baby moving at four months and continued to feel the movement of the baby.

The doctor gently held her hand in his two large hands and softly said, "Mrs. Wixson, you are not pregnant. There is no baby in your womb and the x-rays show there never was."

Now Sue was not only in shock, but she was also flabbergasted. "What, this can't be. I's felt the baby. I's am as big as a house. I's had no periods for ten months. NO, NO, there is a baby in me!"

The doctor reiterated that she was not pregnant and there was no baby. He then went on to explain that some women want a child so badly that they experience a psychological pregnancy or what was called a phantom pregnancy. They are so convinced that they are pregnant that the brain triggers a chemical reaction in the body, inducing a pregnancy-like state.

Sue started to sob. She cried so hard and just wanted to die. This was a nightmare for Sue. She wanted to wake up and discover she and the baby were fine.

The doctor asked her if she wanted them to call her husband to come and get her. She declined. She left the office and wandered away from the base. She did not know how far she walked because she was in a blinded state of shock.

Sue found herself in the village of Faulquemont, eight miles from the base. There was a small stone church there. She walked up the steps and pulled open the wooden door, which felt as heavy as her heart. Sue sat on an old wooden pew at the front of the church. She looked up at the crucifix on the wall. Through her tears, she prayed aloud, "Lord, I's am so heartbroken, ashamed, and scared. I don't know what to do or how to tell Jack. I need your help. I want to have children. I want to give Jack children. Lord, if you give me children, I promise to give you one back."

Sue sat there and quietly sang "Peace in the Valley" until her tears ceased falling and her mind, body and soul were flooded with peace. She then had the strength to walk home and face Jack with the sad news.

Jack was distraught to learn of Sue's phantom pregnancy, but he was more concerned about Sue. He knew this was devastating for her. Jack did his best to comfort her and encourage her. Within a week Sue started to menstruate and her abdomen shrunk to its normal size, but with new stretch marks. No one in the PMQs knew the situation and no one asked why there was no baby in the Wixson household. They assumed the baby had died.

At first, Jack was going to remove the baby furniture from the apartment, but then he decided that might upset Sue more. He was concerned it would push her over the edge if she thought that Jack presumed, they would never have children. Jack removed the cradle from their bedroom to the nursery. He shut the door and left the baby's room as Sue had arranged it.

Sue struggled with depression over the next few months. She was lethargic and cried a lot. She would prepare Jack's meals but did little else. The social butterfly Sue went into a cocoon and withdrew from all friends and neighbours. Jack was at his wits' end and wanted to help his wife, but he had no idea what to do. Things were so bad, he thought she might need psychiatric help. Acquiring psychiatric services was looked down upon in those days.

Jack spoke to his boss about taking time off, but his boss came up with a better idea. "Jack, you know the Air Force will pay for you and Sue to have a maid. It probably would be good for Sue at this time.

Having someone around during the day, she will be forced to talk to someone, and it will give you peace of mind while you are at work."

Jack decided he had nothing to lose, and he applied for a maid. Some of the residents in the building had live-in maids, but Jack knew that arrangement would be too much for Sue. Instead, he secured the services of a maid from Faulquemont. Jack informed Sue that a maid would be coming over five days a week for eight hours. Sue was surprised at the arrangements he made but she did not object. Before the pregnancy incident, she would have protested, but now Sue was indifferent about having a maid.

CHAPTER 52
The Maid

Julie, the maid, arrived on Monday. She was a middle-aged woman. Even though she was only five-foot-four, she looked tall next to Sue. She wore a black uniform, a white apron and a white frilled headband, just like a traditional French maid. Julie understood English but her spoken English was limited. Luckily Sue had picked up some French while living in Quebec.

Sue liked her immediately. Julie introduced herself and went about cleaning the apartment. At ten-thirty she brought Sue a cup of café au lait and some cookies she found in the cupboard.

"Eat. Get strong, Madame," Julie urged as she sat down to partake of the goodies with Sue. Before long Julie and Sue were talking about their families and life in general.

Julie knew about Sue's struggles since her false pregnancy, and she approached Sue with kindness, compassion and diplomacy.

When Jack came home that evening, he was surprised that Sue greeted him at the door. She still had that wounded look on her face, but he could see progress in her condition. At the supper table, she talked about her first day with Julie.

As the weeks passed, Julie and Sue developed a friendship. One day Sue broke down and told Julie about the baby she would never have. Julie listened intently and comforted Sue. When Sue was finished crying, Julie told her, "You, Madame, will . . . how you say it . . . Babies will come. Maybe one, two, tree, or maybe many. I pray and ask le Dieu for dis."

Sue could not help but smile at Julie's attempt to speak words of comfort. Julie's imperfect English reminded Sue of how her dear mother, Grace, spoke.

Sue asked Julie to teach her more French. Throughout the day Julie would point to items and tell Sue the French names and have Sue repeat them. It turned out that Sue had a knack for learning languages. In turn Sue helped Julie advance her English skills.

One afternoon, Julie was cleaning the kitchen floor when she heard a loud horrid scream from the bathroom. Julie found Sue up against the wall opposite the toilet, attempting to pull up her pants. She was as white as a ghost and trembling.

"What, Madame? What is wrong?"

Sue pointed to the toilet. Julie lifted the toilet lid and saw what had horrified Sue: a black rat in the toilet bowl.

Julie laughed. "Oh, Madame, it's a rat. No problem," she said casually. Then she flushed the toilet. "There, Madame, it is gone."

Julie acted as if it was no big deal and a typical occurrence. Sue was horrified by the thought of rats coming up the toilet. The thought of a rat biting her on the backside was one she could not tolerate. Right there and then Sue marched into the nursery and returned with a potty a neighbour had given her for the baby. From then on, she used the potty and dumped it into the toilet.

Occasionally, Sue received letters from home. It was usually her mother or Ruby who wrote. The family had moved to Kirkland Lake, Ontario, in February.

When Sue read this news, she chuckled. "Poor Maw, another winter move."

Bill, Critch, Arthur, and Norm were working in the mine. Grace, Bill, Critch, Arthur, Howie, and Ruby lived in Kirkland Lake. The two older sons rented their own apartment. Marg, Norm, and their boys had moved to Larder Lake, a half hour away from Kirkland Lake. Audrey had met a man named Henry Rude, a schoolteacher from Larder Lake. They were married in June. Howie was in his last year of school. Ruby was enjoying the school she attended, and she had made many friends. Grace had been drinking on a regular basis and

Ruby had to retrieve her from the hotel on many occasions. Ruby was genuinely concerned about her mother. Sue became concerned too, and wished she were there to talk to her and help Ruby. Sue pined for her family. She had always been able to call them or visit them. Now, letter writing was their only form of communication. On the days when the yearning to see her family was strong, she would take out the few photos she had and talk to them as if her family members were in the room with her. Doing this and praying eased her loneliness.

Sue busied herself preparing for their first Christmas in France. She suspected she was pregnant but did not mention it to Jack. She wanted to wait a few more months then see the base doctor. Sue was worried she would have a recurrence of the phantom pregnancy. Julie suspected that Sue was pregnant but said nothing to her. Sue, her employer and friend, would let her in on the secret when she was ready.

Julie and Sue baked and decorated the house. Julie arrived with a small pine tree one morning. Sue was thrilled. Together they decorated it. Amongst the decorations were a few her mother had given her. Sue carefully unwrapped the two sparkle-covered cardboard churches and the two white cardboard snowmen. She held one of them close to her heart, took a deep breath and closed her eyes. She envisioned her mother handing them to her and saying, "Here, girly, when you put these on da tree in France you's remember yours Maw and that I's with you's all da time."

She told Julie the story behind the decorations. A huge smile came across Sue's face as she thoughtfully hung the first church ornament on the tree, and she said, "Maw, I's remember you are with me. Merry Christmas, Maw."

Julie had tears in her eyes. She had lost her mother years prior. Sue's story touched her heart and hearing Sue speak to her maw as she placed the first ornament on the tree had Julie reminiscing about her mother.

Julie took off the week of Christmas and the week in-between Christmas and New Year's. Sue missed her; she found the apartment quiet without the chatter and laughter of her new friend.

Sue loved to take walks outside of the base. She noticed that mistletoe grew wild in the woods. She thought they were beautiful and would be stunning on the mirror above the fireplace mantel. Sue gathered a huge armful and took them back to her PMQ. She draped some over the mirror so that long tendrils hung down on the sides. She used some to make a centerpiece for her dining room table. She wrapped some around the candle sticks on the end tables beside the couch. She was pleased with the results. Her apartment was a vision of Christmas hope. Sue was pleased but she felt something was missing. She could not put her finger on what, but she just felt there was an item needed to pull everything together.

CHAPTER 53

A Special Gift

Two days before Christmas, Jack was shopping in the Canex, the military store on the base. He saw a perfect gift for Sue. It was pricey but he thought after all Sue had been through, she deserved something special. He got one of the store attendants to wrap it and place a big red bow on it. Jack was pleased with his purchase and could not wait to see Sue's face when she opened it. On Christmas Eve Day, to Sue's disappointment, Jack said he had to work. He didn't have to work; instead, he went to a friend's place and made a model wooden stable for the nativity scene figurines to be placed in.

Jack and Sue started their celebration Christmas morning by sipping on a glass of homemade eggnog. Sue read the story of Mary and Joseph and the birth of Jesus out loud from an old Bible the Salvation Army had given her as a kid. Of course, there was some kissing around the mistletoe before presents were opened. Jack passed Sue her present. She knew someone else must have wrapped it because it was perfectly packaged. Sue carefully peeled each piece of tape. She thought the shiny gold and red paper was so pretty she wanted to save it.

Jack was growing impatient. "Sue, for God's sake, just tear it open."

Sue looked at him and smiled. "I'm saving the paper. Hold on, I's almost have it opened."

Sue opened the package and began unwrapping each item wrapped in newspaper. The figurines were made of hand-carved plaster and were hand-painted.

"Oh Jack . . . oh Jack, this is beautiful," Sue exclaimed joyfully. When all the figurines were unwrapped, she ran to Jack and hugged him and kissed him hard. He could not have given her a more wonderful present. Sue's reaction was far beyond what Jack expected. When they were finished embracing, he told her, "Wait, there is something else."

"You've already given me so much. Jack, you're spoiling me."

Jack retrieved the model wooden stable for the nativity scene from where he had hidden it and placed it under the tree. Sue placed the figurines in the rough wooden stable. Sue and Jack stood back from the tree with arms around each other and scrutinized the nativity scene.

"It's perfect, honey, just perfect," declared Sue. "This is what was needed to complete the Christmas decor."

The excitement over Sue's gift consumed their thoughts and Sue almost forgot to give Jack his gifts—a new wallet and pocketknife. He appreciated his gifts, but the best gift was how ecstatic Sue was. Having his happy wife back was worth more than money could buy. That special nativity scene would be placed under their Christmas tree for many years.

On New Year's Eve Day, Sue awoke to a surprise. She had just sat down in the living room with a cup of coffee when she noticed streams of clear liquid with black flecks in it running down the mirror above the mantel. She rushed to the mirror, and, to her horror, she found the liquid was extremely sticky, like a thick glue. The mistletoe berries had burst from the warm temperature, leaving a gooey, gummy, and slimy mess. The black dots in the streaks were the seeds from the berries. Sue checked the tables which she had also decorated with mistletoe and found a similar mess.

Sue knew she had to get the mess off the mirror, mantel, and tables without damaging them. This furniture did not belong to them. Sue tried a pine cleaner and that only smeared it. She tried dish detergent mixed with a bit of ammonia. This smeared it more. Finally, in defeat, she called Jack at work and explained the situation.

Jack brought home a degreaser they used on the planes at the base. With this product and some elbow grease, they were able to clean the gooey mess off. The finish on the tables also came off with the degreaser. Jack was upset because he knew he would have to pay for them. That New Year's Eve was a memorable one, with Jack and Sue attending the New Year's Eve dance smelling of degreaser. The smell lingered on them and the home for weeks.

CHAPTER 54

Déjà Vu

At the end of January, Sue went to see the base doctor. Nervously, she told him that she had not had her periods for four months. Sue was embarrassed to even tell him this because it was the same doctor who diagnosed her phantom pregnancy. She wondered if he thought, *here we go again.*

He examined her and then sent her to the lab at the hospital. There she gave a urine sample, and they took blood tests. The doctor told her to make an appointment for the following week and by then they should have the results back.

Sue made the appointment before she left the hospital. That week felt like a year. Each day seemed to drag as if it had multiplied every hour by two. When the day of the appointment came, she woke up much too early. She was so anxious that she went one hour early, hoping the doctor might see her ahead of her appointed time. This was not possible, so she sat and waited, but she felt better waiting in the waiting room rather than at home.

At last, the doctor called Sue into his office and asked her to sit down. Before he closed the door, he asked the nurse to join them. Sue thought she was going to faint because it was déjà vu.

"Well, Mrs. Wixson, I remember when you were here before. That was a very difficult time. The test results this time show you are about four months pregnant according to the date of your last period," said the doctor.

Sue stared at him for a few moments. She could barely believe what she heard. She was expecting him to say that it was another false pregnancy. Finally, she asked, "Are you sure?"

The doctor smiled. "Yes, according to our tests and my examination, I am certain that you are pregnant. You are due at the end of June. If you like, we can do another test in two weeks."

Sue agreed that they should do one more test. She did not want to make her announcement to Jack, or anyone else, unless she was positive there really was going to be a baby. Sue wanted to be happy, but she was cautious and guarded her heart. She shut off her emotions to protect herself from being disillusioned again. Two weeks went by and she returned to the hospital laboratory to be retested.

The doctor phoned her with the news. "Mrs. Wixson, you definitely are pregnant. The second test came back positive. Make an appointment to see me in two weeks. I am going to prescribe prenatal vitamins. Your iron is a bit low. You can pick them up at the base pharmacy."

Julie was with her when she got the good news. Sue sat down on a chair and cried and laughed. Julie heard her and ran to her and knelt beside her. "Madame are you ok. Madame, talk to me," pleaded Julie.

"Yes, I am ok. I's more than ok. Julie, I am expecting!" shouted Sue.

"Pardon, Madame . . . What are you expecting?" Julie was puzzled by the term.

"Julie, I am going to have a baby . . . at the end of June!" Sue was ecstatic.

They stood up and hugged each other. Julie proclaimed, "Bravo, Madame. I will pray all will be well. You will have a wonderful healthy little one."

"I guess we have work to do in the nursery," said Sue.

"Oui Madame, I will wash all the baby clothes and clean the room," replied Julie.

That evening Sue had a roast beef supper waiting for Jack when he got home. She put candles on the table and had a bottle of wine opened. When Jack came home, he looked around and said, "Wow, what's the occasion? Did I forget the date of something special?"

"No, my love, you did not. But I do have some news. Some wonderful news." Sue smiled from ear to ear. It had been an awfully long time since he saw that sparkle in Sue's eye.

Sue leaned in close to Jack, pulled his head down and whispered, "We are going to have a baby. You're going to be a father!"

Jack backed away and asked, "Sue, are you sure? How do you know this?" He was apprehensive because of the previous experience.

Sue laughed. She understood why Jack was concerned. "Jack, I have had two pregnancy tests done at the hospital and they both were positive."

Jack hollered, "Yahoo . . . I am going to be a father." He hugged Sue, lifted her off the ground and twirled her around. Suddenly he stopped. "Oh, maybe I should not have done that."

Sue gave him a big kiss. "That's fine, my love. I am not fragile, just pregnant."

CHAPTER 55

Baby Daze

On June 29th, 1956, Sue gave birth to a healthy baby girl. They named her Glenda after Sue's friend in Duparquet. She weighed six pounds five ounces, a good size for a tiny woman to give birth to. Once the nurses got the baby cleaned up, they brought the baby to Sue. Glenda had a huge red bow tied on thick long hair. The nurses had never seen a baby with so much hair.

Sue was anxious to get home and take care of her wee one on her own. While she was in the hospital the baby's main care was provided by the nurses. One nurse constantly reminded Sue of her disability and her inability to take care of a baby. This nurse was a tall blonde who wore her hair in braids rolled up on each side of her head. Sue secretly called her Butterballs. A few of the other nurses let Sue bottle feed the baby. But Nurse Butterballs insisted she be the one to feed the baby, treating Sue as though she were inadequate. Sue finally asked her why she would not let her feed her own baby.

"You are never going to be able to care for this baby. You should not have had children since you are a cripple. What were you thinking? Besides, you are nothing but a girl. You mark my words, they will take this baby away from you," the nurse viciously declared.

Sue had not experienced this narrow-mindedness since her first day of school. She never expected a nurse to behave so unjustly and cruelly. Tears were running down her face.

The nurse continued her tirade on Sue's mothering skills: "All the tears in the world will not change the fact that you will be unable to change, feed, bathe or care for this little one." Butterballs left the room.

Jack walked into the room a few minutes after the nurse had left. He found his beloved Sue wiping tears from her eyes and blowing her nose.

"What in the world is going on, Sue?" Sue thought she had pulled herself together, but Jack's sweet concern and his touch made the dam of emotion break, and she sobbed in his arms.

When Sue was at the end of her tears, she told Jack what the nurse had said. Jack marched out to the nurse's station. He demanded to see the head nurse and the doctor. With Butterballs present, Jack was livid and did not hold back his words. He pointed at the nurse who had verbally assaulted his wife. "This nurse has just put my wife through a living hell. She has told her that she will not be able to care for our baby. She maliciously claims that because Sue is crippled, she will not be able to keep our child. Sue is devastated. You are not a nurse, you are a mean, miserable bitch, and you had better never go near my wife again. Sue has been through enough shit in life that this kind of treatment is bullshit!"

The doctor stopped Jack. "She will be dealt with, and I assure you she will not go near your wife again. Jack, come with me while the head nurse deals with her." The doctor then addressed the head nurse, "Once you have dealt with her, go and check on Mrs. Wixson and assure her we have every confidence she will be a good mother."

Sue was given the reassurance she needed, and Butterballs was transferred to the medical floor in the hospital.

Jack and Sue brought their wonderful bundle of joy home seven days after her birth. Sue had no problems figuring out how to bathe her, feed her and change her. After all, she had helped her sisters with their babies.

Sue had practiced changing diapers on the teddy bear Jack had bought the baby before she was born. She would put the diaper on the change table and then the baby on top of the clean diaper. She removed the old diaper by taking the pin off, then held down the clean diaper by placing her right hand on top of it by the base of the baby's bum, which kept the baby from sliding down when she pulled the dirty diaper off. She cleaned the baby, then pulled the middle of the clean diaper up and the sides into the middle before pinning the diaper.

Glenda was a happy baby and easy to care for. Jack loved being a dad and he was amazed at how Sue managed. He should not have been, since her sheer determination and creativity was something to behold. Sue used to tell him, "A disability is only an ability to do things in a different way." She could have been the poster girl for this saying.

Glenda was the apple of their eyes. Her personality was sweet, and her long hair made her look even cuter. At the age of six months, her hair was down to her shoulders.

Baby Glenda walked just before her first birthday. On Glenda's first birthday, Jack got another surprise. Sue was pregnant with their second child. Jack hoped they would have a boy this time.

CHAPTER 56

A Noble Surprise

That summer Jack and Sue went sightseeing in France, Germany, and Spain whenever Jack was off work. Glenda was a content toddler, easy to take on their travels. In Spain, at Getafe Air Base near Madrid, Jack attended training, and Sue and Glenda went along. While Jack was at his training session, Sue took Glenda to a park in the city. She packed a picnic and a blanket, put Glenda into the stroller and off they went.

Glenda loved running around and playing with the other children. When she had exhausted herself, Sue fed her lunch and put her into the stroller for her nap. As Glenda was napping, Sue sat eating her lunch when a young boy around nine or ten ran up to her. He wore a white shirt and black long shorts, white socks and shiny black leather shoes.

"Hello," greeted Sue.

"Hello," he shyly reciprocated and looked around.

"Would you like to sit down and join me," asked Sue.

He flopped down on the blanket beside Sue. "Yes, Ma'am, I surely would."

Sue deduced from his accent that the young boy was British, and he knew she was from another country because of her accent. The young boy introduced himself as Charles, and Sue introduced herself. Sue offered him a sandwich, which he accepted. Charles was curious about Canada and asked many questions. He barely gave Sue the opportunity to inquire about England and his life. Whenever she asked about his parents, he responded in general terms and changed the topic. She was enjoying his company while Glenda was sleeping but she wondered where his parents were. Just as she was about to ask him where they were, four men in black suits, white shirts and black ties ran up to the blanket where Sue and Charles were sitting. They stood at the four corners of the blanket.

Sue was startled and was about to grab Glenda, when one of the men spoke. "We've been looking everywhere for you, Prince Charles. You should not have run off like that. We were worried sick. Time to leave now. Ma'am, I hope he was not a bother to you?"

Sue said, "No, not at all. We had a wonderful conversation."

Charles apologized to the men and thanked Sue for the sandwich and the smashing visit. He stood up, waved and said goodbye. He left with the four men. Sue had entertained royalty and she did not even know it until Prince Charles's bodyguards showed up. That picnic with Prince Charles was one she would treasure all her life.

On December 5th, 1957, baby Janice Ruby was born. Instead of the mass of brown hair that Glenda had, she had dirty blonde curly hair. Jack was not disappointed that the baby was a girl. He fell in love with her the first time he held her. Glenda was happy to have a baby sister. Sue included Glenda in caring for the new baby, as much as an eighteen-month-old could be involved. Glenda held the wet clean clothes to wipe the baby, she brought her mom the clean diapers, and occasionally she would help hold the bottle.

Julie had resigned a few weeks before Janice was born, to take care of her elderly father, so Sue was on her own. She enjoyed her independence most of the time but missed the girlfriend talks.

CHAPTER 57

Explosion

The next few months flew by. At the beginning of April Sue was exhausted. Taking care of two young ones was a handful, but she wondered why she was tired. She began taking afternoon naps when the girls were napping, a new habit which, regrettably, left the laundry to be done later in the evening.

By the beginning of May she suspected she was pregnant. Janice would barely be one when the new baby would be due. Sue was not happy about her condition.

During the next few months Sue was not only exhausted but she frequently passed out. One time a neighbour found Sue passed out on the floor in front of Sue's apartment with a basket of clean laundry spilled everywhere. Another time she had just finished feeding Janice, who was in the highchair, and then she woke up on the floor. Janice had thrown her food on the floor. Glenda was in the kitchen playing with the pots and pans she had taken out of the cupboard. Sue was mortified to think what could have happened. When Jack came home, she relayed the incident to him. The first thing he did was send Sue to bed after supper. He put the children to bed that evening and then went next door to enlist the help of the neighbour. Sue slept sixteen hours, and when she woke, she hurried to the girls' room. The girls were not there. They were in the living room with Jack. Sue had not heard a thing. She told Jack that he should not have taken the day off.

"Sue, sit down. I'll get you some breakfast and a cup of coffee." Jack made scrambled eggs, toast, and a café au lait. When she had finished breakfast, he informed her that Marie next door would be helping her.

Sue was upset with him. "Jack, that is not necessary. You know I am totally capable of taking care of my own children."

"Damn it, Sue, put your pride in your pocket for once. You need help and you need someone checking on you and the children." Jack had made up his mind and Sue was not going to change it. He could be just as stubborn. Sue knew she was defeated in the matter. Sue loved to help others, but she did not like others helping her. When others offered to help her with anything, a little voice in her head would say, "The little crippled girl can't do it." Jack did not realize it was not just her pride, but a survival technique she developed as a child.

Marie knew Sue would not be pleased with the arrangements Jack made, so she made a trade-off with Sue. She would check on Sue if Sue would do some baking for her. Marie's husband would be grateful to have baked goods for his lunch. Marie also told her she had been lonely since she moved into the PMQs and it would be a nice change for her to have another woman to talk to. Sue knew what Marie was doing but she found Marie so sweet for trying to figure out how to help Sue without offending her.

A deep friendship developed between them. Marie was careful not to offer help to Sue when it wasn't necessary so as not to cross a boundary. But as her pregnancy progressed, Sue did allow Marie to do her laundry for her, so she would not worry about passing out in the laundry room. Marie found Sue unconscious several times. Applying a cold cloth to Sue's forehead usually revived her. The last two weeks of her pregnancy the two apartment doors were left open during the day. Jack had purchased a child's safety gate to put across the doorway to keep Janice and Glenda in the apartment. Marie could hear Sue moving around and talking to the children. If it got too quiet, she would check on Sue.

Two months before Sue was due, all personnel were notified to prepare for evacuation to Spain. The families had twenty-four hours to pack minimal belongings.

"Oh no, not now. This can't really be happening," whispered Sue to herself. Jack was at work and in her exhausted state she could not figure out what she needed. Marie assisted her in packing the necessary items including passports and other important papers. Intelligence had been received that Russia was going to bomb the base. They were under evacuation notice for two weeks before it was lifted. This was a stressful time for Jack and Sue. Not only were they concerned about her pregnancy, but also the threat of war had become a reality.

A week before Sue's third child was due, a huge explosion shook the apartments. Plates fell out of the cupboards, glasses fell off tables, the mirror and the fireplace cracked, and the highchair fell over. It felt like an earthquake. Jack was at home and thought they were being bombed. He told Sue to get the children ready in case the sirens went off. Marie was at Sue and Jack's door within seconds. Jack grabbed his movie camera on the way out the door. Marie helped Sue dress the children and prepare bottles and snacks.

Two hours later Jack phoned Sue to tell her that it was not a bomb. One of their own CF-100 jets had crashed into the base hospital. He did not know when he would be home. Although she was relieved that it was not a bomb, she knew people must have died in that crash and she felt horrid and cried. Plane debris was found for miles around the base and the district. All personnel were called in to help gather the debris and keep onlookers away from the main site of the crash.

Marie carried the two sleeping girls to their beds and stayed with Sue for a few hours to make sure the shock had not caused her to go into labour.

Against orders, Jack recorded a video of the crash site. He kept this quiet for years because he knew he would be brought up on charges if his superiors ever found out. Years later, Jack would show his family the movie and describe the events.

CHAPTER 58

A Candlelit Birth

On November 29th, late in the afternoon, Jack and the girls were napping when Sue started having labour pains. Because this was her third child, the baby could deliver quicker.

Standing over her husband, Sue whispered, "Jack, it's time."

"OK, dear, I just want to sleep a few more minutes. Then I'll get up," he mumbled as he turned over.

Sue shook Jack and raised her voice. "Jack, get up. I am in labour. We need to get to . . . Where are we going?"

"Holy shit, you mean it's time for the baby to be born! Ok, I am getting up now. We are taking you to one of the barracks. They have set up a makeshift hospital there," he explained as he pulled his pants on. He ran next door and banged on it until Marie answered. She knew exactly what was going on and followed him back into his apartment.

With Sue and her overnight bag in the car, Jack raced to the makeshift hospital. Sue kept telling him to slow down because they did not have far to go but he paid her no heed.

When Sue entered the barracks, she was taken by wheelchair to the area set up as a maternity ward. The grey walls were not very pleasant, but it was definitely a hospital setting because the smell of disinfectant was so strong that it felt like it was burning Sue's nostrils. While she was in labour, the electricity kept cutting out but would come back on within a minute. Sue was concerned that her baby would be born in the pitch black. The nurse told her not to worry and that they were all set up in the delivery room. When it was time, Sue was wheeled down the hall and just as she was entering the delivery area, the electricity went out. This time it did not come back on. She delivered her third baby girl while two nurses stood on either side of the doctor, each holding a lit candle. Another nurse took the baby and left the room immediately.

"What's wrong? Is something wrong with my baby?" Sue was frantic.

"She will be fine. She looks very jaundiced, well, at least by candlelight she does. She is being put in an incubator," explained the doctor.

"Can I hold her soon?" Sue asked.

"Mrs. Wixson, you will have to wait. I will go and check on her when I am finished here. I will let you know what is happening then." The doctor was overtired and getting impatient.

They had taken the baby to a large broom closet that was set up as an emergency nursery. There were no windows, just two incubators, metal shelves for all the supplies, and a chair for an attending nurse to sit on.

Sue did not see her baby girl for six days. On the sixth day the nurse brought a jaundiced infant to meet her mother. Sue cried because she had wondered if the baby had died, and they were not telling her. Sue and Jack named their new bundle of joy, Sharon Ann. Sue was able to bring her home on the eighth day.

Sue loved to tell the unique story of how Sharon was born by candlelight and was put in a broom closet.

CHAPTER 59
Back to Canada

Two Wings closed in 1960 and all RCAF troops were withdrawn from France. Jack was amongst the first wave of troops that left. In May 1959, Jack was transferred to Exeter, Ontario, Canada. The couple travelled home from France, now with three girls in tow. Jack's motion sickness was as bad this time as it was on his voyage to France three and a half years prior.

Sue's family had all moved to the Kirkland Lake area in Northern Ontario, except for Fran, Wallace and their three children, who had moved to Southern Ontario.

Sue was so glad to be home on Canadian soil she said she would have kissed the ground, but she was holding baby Sharon in her arms. She enjoyed touring France, Germany, and Spain, but she was glad to be away from an area where the threat of war loomed. She felt safer being back in her homeland.

They were used to PMQ living and settled in quite quickly. Exeter was a training base and Jack was an Electronics and Communications Instructor. He enjoyed his new role and found it relaxing compared to the stressful position he had in Europe. Jack and Sue were stationed in Exeter for four years. During that time Sue gave birth to two boys. On November 23rd, 1960, Ross Alan was born, and on October 18th, 1962, Mark Dwayne was born. Sue claimed they had to come back to Canada to have children with handles.

In 1963 they moved to Seaforth, Ontario. There was a wonderful playground beside the PMQs where the three girls played on the swings and slides with other children. Sue never worried about them going there by themselves because it was a fenced area and usually one of the other parents was present.

Sue had no idea the playground had been shut down to be upgraded until the three girls came home with a mixture of tar and powdered cement on their clothing, hair, arms, and legs. When she asked the girls what they had gotten into, Glenda said, "There were buckets of black paint and bags of sand opened. So, we thought we would help, and we painted the swings and then filled the sand box up. Well, we really didn't get the sand box filled because we could only use our hands."

Janice, full of pride, spoke up. "We helped the workers. Now they don't have as much work to do." Janice then repeated one of Sue's sayings: "Credit's due, Mom. When the workers came, we showed them all the work we did to help them."

Sue wanted to cry and laugh at the same time. "What did they say?"

Glenda put her head down and said, "Well, they said they didn't need our help anymore and something about a mess they had to clean up. They told us to go home and tell you about our adventure."

"Credit was due alright," Sue said, shaking her head as she looked over her tarred, cement-crusted daughters.

The girls cried as Sue scrubbed the tar off them with turpentine. Into the tub all three went. The tub had to be filled four times before all the cement residue and turpentine was washed off. It took three hours to clean up those unhappy helpers.

CHAPTER 60

Bullfrogs

When they moved to Clinton, they did not live in the PMQs. Instead, Jack rented a two-story, three-bedroom house in town with a backyard where the children could play. Clinton was close to the Ottawa river and bullfrogs and snapping turtles were in ample supply along the river's edge.

Next door lived the Burrey family, who had a four-year-old girl, Carley. She was Sharon's age. Sharon and Carley became friends and often played together. Carley had three older brothers, aged eleven, twelve and eighteen. The two younger brothers liked to gather bullfrogs and keep them in an old laundry sink which had a makeshift plywood lid. They got together with their friends and had bullfrog races. Sharon and her two sisters were constantly being teased and annoyed by these two boys, which made the girls leery and nervous around them.

One day the boys went too far with their teasing and harassing. They grabbed Sharon when she was outside playing with her sister Janice. One of the boys held onto her as the other put bullfrogs into her clothing. Sharon was screaming and then passed out as the boys put the last frog into her pants. This scared the boys, and they took off running. Janice was hiding behind the old hand pump water well and peeked around the cement base and saw what the boys were doing. She was terrified and stayed where she was. Once the boys had left, she went to Sharon and pulled the frogs out of her clothing and then ran to get Sue.

"Mom, the Burrey boys put frogs in Sharon's clothes and she's not waking up. I took them out. Mom, I think she's dead," said a petrified Janice.

Sue rushed outside and once she determined that Sharon was still breathing, she picked up her unconscious child, took her into the living room and laid her on the couch.

"Sharon, it's ok now. The frogs are gone, and Mom is here," Sue said gently as she wiped her daughter's forehead with a warm cloth.

After half an hour Sharon was still unconscious. Sue called the base and told Jack what had happened. Jack immediately came home, and the base doctor arrived with him. Jack and Doctor James were good friends and he had been with Jack when he answered the panicky phone call from Sue.

After the doctor examined Sharon, he asked Sue and Jack to join him in the kitchen. "Physically she is fine, but mentally and emotionally she has been traumatized."

The doctor instructed Sue and Jack to wash Sharon down, put her pajamas on and put her into bed. If Sharon had any favourite toys or a doll, they were to put these beside her in the bed. Dr. James called the base psychiatrist. The psychiatrist came to the house, and he too examined Sharon and came to the same conclusion.

The psychiatrist was concerned about the degree of trauma this four-year-old had experienced. He felt she had better remain at home for the time being. Sue and Jack were to notify him, any time of the day, when she woke up or if she had nightmares which he suspected would follow. If she did not become conscious within twenty-four hours, Sharon would have to be hospitalized.

"One of you needs to sit with Sharon until she comes around. Reassure her that she is safe now. Talk about her sisters and brothers and things she enjoys doing. Do not speak about the malicious incident. I will call you in the morning," stated the psychiatrist.

That night Sharon would repeatedly sit up screaming and would not stop until Sue or Jack held her and reassured her that she was safe. Then Sharon would fall back into an unconscious state. The next morning Sue and Jack were exhausted and worried that their daughter had suffered permanent mental and emotional damage.

That day Glenda and Janice went into the room and Sue encouraged them to talk to Sharon. But they were not to talk about the frogs, she whispered in their ears. As Janice and Glenda were talking to Sharon, she woke up after being unconscious for twenty-two hours. Sharon said, "Stop talking so loudly. My head hurts." Sue yelled for Jack, and he rushed to the room, thinking the worst had happened. Sue was sitting on a chair in front of Sharon's bed. When he entered the bedroom, she turned around, tears running down her face, and pointed to Sharon. There he saw Sharon with her eyes open and talking to her sisters. Jack turned white and he felt nauseated, but he hurried to the foot of the bed. Tears welled up in his eyes. "Thank God she's awake," Jack exclaimed. Sue and Jack held each other and cried for joy. Sharon was confused and asked her sisters, "Why are Mom and Dad crying?"

Even at their young age, Glenda and Janice knew this moment was special and they too cried and laughed.

The psychiatrist came to see Sharon that day. After speaking with her for about half an hour, he gave Sue and Jack his prognosis. "She does not recall the frog incident. The mind can do that to protect itself. She may or may not recall it. What you need to watch for is recurring nightmares and I suspect she might be terrified of frogs for the rest of her life. In that case, do not make light of it nor make a big deal about it. Provide reassurance that they cannot hurt her and remove her or the frog from the area. I am going to give you some mild sleeping sedation for a few nights. She will need to get some rest without having nightmares. I must be honest; I did not think she was going to regain consciousness."

Sharon did have the odd nightmare and she developed a horrendous fear of frogs and toads. When she saw one, whether it was near her or in the distance, she would faint. This fear remained with her for life. By the time she was in her twenties, although she no longer passed out, she would feel great anxiety and run the opposite way. It would take her about an hour to calm herself down.

The neighbours' boys were severely disciplined by their mothers, and they never again bothered the Wixson girls.

CHAPTER 61

Feather Fun

One morning Sue took her coffee outside to relax before the children awoke. There, sitting on the handle of the hand pump, was a white chicken. It did not fly away when she sat in the lawn chair about one hundred feet away. The chicken flew up and down, hopping on the handle. It did this until water came out of the faucet. When water filled the tiny hole at the base of the pump, the chicken hopped down and had a drink. Sue laughed at the resourceful bird. "What a smart little gal you are." When Sue asked around about the chicken, the neighbours told her there was a poultry farm about one mile out of town.

The chicken hung around the back yard for days. The children were entertained by her antics and friendliness. She allowed the children to pat the top of her head. They called her Whitey. Sue did not want the children to get too attached to the chicken because she knew the bird would be going back to the farm. Sue had to admit she had grown fond of Whitey too. Sue was glad the farmer had not come right away after she phoned. The next-door neighbours had a medium-sized black, shaggy dog. When he was on his rope outside and saw the chicken, he would run to the end of his rope and bark like crazy. The first time this happened the chicken flew onto a lower limb of the elm tree. Whitey sat there and watched the dog. She must have determined that the dog could not reach her, so she flew back onto the pump handle. Whitey would taunt the dog by flapping her wings and clucking loudly. One day the dog ran out of the door before his owner could tie him up. That was nearly the end of Whitey. She escaped just in time, thanks to the dog owner who ran and grabbed the dog before it caught the teasing fowl.

Sue knew she had better call the chicken farm again, before Whitey became the neighbour's dog's dinner. The farmer came to retrieve Whitey and Sue and the children were glad that the bird was going back home, where it would be safe from the neighbour's dog. Nevertheless, they would miss Whitey. For a short period of time, the Wixson's first family pet was a chicken

Bill, Grace, and Ruby had visited Sue in Exeter, when she first came back from France. It had been almost five years since Sue had seen any of her family. The absence of family contact in her life in Exeter made her feel like she was in a foreign country again.

Jack and Sue discussed and agreed that Jack would request a transfer to RCAF Ramore Radar Base in Northern Ontario. Ramore was only forty-five minutes from Kirkland Lake. The other reason Jack and Sue made this decision was Sharon's health. She had chronic bronchitis and the doctor suggested she would fare better in a colder, less humid climate. Northern Ontario fit the bill.

When Jack put the request in to be transferred to Northern Ontario, his superiors were concerned. They asked Jack to see the psychiatrist. Jack was puzzled but attended the session with the psychiatrist.

"So why am I here?" inquired Jack.

"Jack, first tell me why you put in for a transfer to Ramore Base in Northern Ontario?" queried the psychiatrist.

Jack provided his explanation. The psychiatrist started to laugh. Jack was confused. He did not think what he said was humorous at all.

"Jack . . . they asked you to see me because they thought you were having a breakdown. No one has ever asked to be transferred to Northern Ontario before. Usually, it is the last place enlisted men want to go."

Jack had to laugh with him. He now understood the strange reactions of his superiors. Jack was not only required to see a psychiatrist, but he also had to have a complete medical, dental and eye examination. The requirements for being sent to France were not as stringent as these.

Jack had his medical and eye examination. He saw no need for a dental examination since he had false teeth from the age of twenty-two. The dental office called several times to book an appointment and Jack told them he had false teeth. He finally got fed up with the harassment, so he put his false teeth in an envelope addressed to the dentist and through the internal mail. The dentist was furious with him. He did not have the same sense of humour Jack had. The dentist could have brought Jack up on charges, and he did threaten to do so, but he knew Jack would be leaving the base, so he let it go.

CHAPTER 62

Holtyre

In the early summer of 1963, Jack, Sue and their five children piled into the light blue Studebaker and headed towards Northern Ontario. As they travelled, the children were in awe of the forests that went on forever. They wondered if they would ever get to their new home. The nine-and-a-half-hour trip was long. Sue tried to make it comfortable for the children and attempted to keep them occupied by singing songs, playing car games like "I spy with my little eye," and talking about her family.

When they drove into the village of Holtyre, the children were hungry and cranky. Mark, the one-year-old, had a dirty diaper, and Jack was exhausted. Over the crying and bickering Sue began to sing "There'll Be Peace in the Valley." As soon as Jack put the car in park in the driveway, the children scrambled out as fast as they could because when Mom started to sing that song, she was trying to calm herself and needed space.

Holtyre was located twenty minutes from the base. It was predominantly a French-speaking community with a population of five hundred. It had three corner stores, a bowling alley, a hotel, a gas station, post office, telephone office with a switch board, French Catholic school, English public school, and a town community hall.

Jack rented a two-story, three-bedroom home on Euclid Street. It was not a fancy house, but it was big enough for the family. The walls had been freshly painted light beige. The two bedrooms upstairs were large rooms with slanted ceilings and hidden cubby closets behind the walls. The children shared one room and Jack and Sue had the other room. Ross and Mark slept near the window at one end of the room and the three girls' beds were lined up on the opposite wall. Two dressers were set on opposite sides of the room, one for the boys and one for the girls. The stairs led to the bathroom between the two bedrooms. Although the house had been painted, it required a good cleaning. The kitchen was small, so they used the spare room on the main floor as a dining room. There was a pantry in the half-finished basement. The rest of the basement was dim and damp with clay walls and floor—a hospitable environment for the toads Sue encountered there. Sue knew this would be a problem for Sharon. Jack would have to get rid of them when Sharon was sleeping or out playing.

The next day, friendly neighbours, bearing casseroles and desserts, dropped by to welcome the newcomers. They provided the Wixson family with meals for a few days. Jack took Mark and Ross with him to get groceries in Ramore, a village five miles away. The grocery store there filled the needs of the outlying communities.

The three girls put their belongings away and then went out to play. Behind the house was an old empty shed. It looked like it was a chicken coop at one time. Beyond the shed, a trail ran through a small, wooded area to the next street and across the street was a big field. On the other side of this field was a creek that flowed behind Holtyre. The water was deep, and the current was fast. The neighbours told Sue that a child had drowned in this creek, so she sternly warned the children to stay away from it.

Everyone in the village knew that a family had just moved in and some of the village children rode by on their bikes to satisfy their curiosity. One young girl with short black hair rode up on a bike five times her size. When she stopped her bike, she nearly toppled over. It was a girl's bike with a step-through frame and her crotch sat on the top tube of the frame as she stood on her tippy toes. She was out of breath from maneuvering the bike to a stop. She introduced herself as Karen and, between heavy breaths, she asked Sharon, "Do you want to play with me?" From that point on they became good friends.

The two of them made mud pies, ran in the fields playing fairies, had peanut-butter-and-jam-sandwich picnics in the woods, skipped, and did what six-year-old girls do. One day they were playing house with their dolls in the weather-worn wooden shed in Karen's backyard. They decided they should have a stove to cook their mud pies. Karen said, "We have matches in the house." She ran into the house to get them.

In the meantime, Sharon gathered some twigs, straw, and a few pieces of old wood which she piled in a corner in the shed. Karen returned, gave her approval of the fuel collected, and lit a match and *poof*, the fire was lit. In seconds the flames were licking the tinder-dry boards of the shed and spreading out of control. Karen and Sharon bolted out of the shed, their hair singed and their faces pale with fright. At that moment Karen's mother came out of the house to hang clothes on the line and saw the smoke. She grabbed the garden hose and put the fire out before the shed burned down. Karen was sent to her room and Sharon was sent home. Sharon knew she was going to be in big trouble because Sue would receive a phone call from Karen's mother.

Sharon hid in the bushes behind her house for about one hour, talking to herself and crying. "You dummy. You are sure going to get it from Maw. How could you have been so stupid, Sharon."

When Sharon decided she had better face the inevitable, she went home and was sent to her room after a thorough spanking. A lecture about the dangers of playing with matches was given to all the children, thanks to Sharon's escapade. Not only was Sharon embarrassed, but she also couldn't sit down for the rest of the day.

CHAPTER 63

Rite of Passage

The summer months passed quickly as the family adjusted to living in Holtyre. It was easy to develop friendships in the small community. Sue was very content and knew she would love living in Holtyre. It was just close enough to her family without being in each other's hair and business. Jack enjoyed the crew he worked with at the base. There were many couples and the base held family social activities such as Christmas parties, dances on every special occasion, winter carnivals, bowling, curling, baseball, barbeques and chapel every Sunday.

The Wixson family attended chapel at the base for many years. They drove Father Dehay to the chapel every Sunday and helped set up for mass.

Every Sunday Sharon was in the confessional, confessing the same sins: "I stole a dime from my dad, I fought with my sisters and I swore at my brothers!" Father Dehay would tell her to say five Hail Mary prayers and the Lord's Prayer twice. This went on for months until finally Father Dehay was either fed up or amused. He told her, "My dear girl, you need to stop coming to confession and stop doing those things. God will know when you are truly sorry." Sharon was stunned. In her young mind she figured she could keep getting away with it if she confessed every Sunday. From that day on she tried to correct her ways.

Since Sue's right shoulder was sloped and she had one breast smaller than the other, she had to either make her own clothes or make alterations to the clothes she bought. Her dresses and outfits were gorgeous and the women at the dances would ask her where she bought them. They were all stunned when she replied that she had made them. One of her creations was a long sparkly light green evening gown that had one long sleeve and a strap over the other shoulder. When she emerged from the bedroom in this evening gown with her red-dyed hair in an updo, the children were in awe. Janice yelled out, "Mom, you look like a movie star." They could barely believe that was their mother.

Holtyre held many functions at the hall, from school fundraising activities to town wedding showers. When someone was getting married, the women from all the families in town were expected to attend the bridal shower so that about one hundred women would typically be in attendance. Everyone knew that it was not necessary to invite everyone to the wedding, but it would be a faux pas if a family representative didn't show up at the shower, unless they had a good excuse. French and English chattering filled the town hall. One could barely hear oneself talk. The recent gossip was told and as the bride-to-be opened her gifts, they were passed to each person to look over.

Most events were potluck. One of Sue's specialties was her homemade soup and biscuits. Her chicken vegetable noodle soup was to die for. She would simmer the carcass of a chicken for eight hours to make the broth, then add the vegetables and noodles the last hour. The biscuits were light and flakey. Whenever there was a school or community function, she was asked to bring these two food items.

The first year the three girls attended the French Catholic school. The three-story school had one classroom for the English-speaking Catholic children. It was an unpleasant experience for the girls because at the time the French kids and the English kids often feuded. Being pushed around and bullied at recess became too much for the girls. The next year they were enrolled at the English public school. Ross and Mark also attended this school when they were old enough.

Winters could be brutally cold in Northern Ontario, with an abundance of snow. The children loved to play in the snow. Sometimes the two boys would build forts in the six-foot-high snowbanks on the side of the road. They dug a hole in the side of the bank and hollowed it out just enough for the two of them to sit in. A few hunks of snow were rolled in front of the entrance to camouflage their hideout. The next storm that arrived would result in the snowplow coming by and their fort would be filled in.

That winter a young boy was in his snowbank snow fort when the plow went by. He suffocated before he was dug out. Sue took the boys aside and told them about the tragedy. She asked, "Do you boys build snow forts in the snowbanks? I sure hope not and don't because I would not want to lose either one of you."

Both boys responded, "No, Mom, we don't!"

As soon as Sue was finished talking to them, they put on their winter attire, ran outside and filled in their fort hole. If she would have found out they were lying to her, they would have gotten a spanking. Sue's left arm was muscular because it was the only arm she used. When the kids got a spanking from her it was double the pain.

Friends and friends of friends gathered in the backyard of the Wixson home to go sliding. It wasn't unusual for there to be up to twenty kids on the Wixson hill. The steep hill led down to the creek and was slick. A path between the birch and pine trees made it easy to navigate to the bottom. The children used wooden toboggans, cardboard boxes and big garbage bags. Competitions of who could go the farthest was the name of the sliding game. When the snow was powdery you could slide clear across the creek into the gully. The only problem was that you could not steer the cardboard or plastic easily or accurately. Ross found this out one day. He sat on the plastic bag and got one of his buddies to shove him on the back. Ross took off sailing, but he was headed in the direction of a large pine tree. He tried to move his body over, but to no avail. The kids on the top of the hill were screaming, "Ross, get off. Get off!"

Too late. Ross smashed headfirst into the pine tree. It knocked him out cold.

He was no worse for the wear except for a big bump on his forehead and two black eyes. The family teased him mercilessly, calling him a "tree hugger." That was before the term was popular. He wore his injury with pride. Ross thought he looked like a wrestler.

The town boys had a horrible custom that they saw as a rite of passage for each other licking a steel post or pole when it was well below the freezing mark. Mark had licked a metal railing on the stairs at school and he only got the very end of his tongue stuck. When he pulled it off it bled a fair amount, but his injury was minor. Ross, on the other hand, did not realize that Mark had made sure he only licked the pole gently with the tip of his tongue. He had done it so fast that the boys did not notice he had not taken a good lick. The next day some of the boys decided it was Ross's turn and he took a good lick on the steel railing of the school steps. A good portion of his tongue stuck immediately to the railing. He tried to pull it off and it started to bleed, and the blood was freezing and coating his tongue like a bloody ice cube. The boys left the scene of the crime and Mark hurried into the school to get the teacher. The teacher rushed out with paper towel and a pitcher of warm water. The teacher told Ross that he must gently pull his tongue away from the railing as he was pouring the water. Ross did as he was instructed and, although his tongue was freed from the railing, the first layer of his tongue's skin was left behind. The teacher brought Ross into the school and gave him paper towel to absorb the large amount of blood running down his chin.

Sue and Jack were wondering where their boys were. Usually, they came right home after school. Sue was concerned because it was bitterly cold out. Jack went out in the car, looking for his tardy boys. He ended up at the school and when he saw Ross he snickered and said, "Well, did you learn a lesson, Ross?"

Ross was in so much pain, he just stared at his father with tears running down his cheeks. Jack told both boys they should never give into a dare from anyone because it usually means trouble. He also said that no one should ever, ever, ever lick anything metal outside anytime, but especially in the winter.

Ross was not able to eat solid food for a week and the liquid he did drink often stung his tongue. Sue insisted he rinse his mouth out with salt water to prevent infection, which caused additional agony.

CHAPTER 64

Tinker

The neighbours' dog was a Pomeranian who had bred with a medium-sized mutt. She had four puppies. The runt of the litter had long rusty-red fur. He looked like a Pomeranian but was not fluffy. This runt became the family's first dog. All the children fell in love with the small creature. Glenda was especially infatuated and captivated. The family named him Tinker. Sue and Glenda worked together to train Tinker. He was intelligent and within a week he was house-trained and would run to the door to go outside. When outside, he was tied to a rope that gave him room to go down the stairs and wander around. Sue wanted to train him to stay off the road in front of their house because huge ore trucks passed by at scheduled times. Sue picked times when the road had minimal traffic and let Tinker loose. As he dashed towards the road, she yelled, "No, Tinker." Tinker stopped and looked at her and then looked at the road. She yelled firmly, "No, Tinker!" Tinker looked at her as if she were teasing him, but he put his tail down and with sad big brown eyes obeyed his master and sheepishly walked back towards the house. Tinker was always rewarded with a treat of leftover meats from the family meals. The family was entertained by his tricks of playing dead, dancing and rolling over.

A family of skunks lived under the garage. Tinker befriended them. It was common to find Tinker laying a few feet away from a skunk on the back porch. The skunk family considered the back porch their domain and could be found lingering around there late at night. In all the years that Tinker maintained his friendship with the skunks, there was only one spraying incident.

Janice's boyfriend, Johnny, forgot to check the porch for skunks before leaving one dark evening. He was busy laughing and chatting with Sue. As he opened the door he stepped on a skunk's tail. Tinker started barking, Johnny jumped back, and all hell broke loose. The dog ran outside as the skunk was spraying. Johnny and Tinker both got sprayed. The house filled up with the stench and no amount of tomato juice alleviated the wretched odor on Tinker and in the house. It was months before it dissipated.

Although Tinker enjoyed being with the rest of the family, Glenda and Sue were his two favourite family members. Tinker reminded Sue of Tucker. He had the same colouring but was smaller, friendly, and obedient.

At Kreskie's, the department store in Kirkland Lake, Sue bought a yellow and green budgie. He was named "Fellow." When the children were at school Sue let the bird out of the cage and put a treat on her shoulder. The bird would sit on Sue's shoulder and eat the treat. Eventually Fellow would sit on her shoulder without a treat. She would go about her household chores with Fellow on her shoulder.

One morning after Sue let Fellow out of his cage, she prepared red Jello and put it in the fridge to set. Later that morning she noticed that Fellow was missing and searched the house. Sue thought he must have escaped outside somehow. A few hours later Sue was preparing supper and opened the fridge. There was Fellow, headfirst in the red Jello with his rear end sticking up. He must have flown into the fridge as she turned to shut the fridge door. Although she felt bad, she could not help but laugh. Little Fellow became the Jello Fellow.

The Ross family lived down the street. Mrs. Ross was in her late fifties and Mr. Ross was in his early seventies. They had married later in life and had one daughter and then a set of twins. Shirley and Sheila were twins in their early twenties. Shirley was developmentally challenged. She was difficult to understand but did her best to pronounce words. Those who knew her understood what she was saying. Like Sue, she only had the use of one arm and hand. Shirley was excited that Sue had an arm and hand like hers.

Mrs. Ross had difficulty getting Shirley to do much. Sue offered to teach Shirley how to dress herself and do housework. Usually, Shirley enjoyed her time with Sue but occasionally Shirley would get frustrated and scream at Sue.

Sue would stop what she was doing, look at Shirley and calmly say, "Shirley, it's ok. It takes time to learn things. It took me time also. You don't have to scream and yell. We are two grown ladies, and we can talk to each other." With that said, Shirley calmed down.

Eventually Shirley would catch herself before she screamed and instead firmly said, "Wue . . . no . . . no!" This was a cue that it was break time. ("Wue" was how Shirley pronounced "Sue.")

The Wixson children enjoyed playing at the Rosses' and spending time with Shirley. On one occasion, three-year-old Mark wandered onto the road. Shirley saw him and yelled, "No!" She ran and grabbed him just before a car hit him. Then she put him down and angrily yelled at him, "NO! NO!" pointing at him and then the road several times. The memory of her grabbing him and yelling remained with Mark the rest of his life. Shirley saved his life. She probably would have spanked him, except Sue came outside then.

The Gallivan family were also neighbours. Sharon's first boyfriend was Hal Gallivan. Hal was 9 years old, and she was 7 years old. She was smitten with this short young boy, and he was smitten with her. They would go for walks together and hold hands. Her sisters and brothers would tease her, singing the song, "Sharon and Hal sitting in a tree, k-i-s-s-i-n-g . . ." Sharon would chase after them, but she never did catch them. He was the first boy she kissed. They were walking home from school, hand in hand, and talking about their day. Suddenly he stopped and held her hands and kissed her. *Wow*, she thought. Her head was whirling, and her knees got weak. Her heartbeat faster and she thought it was wonderful and at the same time she felt sick.

He asked her, "Was that ok that I kissed you?"

She could barely speak but managed to whisper, "Yes. I liked it."

Hal beamed and replied, "So did I."

They were best friends for the six months that their puppy love lasted. It ended when his father was transferred to another base in Southern Ontario.

Sue used to visit Mrs. Gallivan and fell in love with the house. In the summer of 1964, when Mr. Gallivan received a transfer, and their house went up for sale. Jack and Sue purchased the house for $4000.00. For two years Sue had been praying that the three-bedroom house on the hill would be theirs one day. When they moved in, the first thing Sue did was hang her precious family pictures on the living room wall. "There!" she exclaimed. "Now it is our house, our home." As she marked the wall with nails to hang the pictures, she also marked a new phase in their lives.

In the spring of 1965, Bill and Grace moved to Holtyre. Bill was hired at the local Ross Mine. The mine in Kirkland Lake was struggling so he moved on as he always did.

When they left Kirkland Lake, Grace searched inside and outside for her tabby tom cat, who she called Tom. She had Tom for seven years and he had been in many cat fights, leaving him with half his left ear torn off, a bald spot and scar on his cheek, and half of his tail missing. He was an ugly cat to say the least, but she loved him. Bill didn't care much for Tom so when it was time to leave Kirkland Lake and head to Holtyre, Bill told her, "Forget the cat. We are leaving. The bugger will fend for itself."

One year later, when Grace was hanging clothes on the clothesline, a cat came up the stairs and rubbed himself against her ankle, purring. She almost jumped out of her skin and, when she looked down, there was no mistaking it: it was her old buddy, Tom. How he got to Bill and Grace's house in Holtyre was a mystery. Holtyre was forty miles (approximately 65 kilometers) of forest from Kirkland Lake. Tom spent the rest of his days with Grace. He died three years later from severe injuries after he tangled with another tomcat, younger and stronger than him.

While Grace was living in Holtyre, she had what she called 'spells.' She would feel weak, pass out and come around about forty-five-to-sixty minutes later. Sharon was still in public school and Grace and

Bill's duplex was right behind the school. When Sue could not reach Grace by telephone, she would call the school and the principal would send Sharon over to her grandmother's. Sharon would find Grace passed out on the couch. Sharon would get a cold wet cloth to wipe her grandmother's sweaty brow and sit with her until she regained consciousness. Later, Grace told Sue that she had been having these spells for years. Sue begged her mother to see a doctor, but Grace would always say, "Girly, when me's time is up, 'tis up. I's got no time ta be seein' no doctor."

Grace enjoyed her grandchildren and teased them when the opportunity was presented. Sharon was visiting Grace when Sharon went into a bout of coughing. Grace waited a bit, the coughing subsided, then she said, "Child, ifin you's feel a hair in your throat, don't cough it up; it might be your arse."

That poor kid thought everything her grandmother said was the truth, so she tried to hold back whenever she felt a cough coming on and would choke and almost pass out. Sue thought her daughter's behaviour was strange. "What on earth are you doing? Just cough if you need to. It helps clear your lungs," stated Sue.

Once Sue discovered the reason her daughter was choking and gagging instead of coughing, she smiled and explained that Grandma was only joking.

Grace was full of jokes like this. She used to tell her grandchildren that she went to the round church, so the devil could not corner her.

CHAPTER 65

Upside Down and Inside Out

In the spring of 1967, Jack's rank was Warrant Officer, and he was up for a promotion. Before he received his promotion, he had to have a physical and attend maneuvers at the Military Training Base in Exeter. After only a few days he returned home. He walked into the kitchen and sat at the kitchen table. He was as white as a ghost and looked like he had not slept in days.

Sue was shocked. "Jack, what are you doing home so early? I thought you were supposed to be gone for two weeks."

Jack sadly looked up at Sue, murmuring, "Sue, we have to talk!"

Jack explained that part of the medical and physical was running on a treadmill. He could walk on the treadmill but when they sped it up to a running mode, he was not able to run. They stopped the treadmill and asked him to run across the room. Again, his legs would not cooperate. The military doctor booked him into Sunnybrook Military Hospital in Toronto. In three days, he would be admitted to hospital for tests.

Jack started thinking about the times he sat for over an hour and his legs would feel tingly. The tingling stopped once he walked around. He also remembered having headaches and was feeling fatigued, but he concluded it was stress related to his job. Jack's workload had doubled since he had taken on another sergeant's job.

Jack drove himself down to Toronto and admitted himself into Sunnybrook hospital, where the medical team performed extensive medical examinations. Jack described his experience as "having every medical test known to man!" It was exhausting. At the end of the week, Jack was given his diagnosis and prognosis. He was devastated and knew Sue would be also. On his drive home he cried, screamed, and prayed. Jack barely remembered the drive but when he arrived home, he had gained some composure.

When he walked into the house, he hugged Sue tightly. He hugged the children, which was unusual for Jack. His children knew he loved them, but he was not one to show them physical affection.

Sue knew not to question him in front of the children. His demeanor was solemn, and he was quiet during supper time. The children chattered about what they had been up to while he was gone. Like a robot, Jack smiled, nodded, or said, "Oh, really." Sue could tell that he was not paying attention.

Once the children were in bed, Sue made Jack and herself a gin and tonic and they went to the living room. They kept their voices hushed so the children could not hear them.

Sue sat beside her forlorn-looking husband and waited. At first, all he could say was "Oh, Sue . . . Oh, Sue," as he shook his head, eyes closed, head down and tears running down his cheeks.

He opened his eyes and looked at his wife who was crying. "Sue, I have multiple sclerosis. The doctors told me to go home, get in bed, and I will be dead within six months."

Sue gasped. She felt like her breath was taken from her and the blood had drained out of her body. For fear of fainting, she leaned her head back on the couch and closed her eyes. The cold and dreary silence hung in the air as though death had entered the room. Jack inched closer to Sue and put his arms around her. As tears poured forth from them no words were spoken. This news was too much for either one of them to endure. Their whole world was being turned upside down and inside out.

When their sobbing ceased, Jack got up, got a box of facial tissues and handed it to Sue. They wiped their tears, blew their noses and sat in silence, trying to regain their composure.

Sue finally managed to whisper, "What is multiple sclerosis?"

Jack explained what he knew about M.S. He had been given information pamphlets by the nurse. All he really understood at the time was that it affected the nervous system, it was a rare disease, and he was going to die.

Jack sat up straight and in a determined voice said, "I told the doctors I will be damned if I am going to go home and get in bed. I have a wife and five kids, and I will do everything that I need to do to fight this bastard disease!"

Sue was glad to hear the determination in his voice even though she could see the trepidation in his eyes. The rest of that evening they discussed what their future would look like if Jack lived and what had to be done if he were to die. The flow of tears resumed in spurts from time to time.

That night when they lay in bed in each other's arms, Jack and Sue cried more. They did not know that Sharon and Janice were still awake and overheard their sobs. Sharon crawled into Janice's bed, and they held each other and silently cried themselves to sleep. The two girls did not know what was going on, but they knew it had to be dreadful because they had never seen nor heard their father cry.

The next morning, Jack slept in and, while he was still sleeping, Sue gathered the five children together and told them that their dad was extremely sick and they would have to be quiet and well behaved from then on. The children had a lot of questions that Sue could not answer.

The children were scared and worried that they would lose their dad. Some of the children thought the family would have to be split and they would be sent to an orphanage. It was a gloomy and daunting time for the Wixson family. The uncertainty was unnerving.

Over the next few months, Jack put his affairs in order. He received a medical discharge from the Armed Forces as soon as the medical report went to headquarters. He petitioned the Armed Forces to extend his service for one year so he could receive his full pension. Jack's request was denied. Jack applied for a job at the Canex, the general store on the base, and was hired as a civilian. Being a civilian was new to him and he struggled with the different treatment he received from the enlisted personnel. Going from being in control and in command to receiving orders often frustrated him. All Jack knew was military life. He missed the comradery, special events and his job. Within six months, he realized he was physically incapable of doing his previous job; regardless, he still mourned the life he once knew.

Those years were financially difficult since Jack's pension was two thirds of his wages. Stretching the money was no easy task. The children had what they needed but nothing extra.

The local corner store allowed people to put purchases on credit. Jack and Sue used this service. When pay day came around Jack ensured it was paid off. The owners of the store constantly told Jack and Sue that they wished other customers were as punctual with their payments as they were. When the owners found out that Jack was ill, they asked that his small line of credit be paid right away, and they no longer granted him credit. They made this request in front of several other customers. Jack was so angry that he threw the money on the counter and told them he would never shop there again. Two customers followed Jack out and apologized for the owners. They decided they would no longer shop there either.

Jack retained his driver's license and he and Sue took trips to Matheson, a town twenty minutes away, to do their shopping. Jack went into the drug store and then across the street to the hardware store. Sue picked up the few items she needed at the grocery store and then they headed home. On one of these trips Jack was pulled over by a police officer one mile out of Matheson. The officer said he saw Jack in town, and it appeared he had too much to drink. Although Jack explained that his unsteady gait was part of his disease, multiple sclerosis, the officer wasn't convinced. The officer became indignant and said that he had heard that kind of bullshit before. Then he ordered Jack out of the car and told him to walk the white line. Again, Jack tried to explain he could not walk straight. The officer then called for backup. The first officer told the backup officers that Jack was intoxicated and noncompliant.

Frustrated, Jack loudly said, "What part of 'I have a disease which causes my legs to be unsteady' do you not understand?"

The officers insisted Jack re-walk the white line and do a few other balance tests. Of course, he failed these miserably. At one point, the officer had to stop him from falling over. Jack's M.S. symptoms were exaggerated when he was upset, so the whole situation was a fiasco. They were still convinced he was drunk so they put him in handcuffs and in the police car. Sue did not have her driver's license, so she was permitted to ride in the back of the second cruiser. She was crying and shaking as she always did during confrontations.

Jack was charged with driving under the influence. Six weeks later Jack appeared before the judge. He provided his medical papers and explained his side of the story. The judge was livid and expressed regret to Jack and Sue for the ignorant and unprofessional treatment they endured. The officers were ordered to apologize. The officers were brought up on disciplinary charges and were transferred to another district. That would not be the only time that strangers would presume that Jack was drunk.

Adjusting to her husband's disabilities was challenging for Sue. She tried to protect him and do things for him. Jack found Sue's actions frustrating and humiliating. She was the last person he expected that kind of treatment from since she seldom accepted help from anybody. Even when she was sick, she would not rest, but kept on going until she ended up in bed for a few days. Jack grew frustrated with Sue and the children constantly telling him, "I'll do that for you" or "You can't do that."

One day, ladder in hand, Jack stumbled to the front porch and, after a few attempts, placed the ladder against the wall.

Sue said, "Jack, I'll get up on the ladder and change the light bulb on the front porch. You can't climb the ladder."

Jack lost his cool. "Sue, for Christ sakes, if I can't change a damn light bulb then what use am I. Just leave me the hell alone!"

On the fourth rung he lost his balance and fell on the porch. Sue wanted to rush to him but knew this would probably infuriate him. She stood watching. Jack sat there for a while and then attempted to get up by holding onto the bottom of the ladder. The ladder fell over.

Finally, after several attempts, with nothing available for him to hoist himself up on, he looked at Sue and said, "For Christ's sakes woman, don't just stand there. Help me up."

Sue was furious with him. Not only was he foolish to attempt to climb the ladder but he was taking out his anger about his failure on her. Everything inside of her wanted to tell him off, but instead, she quietly helped him to his feet. He staggered into the house and sat in the living room chair, brooding. "One more thing I will never be able to do again," he mumbled to himself. Neither Sue nor Jack discussed the matter. It was the last time he attempted to climb a ladder.

Near the end of the second year after his diagnosis, Jack was no longer physically able to work at the Canex. He could barely walk because his legs were weak and ached constantly. His headaches were frequent, his hands trembled, and his head shook involuntarily. Eating and drinking was a challenge. Half his food ended up back on the plate or in his lap, and half his drink ended up down the front of him. Jack had fought against the idea of using a wheelchair, but the time came when his legs would not hold him up.

Jack fell into a deep depression. He spent his days either staring out the kitchen window, which overlooked the creek and the town, or sleeping. When Sue would talk to him, he would grunt. Providing her husband with suggestions became futile; he seldom responded.

CHAPTER 66

Awakening

Sitting in his wheelchair, staring out the kitchen window, Jack cried out to God, "I have had it, Lord! I don't see a future. All I can see is what I used to be. I need you to do something in my life. I need to hear from you, or I can't go on! Reach out to me or let me die."

Within a few moments Jack felt a presence with him. His life flashed before him and his past actions became clear. He started to weep and said, "Lord, forgive me. I have been selfish. Up to now I have had a good life. I have Sue and my children. I've had a good career in the service. Give me purpose. You have kept me alive for a reason. I can't stand just sitting here and waiting to die. Show me what you want from me."

Jack had a mental and emotional breakthrough. While he had no idea what his purpose would be, he knew he was left on this earth for a reason.

When Sue came home, Jack was still sitting in his wheelchair in front of the window with tears running down his face. This was not an unusual sight. Sue had seen Jack in this miserable state many times over the past year.

Looking at Sue, Jack declared, "I am ok. I am so sorry for what I have put you through the last few years. Can you ever forgive me?"

Sue was stunned because she never expected Jack to say those words even though she prayed that God would reach out and help her husband.

Jack told Sue about his spiritual experience. "I am done with my pity party, and I am going to do what I can in life. I will need your help Sue, and for you to remind me about this day when I start feeling low."

Jack and Sue started attending the Pentecostal church in Matheson. There he found people who encouraged him, accepted him and assisted him when required. He joined the men's church group and also an international men's spiritual group. Feelings of uselessness and depression were lifting from him. There were days where he wondered if his experience was real. Then Sue reminded him of the day that he felt God had delivered a message to him.

Within the month, Jack called a social worker to assist him with planning his future. She recommended that Jack get involved with the March of Dimes in Timmins. To be involved in the program, he would have to relocate to Timmins, an hour away, but they were not ready to leave their home in Holtyre. To keep Jack's hand functioning and give him a sense of achievement, he learned how to knit and rug hook. His time was spent making afghan blanket and rugs and attending spiritual programs.

The girls were teenagers, and they began to bring their boyfriends home. Jack loved teasing them and the girls. He asked Janice's boyfriend to set the ladder up at the kitchen window. Later Jack told him, "There's the ladder, so if you want to marry Janice you have to elope, so I don't have to pay for the wedding." Jack thought it hilarious when Johnny blushed, and Janice gave him heck for embarrassing her. Each boyfriend who entered the house was subject to Jack's playful harassment. Sue felt his humorous antics went too far at times, but she was relieved that his sense of humour had returned.

While the girls were dating, the youngest brother, Mark, made a fortune off the boyfriends. He would hang around one of the couples and drive them crazy asking questions, bugging them and just being a pain in the neck. When the couple had enough and told Mark to leave, with a smirk on his face, he said, "If you pay me five bucks, I will leave you alone!"

The young men always obliged so they could have time alone with their girlfriends. When the girls complained to Sue, her response was, "Just don't pay him."

The response from Jack was, "That's my boy!"

The ten-year-old blackmailer continued collecting from the boyfriends throughout the girls' dating years. His entrepreneurial spirit stayed with him most of his life.

Mark was eleven years old when he came home with a huge bucket full of chokecherries and told Sue that he was going to make chokecherry wine. Thinking he was incapable of making wine, she gave him permission. Little did Sue know that Mark had gotten the recipe from a friend's dad.

Mark whipped up a large batch and put it in a plastic pail with a cover. When the fruit was fermented seven days later, he strained it and poured it into one-gallon glass jugs which he stored in the basement. Two months later Sue noticed the jugs full of what she suspected was the wine Mark had made. When she opened one of the bottles, the alcoholic fumes made her eyes water. Sue called Mark down to the basement and ordered him to pour out all the chokecherry wine.

Mark argued at first, saying, "I want to sell it. I could make good money from homemade chokecherry wine."

"Oh no, you aren't going to sell it. That is illegal. Pour it out now!" demanded Sue, pointing to the drain in the cement floor. Sue went upstairs, convinced she had gotten her point across.

Sharon was in the kitchen when she heard Mark singing from the basement in a slow muffled drawl. When she went to investigate, Mark was sitting on the floor, the drain between his outstretched legs. He had a gallon of the wine over his shoulder and was drinking it while he poured a gallon of wine down the drain slowly.

Mark was happily singing, "*One drink to go down the drain, one drink for me, one drink to go down the drain one drink for me,*" to the tune of "Ninety-Nine Bottles of Beer on the Wall."

It was obvious he was drunk. He had consumed at least half a gallon of the wine. Sharon hauled Mark to his feet and accompanied the staggering eleven-year-old out of the basement and into her boyfriend's car. She explained the situation to Denis who drove Mark uptown to a friend's house. Mark was not to come home until he was sober. Sharon, in the meantime, poured the rest of the wine down the drain.

When Sharon went upstairs into the kitchen, Sue asked, "Did Mark pour that wine out? The little bugger really made chokecherry wine. I am not sure if it tasted any good."

"Yes, it is gone, Mom, and Denis drove him uptown to his friend's house," Sharon responded.

Mark did not gain any capital from his venture, but he did have a major hangover and went straight to bed when he got home. Sue only heard about Mark's drunken state years later.

When Ross was thirteen years old, he became interested in outdoor activities like fishing, hunting and trapping. He and his friend Danny had become young bushwhackers. They built themselves a rough log cabin, installed a small old wood stove in it and insulated it for the winter. The furniture was constructed from scrap wood they had gathered. In the spring, summer and fall they could walk to their cabin which was about one mile into the woods from a farm. In the winter they rode into their camp on Danny's snowmobile. Ross spent most of his spare time there with his buddy.

Sue was used to Ross coming and going from the cabin and was glad her teenage boy kept busy. It was not unusual for him to be late for supper. No one minded as long as he didn't complain about the small amount left or that the food was cold. Ross did forget about this rule. One night he came home an hour late for supper and sat down at the kitchen table, where his plate setting was still laid out for him. There was plenty of spaghetti mixed with sauce in the pot. Sue served him and he took one bite and said, "It's cold!"

Big mistake on his part because all hell broke loose. Sue glared at Ross. "Did I just hear you complain?"

Ross knew he was about to get a good hard slap, so he jumped up from the table and backed up against the wall. Sue quickly ran up to Ross, grabbed him by the front of his shirt, lifted him off the ground against the wall and started screaming. This was quite the feat since Ross was about eight inches taller than Sue. When she released him, he dropped and landed on his rear end. Mark had witnessed the confrontation and was terrified. He ran out the door and down the hill towards the town. Sharon and her fiancé, Denis, were driving down the road.

Mark waved them down and, with terror in his voice, he shouted, "Mom's gonna kill Ross!" Denis and Sharon drove quickly up the hill and into the driveway and ran in the house. By the time Sharon and Denis arrived in the kitchen Ross was sitting on the floor with spaghetti and sauce dripping down over his head and clothing. Sue was standing there with an empty pot and they both were laughing so hard that they had tears in their eyes.

In the summer of 1972, Sue's mother, Grace, was diagnosed with diabetes. The spells she had been having all those years were low blood sugars. Her diagnosis came too late and her kidneys were failing. She died one month later in the Matheson Hospital. A distraught Sue had lost her precious Maw. Filled with gratitude for all the things her mother had taught her and how she never gave up on Sue, Sue found the strength to be involved in the funeral arrangements. Grace was buried in Kirkland Lake cemetery. As the family stood around the casket in the graveyard on a rainy and dreary day, a chipmunk darted between Sue and Ruby. It jumped onto Grace's casket and left a piece of bread on it. All the mourners were in shock. It reminded them of Grace's habit of feeding the chipmunks at her cottage. It was not unusual for four or five chipmunks to wait for her in the morning near her chair outside. Often, they would even jump into her lap. It was as if the chipmunk was honouring Grace for all her kindness to the animals.

In 1973, the year following Grace's death, Bill retired and moved back to Nova Scotia. He was eventually reunited with his six children who he had with his first wife.

CHAPTER 67

The Spinner

Sue knew the day was coming when Jack would be unable to drive, and she wanted to be prepared. She also knew that Janice would soon be leaving home and unable to drive her around. After studying the driver's handbook, she took the test and passed.

As most spouses know, it is not always a pleasant experience having your partner as a driving instructor. Jack was nervous so he would say things like, "Go ahead, back up."

One time, Sue went ahead before Jack said to back up and ran into a pole. Sue was so angry and told him he had to give her one instruction at a time. After a few months of nerve-racking driving lessons with Jack, she booked her driver's road test.

The day of the road test Sue was so nervous she prayed and sang a hymn to calm herself. After the test the family could tell by her expression that she did not do well. They did not ask any questions. Sue went straight to the bedroom and cried. When Sue came out, she told the family members that she did not pass, but she was not giving up. The next day she returned to the Department of Transportation office and asked the instructor what she needed to do to improve and get her license.

He was exceedingly kind and told her, "Mrs. Wixson, you did very well except for your turns. If you had a spinner knob on the steering wheel you probably would have passed your test, but spinners are illegal. Here is an idea. If you can get a judge to write a letter of permission to install and use one, then you should come back and redo your road test."

Sue was on it like a dog with a bone. She always said, "Where there's a will, there's a way."

Sue made an appointment with a judge in Timmins.

"Mrs. Wixson, how can I help you?" asked the Judge.

"Your Honour, I need a letter of permission from you to get a spinner for my steering wheel in my car. I have as you can see . . ." Sue picked up her right arm with her left hand to show the Judge. "I have limited use of my right arm. My husband has MS and sooner or later he will not be able to drive. I need my license. Without a spinner knob I struggle to make turns with the car."

The judge interrupted her, "Hold on, Mrs. Wixson. Your husband has MS, and you have?"

"I had polio as a child," Sue explained, swallowing her pride. Sue hated to tell the story of her polio and draw attention to her disability, but this was no time to hide details. She confidently continued, "Your Honour, I have raised five children, I help my husband and there is very little I can't do. My motto is 'a disability is only an ability to do things in a different way.' I need this spinner so I can drive."

The judge had a smirk on his face. This little woman, who looked more like a teenager, was a feisty one. He was intrigued that she was not using her disability as an excuse but instead she was stating her need while demonstrating her strong mental ability.

"Granted, I will indeed write a permission letter for you, Mrs. Wixson. You have presented your case in a dignified and respectful manner. All the best to you in getting your driver's license," the Judge declared.

Finding a spinner knob took some time but Randy, Glenda's fiancés. was able to locate one. Sue practiced driving with the spinner. At first it was awkward. It took several tries for her to get used to holding on to and maneuvering the spinner. Her hand kept slipping on the hard shiny plastic knob. She found a solution. She made a leather spinner covering from scraps of an old purse. It worked like a charm, and it was not long before she had mastered it. When she went for her road test the instructor remembered her. She presented the letter of permission to use a spinner in her car.

"Mrs. Wixson, you sure are a go-getter. Ok, let's get on with your road test. I have a feeling you will do very well." The instructor winked at her. Sue passed her road test with flying colours.

CHAPTER 68

Etched in Memory

1975 was a busy year for the Wixson family. Glenda and Randy got married in May and Sharon and Denis got married in November.

When December came along, Sue was glad the major events were over and she could concentrate on preparing for Christmas. While making her delicious melt-in-your-mouth shortbread cookies, she was thinking about how two of her daughters had left home within the year and what a change it had made in the house. The house was much quieter now, which would take getting used to. The two boys and Janice were still home, and in April she would have a grandchild. Sue expected life to change but she did not expect it to happen in such a short span of time.

Sue and Jack were both looking forward to having the whole family home for Christmas. In the Wixson home, family holiday traditions consisted of giving joke presents, playing board games, and feasting on a turkey supper with all the fixings.

Since their children were growing up, Sue and Jack would relish every Christmas they spent together. They had no idea that this would be the last Christmas they would ever spend with all the family members together.

Christmas always began with one family member reading the story of baby Jesus's birth from the Bible and one person putting the baby in the manager. Ross had not participated in this tradition since he was a boy.

That year Ross surprised everyone when he piped up and said, "I will read the story this year."

"Just wait a minute," said Sue, smiling like a Cheshire cat as she retrieved a gift from under the tree. "Then you'll need this." She handed the gift to Ross.

Ross tore open the neatly wrapped gift. The package contained a new shiny black leather, Bible. Ross grinned at Sue as though they had a deep secret that only they were privy to. Flipping through the Bible, he found Luke, Chapter 2. What he said was not the written version. He gave the family a fifteen-year old's interpretation of the birth of Christ.

His rendition went something like this: "In those days, the big wig issued a decree that everybody should be counted in the kingdom. Everyone was to be tagged. Joseph, who was from the town of Nazareth in Galilee and a relative of David, took his pregnant fiancée, Mary, to Bethlehem. There they registered as citizens. While they were there Mary went into labour. The hotels were full, so they ended up in a barn. She gave birth to a baby boy. She wrapped him in swaddling jeans and laid that little dude in the hay, man, in the cows' feeding trough. There were all these cool dudes watching their sheep that night. An angel of the Lord came to them, and the sky lit up like the Northern Lights. The dudes were scared and almost peed their pants but, you see, this angel said, 'Be cool. I have great news. Today in the town of David a Savior is born. He is leader and Lord.'"

The family giggled on and off during his rendition and clapped when he was finished.

Three years prior, Sue had bought each one of her children a Bible. At the time Ross did not want one so Sue respected his wishes. At the beginning of December Ross came to Sue with a request. "Mom, I think I want a Bible this year for Christmas. Don't ask me why. I just do." Sue did not ask but happily made the purchase.

After the nativity story, the rest of the presents were opened, including two joke presents. Mark had made Ross a shaving kit since peach fuzz had begun to grow on Ross' chin and upper lip. Ross opened the case marked "Shaving Kit" in big black letters. Inside was a block of wood wrapped in fine sandpaper, a replacement strip of sandpaper, and a pair of tweezers. The whole family thought it was hilarious. To add to the fun Ross chased Mark around the kitchen, yelling, "I'll get you for that!"

Ross gave Jack twelve presents. He said that it represented the twelve days of Christmas. Each gift was wrapped separately. Jack tried guessing what they were, but he was way off base. The thought of having twelve presents under the tree thrilled him. When Jack opened the first one, he started to laugh. Ross had bought a small case of Pepsi and wrapped each can individually.

It was a wonderful Christmas for all, one that would be etched in their memories.

CHAPTER 69

Too Much

On the evening of March 16th, 1976, Sharon and Denis were visiting Sue, Jack, Ross, and Mark. Jack and Ross both had a virus. They were running fevers and vomiting. Ross was groaning as if he was dying. He seldom got sick but when he did, he acted like a big baby. Sue was tired of listening to him, so she asked Sharon to check on him.

Sharon went into the boys' bedroom and saw a very pale Ross. "Hey there. You don't look too good," she declared.

Ross looked up at Sharon with bloodshot eyes and weakly said, "I feel really sick, Sharon. My head feels like someone hit it with a hammer."

"Ok, I'll let Mom know. Do you want some aspirin?"

"Yes, with ginger ale, please. Don't tell Mom what I just said. She'll only get mad. You know how she hates complaining," moaned Ross.

Sharon felt sorry for her poor brother. He really did look sickly. "Well, Ross, you know how you are when you're sick. You act like you're dying, but I do believe you are sick. I will speak to Mom anyways."

After giving Ross the aspirin and ginger ale, she spoke to Sue. Sue did not appreciate Sharon expressing her observations of her sick son. She firmly told Sharon, "I have two sick men in the house right now. Your dad is the priority, and I may have to take him into the hospital and I will bring Ross in at the same time."

Sharon's husband Denis drove them to Matheson. By the time Jack and Ross attended their doctor's appointment, they were dry heaving.

Both were admitted and put on intravenous Gravol and saline. It worked for Jack and he stopped vomiting within fifteen minutes. Ross, on the other hand, slipped into a coma within five minutes. Within an hour he was rushed to a larger hospital, St. Mary's in Timmins. As soon as he arrived, he was put on life support.

Denis and Sue followed the ambulance to Timmins. Jack was informed that his son had been rushed to the Timmins hospital because of a bad reaction to medication. That evening Denis stayed with Sue in Timmins. Sharon was given the job of informing her sisters and Mark.

The next morning Sharon received a call from Jack. He was crying. "Come get me out of the hospital, now . . . I need to see my son!"

Sharon was not sure what had changed but she knew her father needed her. Before Sharon went in to see her father, she decided she had better talk to the doctor to find out what was going on.

As soon as Sharon walked into the office the secretary recognized her as Jack Wixson's daughter and ushered Sharon to the examination room immediately. Dr. Smith entered the room moments later and closed the door. He looked frazzled and exhausted. He moved his chair beside Sharon and took her hands in his and quietly said, "Sharon, you know that your brother is probably going to die."

Sharon did not hear anything he said after that. "What . . . he's dying. What?" Her head was spinning. She knew Ross was sick, but dying . . . How could that be? She felt faint but knew she had to deal with her father, so she took deep breaths, and the doctor got her a glass of water. Once she was able to compose herself, he explained that Ross was in a deep coma and his brain may have been affected. Timmins hospital would run more tests on him later in the day. Dr. Smith felt horrible and kept apologizing for giving him the Gravol which might have caused Ross' condition. He was blaming himself.

After Sharon reassured the doctor that he did what he thought was best for Ross, she went to see the chaplain, who knew her father. The chaplain volunteered to drive Jack to the hospital in Timmins.

Sharon knew Sue would be pissed at her for arranging Jack's travel to the hospital. Sue said she did not want Jack there because she had enough to deal with without Jack falling apart. Even though her mother protested, and a long guilt-inducing lecture would be the consequence, Sharon felt Jack had a right to see his son before he died.

The test results revealed that Ross did not have any brain activity and the life support machinery was keeping him alive. The sisters and Mark were devastated. They had arranged for a ride to Timmins. Sharon was left behind because her husband and mother felt her pregnancy was too far along to deal with the trauma of seeing her brother in his dying state. The people driving her siblings had been contacted by her husband and told not to drive Sharon to Timmins, no matter how much she begged. Sharon was furious and deeply wounded that she did not have a chance to say goodbye to Ross. That wound would cause her pain for many years.

The next day the siblings gathered at Sue and Jack's place and waited for their parents and Denis to come home. Mark went into his and Ross' bedroom and packed Ross' belongings in a big paper grocery bag. Then he unpacked it. He repeated this ritual for over an hour. He was working out his anguish in his own way.

Ross had brought a six-month-old jet-black puppy home a few years after Tinker died. He called him Blackie. He was a medium size dog. Blackie sensed the tense and desolate atmosphere that surrounded the family and he lay at the back door with his head on the floor. He only looked up when a person passed by him. His joyful big brown eyes were now filled with sadness. When Sue, Jack and Denis came home, the dog moved out of the way for them, then resumed his post laying in front of the door.

The family all sat at the kitchen table and Sue, through tears, gulping and shaking, told them that she signed the papers for the doctor to turn off Ross's life support. There was no hope he would ever recover because he was brain-dead. The hospital would call when they turned the machines off. Five minutes before the hospital called, Blackie sat up and howled for about one minute, then he left the room and went to lie beside Ross's bed. Everyone at the table just stared at the dog. The eerie silence was broken by the ringing of the phone. It was the doctor from Timmins. He told Sue that they had taken Ross off the life support five minutes prior, and he died immediately. The family already knew because of the dog's reaction.

Sue reflected on the time in France when she asked the Lord to give her children and she would give one back to him. In Sue's mind the Lord was keeping her to her promise made twenty years prior. Because Sharon had been a sickly child, Sue was prepared to lose her one day but not her son.

Depression fell over the house like a heavy cloak. Jack and Sue only spoke to each other when necessary. Mark went about his daily life in silence. Janice spent as little time at home as possible. All were trying to grasp the reality of their loss.

Sue not only struggled with the loss of her eldest son but also with guilt for signing the papers that ended her son's life. Even though Sue put on a brave front during the situation, she did not have it in her to be strong for anyone. Because her eyes were blurred with tears and her hand shook, the nurse had to guide her hand to the signature line. Every time she thought about signing that paper, she felt faint and sick to her stomach.

The birth of their first grandchild one month later did not soothe the deep wounds. Sue did her best to show joy on the occasion, but Sharon saw through her attempts.

The autopsy report revealed that Ross had died from the rare Reye's syndrome, which has been linked to children and teenagers taking aspirin when they have influenza. The syndrome can cause swelling of the liver and brain. This information was unknown to most families in that day. Aspirin (acetylsalicylic acid) was a common treatment for pain and fever at any age. According to the report, the Gravol (dimenhydrinate) given to him for nausea, may have sped up the progression of Ross's condition.

It took years for the family to come to grips with their grief and, as they did, the unshed tears, sorrows and memories were shared amongst them.

Ross Wixson November 1960 - March 1976

CHAPTER 70

Timmins

Janice was enrolled in the nursing course at Northern College in Kirkland Lake, one hour away from home. Part of the course involved several hours of clinical experience in the hospital. All the nursing students were assigned one or two patients while they were on their shift. They worked under the authority of a registered nurse. Janice was asked to feed an older man green Jell-O. They told her he seldom opened his eyes and to go ahead and feed him the Jell-O anyways. Janice went into the room and introduced herself to the senior patient. The nurses were right: he was not a talker. His eyes were closed, and his mouth partly opened. She explained what she was there for as she put an adult bib on him. He was not eating very fast so after thirty minutes Janice told him that she would give him a break for a while and she left to assist another patient. In the meantime, one nurse went to check on Janice to see how she was doing with the older gentleman. The nurse discovered the man was dead. Janice had been feeding green Jell-O to a dead man. When the autopsy report came back, it said that there was a green residue in his throat. Janice was horrified to say the least, and relieved that the green Jell-O was not the cause of his death.

Meanwhile, Jack was getting bored and needed something more to occupy his time, so he and Sue visited the March of Dimes in Timmins.

On their way home, Jack said, "Sue, what do you think about the place?"

Sue looked over at him. "Jack, it isn't what I think that matters. It is what you thought of the place that counts."

"Well, it appears to be a place to learn new skills. It has a good atmosphere. I was impressed with the counsellors and their knowledge. Sue, I . . . I just have a good feeling about it," Jack confirmed. "You know that will mean leaving Holtyre?"

"Yes, I know." She turned her head to look out the window and hide the sad expression on her face. Then, with a weak smile, she turned to Jack again. "That's ok, Jack. This is important for our future so we will do what we have to do."

It was not an easy decision to move but she knew it was the best thing for Jack. Eventually Jack would need more medical attention and living in Timmins would provide easier access to this.

With the help of church friends, Sue was able to find an apartment that fit Jack's needs. It had a bedroom and bathroom on the main floor and was wheelchair accessible.

On the day of the move when everyone else had left the house and Jack was in the car waiting for her, Sue walked around the house and stopped in each room. This home held such special memories. A few tears ran down her cheeks when she stood in Ross and Mark's bedroom. "Life does not stand still. Time to move on, but you gave me special memories in this home. Thank you, Lord, for the time you granted me here," Sue sadly whispered.

At March of Dimes, one of the counsellors suggested that Jack train on the rock tumbling machine. However, Jack wanted his training to lead to a job, and rock tumbling, in his opinion, did not provide that. Besides, he had a feeling he would grow bored of it and, indeed, it did not take long before he found it mundane.

At the supper table, Jack told Sue he had grown tired of rock tumbling.

"Well, Jack, tell them you want to try something else," Sue insisted.

"You know, Sue, they try so hard to help me out that I don't want to upset them or disappoint them."

Sue gave Jack one of those "Oh, stop it" looks. "Jack, for Pete's sakes, it is their job to help you find something you enjoy and can do. Do you know what you want to try next?"

Jack explained that he had watched a few of the other clients using the engraving machine and he developed a keen interest in engraving. The workers told him he would never be capable of running the manual engraving machine because his hands were too shaky.

"What do you think, Sue. Do you think I can do engraving?"

"You're asking me . . . You know I don't take no for an answer. I always figure out how to do something when I really want it. Jack, you can do anything you set your mind to. Give it a try and see if you enjoy doing it."

The next day, Jack convinced one of the counselors to give him an opportunity to work the engraving machine. Using one hand to sturdy the other hand, he was able to work the machine. To all the workers' surprise, Jack excelled on the engraving machine. He had found something that kept his interest and provided an opportunity to expand his knowledge. Within two years of being trained on the engraving machine, Jack started his own engraving business, J & S Engraving, in a shop set up in the backyard. From his training in the Air Force, Jack had good business and financial sense; his business thrived.

Because of Jack's weak immune system, it was common for him to catch colds and viruses which landed him in the hospital a few times a year. When he got ill, it took a lot out of him and he had difficulty transferring himself from the wheelchair to the bed, living room sofa, or the toilet. Those times Sue would help him.

If he fell, Sue helped him get up by moving the wheelchair in front of him and putting the brakes on while Jack held on to the handles and got up on his knees. Sue braced her feet sideways against the back of Jack's feet and, on the count of three, she pulled up on the back of his pants and Jack would attempt to lift himself. Sometimes this took several tries before he stood. Once he was up, he could turn himself around to sit in the wheelchair. This was difficult for Sue, not only because she weighed one hundred pounds soaking wet, but it put a strain on her left side. Jack was deadweight. It was amazing that she could even assist him physically.

When Jack vomited, it would advance to continuous dry heaving. He would be transferred by ambulance to the hospital and usually admitted for a week to ten days. Sue visited Jack in the hospital a few times a day. She was already exhausted from caring for him at home. Occasionally she would tell Jack she was staying home that day to rest.

On one occasion, when Jack was released from the hospital, the doctor had prescribed several medications which included extra strength Gravol. On his second day back home he was feeling nauseated, so he took a Gravol.

Sharon and her son, Danny, were visiting. They could hear Jack vomiting from the bathroom.

A discouraged Sue said, "Oh no. Here we go again."

Sue opened the bathroom door to check on Jack. "Are you alright?"

When Jack stopped vomiting, he weakly replied, "No. Those pills the doctor gave me are no damn good. Besides, they are so big, they are a bugger to swallow."

"Jack, what pills are you talking about?" She knew that the medication Jack was given did not contain any large pills.

"Those damn things on the counter . . . the Gravol."

Sue picked up the box. "Jack, did you swallow one of these?"

Jack impatiently replied, "Yes, is there any other Gravol on the counter?"

Sue burst out in hysterical laughter; she could not contain herself.

Jack kept asking her, "What's so damn funny?"

Laughing so hard that tears were running down her face, snorting and holding her stomach, she motioned him to wait. When her laughter subsided, she explained to Jack, "These are suppositories. They are not supposed to go in your mouth. They are supposed to go up your bum!"

Jack had never seen suppositories before, and he could not help but laugh at his own error. "Got my ends mixed up." This sent Sue into hysterics again.

Sharon and Danny could hear Jack and Sue laughing. Their curiosity was piqued. "Hey, you two, what is going on? Share the joke," said a curious Danny.

Sue came out of the washroom after handing Jack another suppository and instructing him on how to insert it. The laughter continued as Sue relayed the situation.

Jack and Sue were active in Timmins. They were on the original committees to start the handi-trans bus in the city. They helped establish the Multiple Sclerosis Society in Timmins and were key players in the MS Carnation Campaigns.

Jack and Sue turned their tragedies into triumphs, getting involved in their community to help themselves and help others. Because Sue had been through so much in her life, she had little tolerance for people who complained about illnesses or tragedies. It is not that she lacked compassion; the major trials and hardships of other people seemed minor to Sue when she compared them to what she had been through. Early in life Sue learned not to pity herself, not to complain, to keep her fears to herself, and not to allow herself to feel too sad. This approach to life's challenges made Sue highly functional and resilient, but the suppression of negative feelings led to a few bouts of depression throughout her life. She kept it hidden so well that only Jack and the children knew.

CHAPTER 71
Shenanigans

Over the years all four of the Wixson siblings got married. Glenda had two children, Janice had four, Sharon had three, and Mark had three.

Every holiday, members of the Wixson clan would get together for a meal. The joy of spending time with their grandchildren gave Jack and Sue reprieve from their daily hardships.

Jack would get his grandchildren involved with his shenanigans. At every family gathering, he asked the grandchildren to join him at the table before the meal was ready and instructed them to pick up their knives and forks.

"Ok, are you all ready? Do what I do," Jack snickered. "We wanna eat!" yelled Jack as he banged his knife and fork on the table. The children followed suit. An endless round of 'we wanna eat' and the banging of utensils echoed throughout the house. It was enough to rush the hostess to get the food on the table. Once the food was on the table, the grandchildren and their grandfather laughed. They had succeeded at their mission.

One Easter the grandchildren were all sent to the basement while Sharon's husband hid Easter eggs. Denis was hiding the eggs but, unbeknown to him, Jack was following behind him and pocketing the eggs. Sue was watching Jack do this and she started to snicker. At one point she said, "Jack . . . really?" Jack just smiled like the impish young man she knew many years ago.

When Denis was finished, he called the children upstairs. They rushed upstairs and began their frantic search. Denis was puzzled since he knew he had hidden eggs where the children were looking. Yet they were not finding any eggs.

John, one of the grandchildren, folded his arms in frustration. "Hey man, what's up? We can't find any eggs."

Denis scratched his head while Jack was in the corner of the room chuckling, his pockets bulging. The grandchildren looked at Jack and yelled, "Grandpa, you have the eggs."

When playing cards Jack would take every opportunity he could to cheat. He did not cheat to win, but just to see if he would get caught. The card players always knew when he was cheating because that familiar smirk crept over his face. The challenge was to figure out *how* he was cheating. Once caught he would roar with laughter and so would everyone else.

In the year 1994, Sue had weak spells and would fall over on her right side. When she had these bouts, she was so weak she could barely speak, she couldn't walk and moving her arm was a chore. Her family doctor was puzzled. Sue went through a battery of medical tests that were inconclusive. The doctor booked an appointment with a neurologist who came to Timmins. Sharon and Jack attended the appointment with her in the emergency department at the hospital.

Sue explained her symptoms to the neurologist. She also warned him to be careful when he examined her right arm and shoulder. The neurologist was irritated with Sue and loudly said, "Lady, don't tell me how to do my job. I have had hundreds of polio patients and I know how to examine someone with polio. Now be quiet and let me do my job."

His rudeness and lack of bedside manner brought back horrible memories of Sue's childhood experiences with doctors. Sue sat there stunned, tears running down her face. Sharon was growing impatient and angry at the neurologist. The straw that broke the camel's back for Sharon was when the neurologist pulled on Sue's right arm. Sue screamed. He had dislocated it.

"Get out of here now. Don't lay another hand on my mother," Sharon yelled at the neurologist, infuriated.

Jack started shushing Sharon. He was embarrassed by her outburst because he never confronted doctors. Sue was not shy to question doctors when it involved Jack's medical health. However, when it involved her health, she often became that emotionally shocked little girl sitting on Dr. Slabberly's table so many years ago. Sharon did not care that her father was not happy she spoke up. The neurologist was being rough and disrespectful to her mother.

The neurologist glared at Sharon. "You, young lady, need to shut your mouth. I don't have to put up with this!"

Sharon repeated her command firmly. By this time Sue was sobbing in pain. Two nurses and one of the emergency doctors rushed into the room as the neurologist stormed out. One of the nurses had heard everything and she took Sharon gently by the hand and whispered, "Good for you. He was horrible."

The other doctor apologized to Sue for the rough treatment she had received. Although he carefully put her arm back in the socket, she winced and almost passed out.

When Sue saw her family doctor, she explained to him the dreadful treatment she had received from the neurologist. He arranged for a neurologist who was a friend of his to see Sue. This neurologist was booked up and her appointment was six months away in Toronto at Sunnybrook Hospital.

Sue's independence and stubbornness kept her going in life but also made it difficult for her family. When she was physically weak or ill, she would reluctantly accept assistance and was grateful at the time. She really disliked receiving help, especially from her family. Once she was stronger, she resented them and claimed that she did not need help or that those who had assisted her were exaggerating. Sometimes Sue would imply that the person was lying. Some family members found this too much to deal with and backed away from her because she appeared ungrateful. Sue had to be in control in every situation that involved her and Jack. When Sue thought that her control was threatened, she came out fighting like a tiger. Others understood this was her survival mechanism. To be perceived as having a weakness or to be pitied infuriated Sue. Sue seldom showed these sides of herself to friends or church members.

Many years later, Sue confided to Sharon that, in her mind, if she accepted help, she once again was that poor little cripple girl that was not going to make it.

At the start of 1995, Jack had a major heart attack. The cardiac tests revealed partial blockage of the four main arteries. He needed quadruple bypass heart surgery. Sue was barely coping with her own physical affliction and yet she still thought she had to do everything for Jack. Jack told her there were things he could do on his own. Sue struggled with the fact that if Jack made his own meals, he would make a bit of a mess. Instead of waiting and letting him clean it up, she would get up and clean it. He did not do things on her schedule. When Sue wanted something done, she usually wanted it done now, or yesterday.

Glenda was living in Matheson, forty-five minutes from Timmins, and was busy helping her husband run their scrap yard and towing business. She was not able to come to Timmins often, but whenever Glenda could, she gave a hand. Janice's husband had been diagnosed with Lou Gehrig's disease and she had become his caregiver. Mark lived in Chapleau, two hours North, and spent time with his parents when he could and helped as much as was possible. Sharon was the only sibling living in Timmins, and she assisted Sue and Jack when needed. Daily visits and phone calls became part of her routine. Sharon and Denis would take Sue to her medical appointments out of town, and Mark would take Jack to his medical appointments in Sudbury.

Sue became irritable with Jack and began to resent all the care she had to provide for him. Family members insisted that Sue call Red Cross Home Services to obtain help. Eventually she gave in and called the Red Cross. Red Cross Home Services came to Sue and Jack's home, twice a week for four hours, to help Jack in and out of the bathtub and to assist with the housework.

The four siblings were extremely concerned about their parents. Sue had an undiagnosed condition that seemed to be progressing, and Jack was facing open heart surgery with a twenty-percent chance of surviving because of his multiple sclerosis.

CHAPTER 72

MS and PPS

In-the spring of 1995, Sue was diagnosed with post-polio syndrome, a condition of the nervous system that affects polio survivors from fifteen to fifty years later. Symptoms include weakness, fatigue, and muscle or joint pain. These chronic episodes can come on suddenly and last one day or up to two weeks.

Sue's post-polio episodes usually lasted one day, and it took a few days to regain her strength. Some months she would have a few episodes and other months would go by episode-free. Since there was no treatment for this condition, doctors usually treated the signs and symptoms. She had a sensitivity to medication, and one adult ASA would knock her out for a day. Sue would fight with this condition the rest of her life. Medication, in her mind, was not an option.

At the same time of her diagnosis, Jack was booked into Sudbury Memorial Heart Hospital for his bypass surgery. Both Sue and Jack were convinced that he would not make it through the surgery. Sue made an appointment with a lawyer and Jack updated all his legal papers and made funeral arrangements.

On the day of the surgery, Sue, Sharon, Denis, Glenda, and Mark were at the hospital.

Before Jack went into surgery the surgeon took Sue aside and somberly explained, "Mrs. Wixson, your husband's MS is further advanced than I was given to believe. You understand that this is a risky surgery to begin with but, in his condition, it is extremely risky. I just want to make sure you know the facts."

"Yes, I am aware that he might not make it," was all Sue could say. She had a lump in her throat. Sharon and Glenda were standing nearby. They hugged their mother and led Sue to the room where Jack was. Sue put on her happy face and entered the room. "So today is the big day, Jack."

Jack was worried and told Sue, "I am not looking forward to this at all, Sue." This was his way of saying he was afraid and nervous.

A nurse came in and gave Jack a sedative to relax him. Before he was wheeled out to pre-op, Sue kissed him and lovingly said, "We are praying, Jack, and we will see you later. I love you."

The girls and Mark gave their father deep meaningful hugs and kisses on the cheek and said, "See you later, Dad."

While Jack was in surgery, the family reminisced over their childhood and Jack's antics. They laughed and, at times, they cried.

Sue braced herself for bad news. One of Sue's coping mechanisms was to always prepare for the worst scenario. Then if things turned out well, it was a surprise, and if they didn't, she was prepared emotionally. Part of this preparation was to numb her feelings, a practice she began after her first day at school so many years before. Sue had raised her children this way. Every time their father ended up in the hospital, Sue convinced her children that their father was probably not coming out.

When the surgeon came to the family room and called for the Wixson family, they all rushed towards the surgeon in anticipation. He addressed Sue, "Your husband did well. He is now in the cardiac intensive care unit. The next forty-eight hours are crucial. We will know more once that time passes. In three hours, you can call the ICU floor and ask if you can see him."

Sue was in shock; she could barely believe that Jack had survived the surgery. The children were so relieved, and tears of joy were shed.

Sharon and Mark decided then and there that they would no longer live each day as if their father was dying. Instead, they were going to enjoy the days he was alive. From that point onward they did not view any of Jack's hospital stays as him being at death's door.

Recovering from open heart surgery was painful for Jack, and, at times, his complaining got on Sue's nerves, but she never said anything.

Instead, she rolled her eyes at him. Jack got the hint of her displeasure. She hovered over him and helped nurse him back to health. Because Jack was weak from the surgery and his MS attacks, Sue had to give Jack extra help transferring. She put her left hand under his armpit and held him up while he put his other hand on the wheelchair and twisted to turn around and sit on the couch, toilet or bed. This caused strain not only on her arm but also on her left leg and knee. Jack was too shaky to feed himself or hold a cup. Sue fed him and held his cup up to his lips to drink. Eventually, Sue purchased cups with lids with straws. He was able to hold these cups and drink on his own. Each MS attack caused more damage to Jack's nervous system.

In the early mornings, at about two, Jack would wake up and need to use the washroom. Sue would get up, move the wheelchair close to the bed, help him transfer into it and, once in the washroom, she would help him onto the toilet. When he was done, Sue helped him transfer from the toilet to the wheelchair and back to bed. Sue had not been sleeping well for years, not only due to these nightly washroom trips, but also because Jack had developed restless leg syndrome. Several times a night, when Sue had just drifted into sleep, Jack's legs would involuntarily move and jolt her awake.

Sue was resourceful and found ways to make life easier. She bought a hospital bed for Jack, then moved their bed into the other bedroom. Sue moved and rearranged furniture by herself and set up both bedrooms. Jack's bedroom was the main bedroom and the room at the front of the house became Sue's bedroom. A monitor system was put in place so that Jack could call Sue if he needed her in the middle of the night, and a urinal jug was placed within his reach. She worked with the March of Dimes to get Jack an electric wheelchair. Sharon or Glenda would stay with their father while Sue ran errands or took a break.

Jack recovered from his heart surgery and Sue's post-polio episodes came and went.

Sue did not like all the medications that the surgeon and cardiologist had prescribed for Jack and kept questioning Jack on whether he should be taking certain pills. Jack grew frustrated. He knew Sue did not trust doctors and often thought she knew more than the doctor did. Finally, he told her, "Sue, they know what they are doing. Just give me the damn pills."

With Mark helping at J & S Engraving, Jack was able to travel around Ontario with the International Full Gospel Businessmen's Fellowship. He had become the president of the chapter in Timmins. Jack and Sue were often asked to give their testimonies or be the main speakers by several Ontario chapters of the fellowship. Sue would share her story about being a shoe box baby and how she survived. Jack would give his testimony on dealing with MS.

In the spring of the year 2000, Sue was beginning to show signs of caregiver burnout. Her daughter, Sharon, grew concerned about Sue's irritability towards Jack. Sue was overreacting to minor incidents, such as dropping food on the floor, which he had done for years. Jack seldom asked Sue to do anything because if he did, she would snap at him. When he did fend for himself, she would get upset and angrily say, "Why didn't you ask me to help?" He was damned if he did and damned if he didn't. She was exhausted, had lost weight and showed signs of depression.

Between constant complaints of how much work it was to care for Jack, she spoke of dying before him. She would say that the rest would be nice. When Sharon asked Sue about her weight loss, Sue said she was too tired to eat or had forgotten to eat. In Sue's own strange way, she was calling out for help, but she could never admit that caregiving had become too much for her. Yet it was evident that she had come to the end of the line.

One day Sharon phoned her mother. "Mom, I am calling you back because you sounded so exhausted and worn out. I need to know something."

"What, Sharon?" softly replied Sue.

"Do you need Mark and me to make the decision that Dad needs to go into a home? You've done all you can and now it is time." Sharon had to choose her words carefully. Sue was very sensitive and easily upset.

In a quiet sad voice Sue answered her daughter, "Yes."

Sharon repeated her question to make sure her mother was making this decision and not her. Sue's response was the same.

Mark knew that Jack would be upset and met with him in the living room. Sue was crying in the kitchen as she listened to the conversation between father and son. Jack suspected that one day he would have to leave his home and be admitted to a facility that could provide care for him, but he did not realize Sue was at the end of her rope. He knew she had been curt with him and, at times, passive aggressive, but he had no clue that her mental, emotional, and physical condition had become fragile.

Jack felt bad for Sue and was angry that she had not spoken to him about it. He was also sad to leave his home. Sue diverted his anger towards Sharon by telling him that Sharon was adamant that he moves to a facility. Sue took no responsibility. Sharon knew that was the way it had to be, so she endured her father's indignant and hurtful looks. Sue did not want to look like a quitter in anyone's eyes, especially in her own.

Jack, Sue, and Mark visited a few facilities in Timmins. Most places had a long waiting list, but a new facility had just opened, St. Mary's Manor. There was a room available. Jack could move in within a week. On the day Jack moved out of his home, tears flowed and deep sorrow was felt by all. The family knew this day would come, but it was one they dreaded.

Sue's emotions were mixed. She was sad to see her husband leave, but, on the other hand, she was relieved to retire from the lifting and other physically demanding jobs that had been required. Her children reassured her that she had done a wonderful job and now it was time to take care of herself.

At first, she missed Jack. It was strange not having him at home. She would get up in the middle of the night to check on him and would be standing in his room, staring at the empty bed, before she realized he was not there. Her role had changed, and she was unsure what her new role was. She felt lost and out of sorts for months.

Sue visited Jack every day. At the beginning Jack was annoyed with being "placed" as he called it.

Finally, one day Sue was fed up and said, "Jack, no one is happy that you have to be in here. So we both have to make the best of it." With that said, Sue left the building, got into the car and put her head down on the steering wheel and cried.

The next day, Jack's disposition was better. He told Sue that she was right and that he would try to make it his new home.

Jack was able to go to work at J & S Engraving every day, when the weather permitted him to use his wheelchair. The facility he lived in was right across the street from the mall where J & S Engraving had relocated the year before.

Jack continued to hold resentment towards Sharon, which made her visits with him uncomfortable, but that did not stop her. She hoped that her mother would one day tell Jack the truth about how he came to be in St. Mary's Manor.

CHAPTER 73

Déjà Vu

In 2001, rumours that St. Mary's Manor would close set Sue in motion looking for another place for Jack to live. Again, she visited care homes in the city. When she visited Spruce Hill Lodge, she was impressed with the friendliness, homemade meals, and the size of the residents' rooms. The next day Jack went with Sue to see the lodge. Jack was impressed with what he saw and the friendly atmosphere. A room was available. Sue and the family once again moved Jack.

During this time Sue was diagnosed with type 2 diabetes. Sue was infuriated because she had a healthy diet and was physically active. Her anger towards the disease was puzzling. It was as if she was saying, "How dare you infringe on my life. I have had enough to deal with and now this."

Sue continued to visit Jack regularly, but because Spruce Hill Lodge was twenty minutes away from home, she would visit three or four times a week instead of every day. The new visiting schedule she incorporated with Jack gave her time to be more involved with the church and to do volunteer work. She was able to attend Wednesday night Bible studies, became involved in a young mothers' group as a mentor, and assisted at church banquets and gatherings. Sue volunteered at the hospital doing visitations for the church and worked at the Salvation Army thrift shop.

One day, she was in the basement of the Salvation Army sorting clothing donations, when a friend yelled down the stairs, "Sue, it's time!"

Sue froze, felt weak and sick to her stomach. In those few moments she was transported back in time to when her mother called out, "Sue, it's time. Time for your shock treatment." Sue reminded herself that she was older now and it was just a flashback. She no longer had to have shock treatments.

Her friend bellowed down the stairs again, "Sue, lunch time." When Sue had calmed herself down, she went up the stairs and sat with her friend.

"You look like you saw a ghost," stated her concerned friend.

"No, not a ghost but an unpleasant memory from the past." Sue's voice quivered as she explained what had happened. Her friend said that she would try to remember not to say those words again.

Spruce Hill Lodge was a good fit for Jack. He became involved in the residents' committee, submitted jokes to their newsletter and partook in the activities. The other residents nicknamed him the Computer Man, because he was the only resident who had a computer and knew how to use it.

Sue's visits with Jack were pleasant and she was glad to see how he adjusted to his new home. Even though Jack stayed busy he had plenty of time to think. On one visit he asked her to sit down beside him on the bed.

"Sue, I now realize how much work you had to do since I've been sick. I never ever told you how much I appreciated you and everything you have done. I have had a lot of time to reflect on things and I see now how difficult it became for you. I am amazed that you were able to care for me as long as you did. I appreciate everything and who you are. You, my love, are an amazing lady. I love you very much!"

Tears were running down Sue's cheeks. Hearing these words from Jack meant the world to her. Jack's words also confirmed that she had made the right decision for both. "Thank you, Jack, that means a lot to me. So, let's stop our blubbering and go get some lunch."

Through the years when Jack became too serious and complimented Sue, she would turn it into a joke. At first Jack was insulted, but then he realized she was protecting herself from feeling his love because she knew she would lose him. Jack continued to compliment her always. Sue seldom verbally reciprocated his love.

Most people thought Sue was an amazing and sweet older lady. She was generous, kind, and compassionate, and had a wonderful sense of humour. Most people just loved her to bits. Her family loved her but at times she could be harsh, and her defense mechanisms were obstacles to the cultivation of deep meaningful relationships with her children. If Sue made a mistake or offended her children, her apologies were half-assed. She would say, "I am sorry you were offended by what I said or did," or, "I am sorry you took what I said the wrong way."

Sue never took full blame for any of her errors with her family. Yet she instilled in them the importance of admitting one's mistakes and asking for forgiveness. Her ego and self-esteem were fragile and even coming close to admitting an error was psychologically devastating for her. When this occurred, she would be overwhelmed with grief and confusion. No number of supportive words from her loved ones helped. Her anguish would go on for days until she arrived at a different perception by changing the facts in her mind. The family came to realize that Sue was not emotionally capable of dealing with painful issues. All her life she felt she had to prove to others that she had the right to be alive and be part of society. Even though she often said, "No one's perfect," the standards she set for herself were unachievable for any human being.

Mark frequently visited his father and kept abreast of things that were happening at the engraving shop. Mark also ran errands for Jack. They kept in touch almost every day. This gave Sue a reprieve.

Mark got a frantic call from Jack one day. "Mark, I'm stuck! Come and help me."

Mark did not know where Jack was stuck or what he meant. "Dad, where are you stuck?"

"In my bed . . . the damn thing folded up with me in it," replied a distressed Jack.

Mark picked up Sue at home and they drove to Spruce Hill Lodge. They rushed to Jack's room. The bed had folded in half and Jack was sandwiched. Mark and Sue could barely help Jack because they were laughing so hard. The electronics on the hospital bed had gone haywire. Jack was stuck in the bed for over an hour. The phone was out of his reach but with some twisting and reaching he was able to grab it. With the door closed no one at Spruce Hill could hear him yelling. It was a story that the family would tease Jack about for years.

In 2006, Sue and Jack celebrated their fiftieth wedding anniversary. The family held their party in the family room at Spruce Hill. The hall was all decked out with gold and black balloons. Old photographs of their lives together lined the walls. A special cake with their original wedding cake topper was on display. Old friends, new friends and family members attended. Sue told old stories about her and Jack and, for the first time in a long time, Sue was showing a greater degree of affection towards Jack. They laughed a lot and enjoyed the day with friends and family.

The engraving shop in Sue's backyard was converted to a small apartment. Mark's son and Sue's grandson, Ross, rented it from her. He would check on Sue and do small chores when she asked him. The rest of the family was grateful that Ross was so close by because he would notify one of them when Sue had post-polio episodes.

At the end of January 2009, Sue was having renovations done at the house and the contractor had left blankets on the floor to protect it. Ross was visiting her. When Ross got up to get a drink from the fridge Sue got up from the table and headed to the living room. Within moments Ross heard a thud and rush to Sue. She was prostrate on the floor. She had tripped on a blanket. The fall and stabbing pain radiating from her thigh down her left leg had taken her breath away and whispered to Ross to get a pillow. He called an ambulance. Within a few hours she underwent surgery to repair the broken femur in her leg.

During her hospital stay Jack was extremely concerned about Sue. His anxiety brought on chest pains, and he ended up in the hospital too. Sue's hospital room was a few doors down from Jack's. Sue knew that her accident had worried Jack and was a catalyst for his heart attack. A few years after Jack's heart by-pass surgery, he began to experience angina and mild heart attacks. He had been diagnosed with congestive heart failure four years prior. Jack's legs were severely swollen and bluish in colour. His blood pressure and pulse were high. The nurses gave him nitro, but it only worked for a short period of time.

Mark was in the room when the doctor came in to speak to Jack. She told Jack that she was making arrangements to send him to Sudbury District Hospital to see a cardiologist. Jack's adamant response was, "No! Doctor, you and I both know there is nothing more they can do for me. It will be a wasted trip. No more tests and no more surgeries. I am done. I am tired and I am ready to go home and meet my Lord. I am done now. No more. No more."

Tears filled Mark's eyes as he listened to his father make his last wishes known.

The doctor questioned Jack further to ensure she understood that Jack was saying he was ready to die.

With compassion the doctor looked at Jack and acknowledged his wishes. "We will make you comfortable, Jack. If you at any point change your mind, you let one of the nurses know." The doctor was amazed at how calm and unwavering Jack was in his decision.

Mark sorrowfully asked, "Dad, are you sure this is what you want?"

Jack nodded. "Yes, son. I am tired. I am ready to go."

Mark told the family about Jack's decision. Sue immediately asked that a wheelchair be brought to her so she could see her husband. The news was difficult for her. Although she knew this time would come, it still was not easy to digest.

Before Jack was given morphine to make him comfortable, Sue and each family member got to talk to him.

Sue joked with him, "You picked a heck of a time to do this, Jack."

Jack smiled and replied, "Well, you don't have far to visit me."

Sue grabbed his hand and squeezed it tightly. She smiled down at her dying husband.

During his sedated state Jack drifted in and out of consciousness. One time, he drowsily asked, "Why is everyone here? Am I on my last legs or something?"

Sharon answered, "Yes, Dad, you are!"

"Oh, yeah, that's right. Only three more days," Jack said faintly.

Once again Mark spoke to his father and asked him if he was sure this is what he wanted. Jack's response was a nod.

On another occasion Jack was singing but no one could decipher what he was saying. Mark got close to his father. "Dad, can you speak up. We don't understand you."

Jack opened his eyes slightly and slowly chanted, "Dad's going to give me this and Dad's going to give you that . . . but all I'm going to give you is bills." Then he winked and chuckled. Those were his last words. The family roared because Jack had sung that little ditty for years, joking around with his kids. Right until the end, he joked to ease the sorrow and difficulty.

For four days the family members and Sue took turns by his bedside. Late every night Sue would be wheeled down to her room and helped into bed. She made the children promise that they would come and get her if there was any change in Jack's condition. Lying awake, Sue thought about their life together and how she believed she had prepared herself for his death. She realized that all the preparation in the world did not stop the sadness and pain.

On the fourth night at midnight, the nurse had just helped Sue into bed when Sharon ran to get her mother. Jack had taken several long deep breaths. Tearfully, Glenda spoke into Jack's ear, "Wait, Dad, Mom is coming. She'll be here any minute."

The nurse quickly assisted Sue back out of bed and into the wheelchair. The nurse pushed her into Jack's room and up close to the head of the bed. Sue leaned over and rubbed Jack's cheek. Softly, she said, "It's ok, Jack. I am here. You can go and be with the Lord. I love you."

With those words said, Jack took his last breath. He had waited for his Sue to say goodbye. Everyone in the room stood in silence for about one minute. Sue sat in the wheelchair with tears running down her face, no sobbing, just a steady stream. On February 1st, 2009, at the age of 79, Jack went to be with his Lord and Saviour, just as he predicted three days prior.

Jack lived 45 years after he was given his diagnosis of MS.

CHAPTER 74
Age of Changes

Jack's funeral was held on a frigid, frosty, windy, and gloomy day. The weather suited the mood of the family and friends. Because Sue was still recovering from her surgery, she was not able to attend the visitations at the funeral home. Sue was extremely saddened that she was not with her family, but she needed to save her strength to attend the funeral.

Arrangements were made for Sue to attend her husband's funeral. She was given a four-hour pass from the hospital. Sharon's dear friend, Brenda, arranged to pick Sue up at the hospital and return her when the funeral was over in a wheelchair-accessible van owned by Community Living. The Pentecostal church graciously agreed to hold a one-hour visitation with an open casket before the funeral, so Sue could see Jack for the last time and say her goodbyes.

Sue was wheeled into the church and to the front near the altar where Jack's casket lay open. She sat for several minutes looking at him and reminiscing. The family stood back and gave her that time.

Jack would have loved his funeral because there were not only tears but also laughter when the tales of his antics were told in his eulogy.

When the funeral concluded and his casket was placed in the hearse, all who attended went inside except Sue and Sharon. Sue sat in her wheelchair and Sharon stood behind her. Gently, Sharon placed her hand on her mother's shoulder and Sue grabbed her hand. Together in the bitter cold they watched as the hearse left the church driveway and made its way down the road out of sight. Under Sue's breath, she whispered, "Bye, Jack."

One week after the funeral, Sue was released from the hospital. Glenda stayed with Sue to help her do the necessary paperwork concerning Jack's death. That was the excuse Glenda used, but she was also there to help Sue since she was still in the wheelchair. Even though she was told to use the wheelchair for two more weeks, Sue only used it for three more days and then she started bearing weight on her left leg. Sue rarely listened to doctors' advice, nor did she take most of the medications prescribed to her.

It was not difficult for Sue to go home after Jack's death, because Jack had not lived at home for eight years. Not visiting the Lodge was strange since it was part of her routine for years. When she was out shopping, she would see something she thought Jack could use and occasionally get to the cash register before she remembered Jack was no longer here.

Glenda eventually moved into the back house on Sue's property and was good company for Sue. The two of them were out and about visiting, going to church, going to the church camp in the summers, and doing projects around the two houses. Both were crafty and tackled many do-it-yourself projects, such as framing a door, making a screen door out of a solid wooden door, or changing kitchen taps.

Sue had a black and grey miniature poodle, Lacey. Lacey was more than a pet to Sue; she became a warning dog. A few years prior, Sue developed mild dementia and it was not uncommon for her to forget a pot of food that was heating up or cooking on the stove. If Lacey smelled the food starting to burn, she would go to the stove and let out high-pitched barks until Sue went to the stove. If Sue did not close the back door properly, she would use the same high-pitched bark until Sue yelled, "Well, Lacey, close the door." Lacey would repeatedly jump on the door until she heard it click closed.

At bedtime Sue said, "Lacey, it's bedtime." Lacey would retrieve each toy she had strewed around the house and put them in a box. Then she would jump onto Sue's bed. Although Lacey was highly strung and constantly jumping, running and playing with her toys, when Sue told her to lie down, she did. Lacey sensed when Sue was not feeling well and she would be calmer on those days and spend most of her time lying beside Sue.

In the winter of 2015, the doctor suspected that Sue had pancreatic cancer. She had lost a considerable amount of weight and had chronic sharp pains in her upper left side. Her blood sugar levels were unstable. The doctor and Sue agreed that she was too fragile to go through the testing and biopsies needed to confirm the diagnosis. That evening she asked Glenda to call the family and let them know the results of the doctor's appointment. The next day when family members raised the subject with Sue, Sue was livid, proclaiming she had never seen the doctor and that she certainly did not have cancer. Sue had no recollection of the visit to the doctor and, as much as Glenda tried to convince her, she was adamant that Glenda was making up stories. It appeared Sue's cancer, unstable blood sugars, and post-polio syndrome were advancing her dementia.

At times, Sue became paranoid and would accuse Glenda of stealing her money and belongings. Glenda would often find items, such as one of Sue's socks, in the fridge or food items in the dryer. If Sue discovered the misplaced items, she would accuse Glenda of trying to drive her crazy. When reminded of events or appointments, she would get angry and say something like, "I know. Do you think I am stupid?"

Sue took most of her frustrations out on Glenda. Glenda watched her fun, loving and strong mother, who had treated her so kindly, occasionally turn mean-spirited towards her. Yet Glenda's love and appreciation for her mother kept her by Sue's side.

CHAPTER 75

The Party

Sue's three daughters planned an eightieth surprise birthday party for Sue on the September long weekend of 2016. They held the party two months before her real birthday so her only living sibling, Ruby, could attend. Sue had kept in close contact with many of her siblings throughout her life, except for Arthur and Howie, however, she had remained closest with Ruby. Approximately fifty people were invited which included Sue's children, grandchildren and their spouses, great-grandchildren, and friends. The party theme was Nova Scotia. The food, the pictures, the videos and music were all centered around Sue's dear homeland.

The sun was shining and there was barely a cloud in the sky. The wind kept blowing the tablecloths off the tables that were set up for the party. The driveway was vacant when Glenda drove up with Sue in the car. The partygoers had parked their cars down the street and in the next-door neighbour's yard. Fabric shower curtains were hung on a wire that ran between the house and garage, hiding the crowd waiting in the backyard. Glenda parked close to the house and brought Sue's walker around to her. Sue got out of the car, looked at the curtains and said, "What the heck is that up there for?"

Janice and Sharon came out from behind the curtains and stood with Glenda and Mom.

Janice waved her arm and said, "Mom, because we could not bring you to Nova Scotia, we brought a little bit of Nova Scotia to you."

One of the grandchildren opened the curtains and everyone excitedly yelled, "Surprise, Sue!"

Sue was more than surprised; she was confused because she had no idea why everyone was yelling "surprise." She started to get angry because she thought someone was pulling a prank on her.

Janice noticed her scowl and explained, "Mom, this is your early eightieth birthday party. We are having your party now because the weather is so unpredictable in November. This way everyone from out of town could attend."

Sue's mood switched to being overwhelmed and tears welled up in her eyes. As she entered the backyard, she saw a mock ocean beach with a pool of salt water. Janice helped Sue to a chair beside the sand and pool. Sue removed her sandals and closed her eyes while she rubbed her bare feet in the warm sand. As she slipped her feet into the salt water, a smile and expression of total contentment washed across Sue's face.

With her eyes still closed she gently spoke, "I can picture myself back home with my feet in the sand and then in the ocean. I loved just sitting there and letting the water wash over my feet and breathing in the salty air."

Ruby was in disguise, with a long blonde wig and dark sunglasses. She had fooled many family members as she introduced herself as Mary Jennings, "a long-time friend of Sue." Sue asked who the blonde was. Glenda fetched Ruby and introduced her to Sue as Mary. The minute Ruby spoke, despite her attempt to disguise her voice, Sue knew it was her baby sister. "Ruby!" screamed Sue.

Ruby laughed and hugged Sue. "Can't get anything by you, Sue, can we?"

Then Sue turned to the task of greeting the many people gathered in her honour. She was thrilled that her nephew, Sunny, and his wife, Yodja, were present. Ruby and Sunny were the only two living relatives from their age group remaining and had not seen each other for years.

It was a day filled with laughter, reminiscing, and speeches about Sue, topped off with a lobster supper. Sue said she would never forget it. It was one of the happiest days she had in years.

CHAPTER 76

Homeward Bound

In the months following her birthday party, Sue continued to lose weight and the sharp pains in her left upper side became more frequent and often took her breath away.

In the middle of February 2017, Sue turned jaundiced and the pain in her side increased. She asked Glenda to take her to the hospital. The doctor in the emergency department looked over Sue's chart and listened to Sue explain why she was there.

The doctor pulled up a chair beside the bed Sue was sitting on and took her hand in his. "Mrs. Wixson, it seems the pancreatic cancer has advanced."

Either Sue had chosen to forget the grim diagnosis given by her family doctor the year before or her dementia had robbed her of the memory. Sue stared straight ahead, eyes filling with tears.

The doctor wanted to prescribe pain medication, but Sue refused. Sue told the doctor that this pain was no worse than when her shoulder was dislocated and had to be put back. If she could tolerate that pain, she could tolerate the pain in her side. The doctor warned her that the pain would become unbearable as time went on. Since she wanted to go home instead of being admitted to the hospital, the doctor instructed her to see her family physician within a day or two.

On the ride home, not a word was spoken. Once they got home, Sue, in a very controlled voice, said to Glenda, "You should call your sisters and brother and let them know. I will call Ruby."

Sue phoned Ruby and they chit chatted, joked, and talked craziness as they always did for the first fifteen minutes. Then Sue's voice became serious. "Ruby . . ."

"What's wrong, Sue? I haven't heard you say 'Ruby' like that in a long time . . . well, since you called me to tell me that Mom died."

"I have pancreatic cancer, Ruby. The doctor said I have only a few weeks or months to live. I have jaundice pretty bad," Sue said nonchalantly.

"Oh, Sue, I am so sorry!" replied Ruby sorrowfully.

"Ruby!" Sue snapped angrily. "Don't you be feelin' sorry for me. You know how I hate that!"

Ruby knew her sister well enough that she had better come back with a smart aleck reply or Sue would be very hurt. "Ok, you yellow-bellied lady. So, do you look like a lemon or a banana?"

Sue roared and retorted, "I always was a sour puss, so I guess I am a lemon."

The two joked and teased each other as they always did. When Sue hung up the phone life seemed normal, and her cancer appeared surreal.

Glenda did as her mother had asked and called Janice, Mark and Sharon. Janice lived forty-five minutes away and Mark lived in town. Sharon had been in Florida for three months when Glenda phoned and told Sharon the heartbreaking news. Sharon wanted to know if she should fly home to Timmins. Glenda did not feel it was necessary at the time.

The next morning Sharon felt very unsettled about whether she should go home and be with her mother. Something in her gut told her she must go. She phoned Sue and compassionately inquired, "Hi, Mom, how are you doing today?"

Sue put on her best front: "I am okay. I guess you know I am not going to be around too long, but you really don't need to come home."

Sharon got noticeably quiet and then in a genuine voice said, "Mom, it is not about needing to come home. Do you want me to come home?"

This time Sue grew quiet. Sharon did not break her silence. Then in a weak whisper, as tears rolled down her cheeks, she answered, "Yes, Sharon, I think you better."

Sharon booked her flight and in two days she arrived in Timmins. When Sharon walked in and saw her mother, she was stunned. Her mother was asleep in her recliner, wrapped in a blanket with Lacey lying beside her. The colour of her mother's skin reminded Sharon of an old yellowed waxed floor. Sharon took a deep breath to hold back her tears and shock. As she approached, Sue opened her eyes. Sharon managed to muster a smile because she knew if Sue saw pity in Sharon's eyes, she would be upset with her. "Mom, I made it," Sharon said, kissing her mother on the cheek.

Sue gave Sharon a weak smile as she sat down beside her.

"If you don't mind, Mom, I'll stay here while I am in Timmins."

Sue nodded her head and feebly said, "That's a good idea. You know, Sharon, they gave me up to three months, but I know I don't have that long." Sue then closed her eyes and fell back asleep.

Sharon sat there for a few minutes, holding her mother's hand.

"She had a rough night. She is very weak and exhausted this morning," spoke Glenda softly. After giving each other a big hug and shedding tears, the two sisters sat down in the kitchen to talk.

Sue wanted to die at home. Glenda notified the doctor of her mother's request and in-home palliative care arrangements were made.

"Glenda, do you think you and I can do this . . . take care of Mom while she is dying?" Sharon gulped to repress the lump in her throat.

"I think we can if we work together. Do you want to do this, Sharon?" Glenda genuinely inquired.

"Yes, I do, and we can do this together. We all know how much mom hates hospitals and how afraid she would be, especially during this time.".

Glenda nodded. "This way she will still have some form of control as long as she can. We will do our best and hope we can fulfill her wishes."

Sharon and Glenda were thankful that they had mended their strained relationship five years prior.

The next day Sue requested that friends and family visit. Glenda was concerned about this request. "Mom, you know that visitors would really tire you out. You need to save your strength."

Sue chuckled and said, "Glenda, what am I saving my strength for? I'm dying."

Glenda laughed. "That's true, Mom. Okay, we will call the family and I will get the pastor to announce in church that you would like to have visitors!"

Over the next eight days, family and friends visited to say their goodbyes to Sue. Anytime visitors arrived, Sue would perk up and she sounded and acted like her old self. It was as if her dementia took a backseat and the real Sue stepped forward. She talked openly with her children and grandchildren about dying and joked around about it. The family playfully teased Sue, recollecting funny stories involving her. It was a joyful time for Sue and those days made for wonderful memories.

Memories such as when Janice was learning how to drive. She asked Sue what a "Pernadl" was. Sue had no idea what she was talking about.

Janice said, "Yes, you know, Mom. You know, beside the gear shift."

Sue burst out laughing. "You mean the P R N D L?"

"Yes, the 'Pernadl.' What is it?"

Sue told her it was park, reverse, neutral, drive and low gear. The family still calls it a pernadl.

Then there was the time that Jack was bringing in the groceries and his pants fell and he tripped. The groceries went flying towards Sue. She tried to duck but was hit in the head by a box of Kraft Dinner. Shaking her head in surprise, she looked down at Jack who was lying flat on his face in front of Sue. "Jack, I wish you would not worship me like this, at least not in front of the kids." Everyone roared.

And who could forget when, on a Saturday evening, Sue dyed her hair and the roots turned a fluorescent green. There were no hairdresser shops open, so she had to wait until Monday to fix the dye job. Sue never missed church service and she was not going to let green roots stop her from going to church. The teens thought she was the coolest grandmother.

The last week Sue was alive she struggled to eat because she was experiencing severe nausea. When her granddaughter Angela arrived, Sue asked her to make a chocolate cake with buttercream chocolate icing. The next day Angela brought the requested chocolate cake, made from scratch to her grandmother. Sue loved it. She ate a big piece and downed a half-glass of milk.

When the company left, she was exhausted and slept for hours. Sue was doing what Sue did best: putting up a good front. The friends from the church who visited found it hard to comprehend she was dying. One person said, "If she wasn't so yellow I would not believe it."

During those days, Ruby called her twice a day to see how she was doing. Sue asked Ruby when she was coming to see her. Seeing Ruby one last time was important to her. Ruby had decided she did not want to see her sister dying and Sharon had to tell Sue. Sue was disappointed.

On the ninth day Sue could not take the pain anymore and requested that the nurse from palliative care be called.

While Glenda and Sharon waited for the nurse to arrive, Glenda's daughter, Sherise, and her eight-year-old son, Kegan, arrived to visit Sue. Kegan called Sue "Grama-grama." When Kegan stepped into Sue's room, he appeared nervous. Because Sue was dying, he did not know what to say, but he wanted to see her. Sue sensed his anxiety and held her hand out to him. "Come here, Kegan."

Reluctantly, Kegan walked over to the side of the bed and held Sue's hand. It took a lot of effort, but she smiled anyway and said, "Kegan, don't be afraid. Grama-grama isn't afraid. I am going to be with Jesus, Grandpa Wixson and my son Ross. I will be so happy there."

Tears ran down Kegan's face as his Grama-grama spoke to him. She told him that she loved him, and he hugged her, and she kissed him on the cheek. Tears flowed in streams down the cheeks of Glenda, Sherise, and Sharon as they witnessed this precious heart-moving moment between a great-grandmother and her great-grandson.

That afternoon the nurse arrived with syringes filled with pain medication. She inserted a PICC line in Sue's abdomen so the daughters could administer the medication. To relieve her pain, Sue was put into a medication-induced unconscious state. Lacey stayed at the foot of Sue's bed, laying by Sue's feet. Lacey left this spot only to eat, drink or go outside. Lacey was calm and yet the sorrow in her eyes revealed her awareness that death hung in the air.

On the tenth day Ruby called and said she was heading down to Timmins and hoped she was not too late. Ruby had changed her mind and decided her sister Sue needed her.

Sharon whispered in Sue's ear, "Mom, Ruby is on her way. Ruby is coming, Mom." A faint quick smile crossed Sue's lips and she moaned. She had not made a sound since she was given the medication.

The next day the whole family was at Sue's house. The nurse gave instructions that those who visited Sue during her last days should talk softly and the house should be kept quiet. The room was softly lit and gospel music played gently in the background. Sue was slightly propped up and covered in a bright yellow and orange blanket that Jack had knit. On the wall above Sue hung pictures of Jack and Sue on their wedding day. On the dresser beside her was a picture of her mother Grace and a picture of Ruby and Sue when they were teens. Each family member took turns sitting with Sue. Jessy, her granddaughter, wanted to bring comfort to Sue so she sat and read the Bible to her for an hour.

Ruby arrived close to six o'clock that evening and went straight to see Sue. Holding her hand, she whispered in Sue's ear, "I'm here, Sue. I came." She sat with her for thirty minutes, talking to her quietly and gently. At around six-thirty Ruby left the room and said goodbye to the family members who were heading home.

Glenda, Sharon, Mark, Ruby and Ruby's grandson stayed behind. Ruby went back into Sue's room and noticed her breathing had changed. Ruby called for the others. Sharon sat on the bed by her mother's waist. Glenda sat in a chair by her mother's head. Ruby sat in a chair beside the middle of the bed. Mark sat behind Ruby.

Sue took another deep breath and Ruby gently said, "Sue, you can go now. It's okay to go. I love you, Sue."

Glenda and Sharon, with tears flowing down their faces and holding onto their mother's hand, took turns saying, "Mom, it's okay. We are all going to be okay. You did a good job raising us, Mom. Go be with Jesus."

Sharon gave Sue a kiss on the cheek and very softly whispered in her mother's ear, "I love you, Mom."

Sue died in that moment. She left this world the way she wanted to, at home, at peace surrounded by family, with her dear dog by her feet.

Sue's funeral was held on March 5th, 2017. It was a snowy, blustery, frigid winter's day, much like the day of Sue's birth in Nova Scotia and the day of Jack's funeral. The service was held at the Timmins Pentecostal church, where Sue was a member for over twenty-five years. The funeral was short and sweet like Sue, and the way Sue asked it to be. Sue asked that the song "Farewell to Nova Scotia" be played at her funeral.

"There Will Be Peace in the Valley" was the last song played at her funeral service, the song Sue comforted herself with for years.

When the pallbearers put Sue's casket in the hearse, the weather was still below minus 30 Celsius. Hand in hand, Ruby and Sharon stood outside and watched the hearse drive down the road. Just as the hearse left her sight, Sharon whispered, "Mom, I waited to say my last goodbye as you did for Dad when the hearse drove him away. I love you, Maw."

That sweet tiny Shoe Box Baby grew and survived; she survived her premature entrance to the world, polio, being ridiculed and humiliated because of her disabilities, years of daily intense pain in her childhood, caring for a sick husband for years, the death of her oldest son, raising five children and being struck by post-polio, dementia, diabetes, and pancreatic cancer. Although she had built walls to protect herself to survive, she touched the lives of those around her by her compassion, her faith, her kindness, her generosity, her sense of humour and her phenomenal determination to press onward regardless of what storm hit her life.

From the shoe box to the casket, Sue Fenton Wixson lived a full life with greater purpose than she will ever know. She personified the fortitude of the human spirit and the multiple positive impacts one life can have on others.

CHAPTER 77

Letters

Dear Maw,

You left to go to heaven a few years ago and I do miss you so much. I know that your departure is part of the circle of life, but regardless I still don't like it. I probably never will.

You and I struggled in our relationship for years, but I am so glad that we sorted it out. Maybe we were too much alike or maybe we were too different. None of that matters now. I learned to appreciate you for who you were, and I admired all you had accomplished in life.

One Christmas when Dad was not doing well, we all had to be quiet because he was sleeping. Glenda, Janice, you and I were sitting at the kitchen table. You took out a bottle of wine and poured us all half a glass. We were just teens then, but you said that once won't hurt and it was Christmas. We sat and chatted, laughed until we cried, and I think maybe one of us peed ourselves, which made everyone laugh even harder. None of us girls had wine before, or at least I don't think we had.

We got a buzz and were relaxed. I believe you knew we all needed that time to just "be."

When Glenda, Janice and I get together we have so much fun and laugh so hard. Those times remind me of that Christmas day. They also bring back memories of you and Aunt Ruby. You two were 'kooks' as Ruby put it. You laughed, roared, cried together, knew how to be silly at times, and were there for each other. We have been left with a wonderful example of what sisters should be. It does not mean we always agree with each other, but we have learned we can disagree.

Not every daughter can say they have a mom who showed them how to do things" single-handedly." To this day I still use a broom and mop with one hand. I know you used to say, "God gave you two hands; use them," but I have to say when I find myself using just one hand for a two-handed task, I think of you.

You were probably the most resourceful person I have ever known. I know it came from you determining how to use one hand to do two-handed tasks. You could have just given up and said" I can't" but that was not your nature. I can still hear you firmly saying, "If I hear you say 'I can't' one more time, I am going to lose it." Now your voice echoes in my mind when I say those forbidden words, lol. I can still see you maneuvering that heavy wooden four-drawer dresser down the twelve steep basement steps in Holtyre. There was no way to help you because you had it all figured out. You were the 'one arm wonder.' You didn't say it's too heavy or I only have one arm so I can't do it.

Maw, thank you for encouraging each one of us to use and develop the gifts and talents we had: Glenda and Janice with their artistic ventures; me with my writing; Ross with his love of nature, hunting and trapping, and Mark with his entrepreneurial skills.

I can't help but smile as I am writing this letter to you because you enjoyed writing little sayings down and stories you had created. You also started doing scenic oil paintings in your seventies. You loved nature and animals. When it comes to Mark, I am sure he got his entrepreneurial desires from Dad, but he got his creativity and problem-solving abilities from you. You have left a deposit of yourself in each one of us.

I am indebted to you for all the stories of your childhood that you shared with me. I know you did not tell them so that I would pity you, God forbid I ever do that, since pity shown towards you was something you detested. Those stories gave me greater understanding of who you were and why you did the things you did. They also helped me to understand why you put walls up to protect yourself. They were your survival mechanisms and they kept you sane.

When you were tired of the endless questions and demands from all of us kids, you used to say, "Call me Jill, Jane, or Joe . . . Just don't say mom one more time." Then you would disappear for a few hours. I realized later that you went for a walk to collect your thoughts and recharge your energy. As a mother I found myself saying the same thing and discovered the importance of taking time to do likewise.

You showed your kindness in acts for others. I will never forget when a family moved in down the street. They had seven children and struggled to make ends meet. You often sent us to their home with groceries. If their children needed clothing, you found some for them. You were a good friend and neighbour.

Your faith was inspirational. It carried you through, around and above the harsh realities of life.

I just want to tell you that you were an amazing person. You have left me with so many wonderful memories. Memories that make me laugh, make me cry and make me grateful.

You deposited a wealth of knowledge, compassion, and love for others in me. You taught me not to give up and that when the storms of life come along, they will pass and there is always a rainbow at the end, even if it is hidden. I learned not to quit. If there is a will, there is a way. You inspired me to grow personally and not to settle for less than what I am capable of.

Maw, my dearest mom, I am so glad you are my mother. Even though you have left this earth, your memories and imprint are deep inside of me.

I love you, Maw,
Sharon A. (Wixson) Bruce
(Author)

Dear Mom,

There are so many things I wanted to write. As you read this it will become quite clear that I am not the writer of the family. You will notice that I use "we" a lot, simply because us kids have the best parts of you. Everything that we do, every challenge that we have overcome, and the simple things that make us smile all come from you, Mom. The silly ways we have fun, the way we can laugh at ourselves, our compassion for all kinds of people, our warped sense of humour and, of course, our height. There goes that sense of humour. Mom, if you took all our attributes and our faults, there would be you. I remember you getting very upset and no wonder, 5 kids to contend with. We knew not to provoke you when you were in that mood. There is one awesome gift that you passed down to each one of us and that is the gift of appreciation for music and dance. This is one that I am truly grateful for. You taught me a lot and without these lessons, I could not have overcome some of my most difficult times. I know this letter will get to you somehow. You had two phrases that were used quite often, "God moves in mysterious ways" and "Where there is a will, there is a way." Thank you, Mom, for all the gifts that you gave unconditionally and for your love. Miss you lots.

Love you and miss you,
Janice

Dear Mom,

It was hard when you died. I lost my best friend, but I do have wonderful memories. The many trips we took together, our time at comp and going to Manitoulin to visit Aunt Ruby. We always had fun doing things together and I miss that. I miss going out shopping or eating out. We acted silly and joked just to make the cashiers and waiters smile.

You always encouraged me with my art and I owe you for that. We shared our love for painting, and I really enjoyed that. You taught me to never give up, to keep on trying and that the words "I can't" was just an excuse to not try.

I watched as you lived your live as if nothing could hold you back. People would try to tell you that you couldn't do certain things but you proved them wrong. You had to do it differently but you did it. That determination has stayed with me, and I've been able to accomplish things that others said I couldn't.

You taught me not to judge others. You would say, "to walk in their shoes' before judging." I've tried to live by that.

I miss talking to you, sharing my thoughts and dreams. I miss how we would laugh until we cried over silly things.

There is so much I want to say and share but this last statement sums it up: You struggled through polio, having a disability, losing a son, dealing with a sick husband and your own illness. Yet, you never gave up even when it was hard. You had a strong faith and that kept you going. What a legacy you have given me. Thank you, Mom.

Love Glenda

Since the publishing of this book all the Fenton family characters have passed away.

AUTHOR BIO

Writing has been Sharon's passion since childhood. At seven years old she won first prize, at a local fall fair, for her story about a stuffed pink elephant. Since then, she was hooked. Articles, poems and the book *Beyond the Forests of Yesteryears*, are part of her publishing portfolio.

Curiosity mixed with a love of hearing and writing unique stories about others is the subject of her work. Some call it being darn right nosey, others call it vivid creativity.

During her career she worked in the social services field with individuals, families, groups and organizations to address social and cultural issues. A significant part of her job included inspirational speaking and sharing stories.

Sharon was raised in Northeastern Ontario, Canada, where she resides with her husband. Together they both enjoy retirement, organizing activities for seniors, which includes writing and acting out comical skits for small audiences.